Attendees' Comments on Ra Market Economics
(for which this book is pre- and supplementary reading)

MW00946304

Many more reviews are available at gmsinc.us, including how to access original sources of these comments.

- Dr. Deonaraine has very profound knowledge…. The practical perspective of economics was a welcome relief from the volumes of textbooks I have read prior to attending the session. Bravo!

- My understanding of the subject increased manifold because of Ramesh's teaching. Great knowledge imparted in laymen terms making it very easy to grasp.

- As a non-econ, non-business major, I greatly benefited from Prof. Deonaraine's lecture—he was extremely clear, easy to follow, knowledgeable, and funny. I took a few econ classes early in my college career, and probably would have been an econ major if my professors had been as good as Prof. Deonaraine.

- Fantastic. His efforts to apply theories to the real world were outstanding. Impressive and seemingly exhaustive knowledge of all related material.

- An incredible presenter. Ramesh has an amazing ability to recall facts, dates, and events and incorporate real-life examples of economic principles and relate them in a thorough, lucid way.

- Thoroughly impressed with the way he brought economics to life in a practical way. His knowledge was very applicable to the public markets that we will deal with.

- The professor was extremely interesting and easy to learn from. The course was extremely enjoyable. He possesses an impressive grasp of macroeconomic data. He is really brilliant.

- By far the best teacher quality and content that I have enjoyed over the years (includes trainings during internships).

- Excellent instructor and one who I wish I had had at university.

- The professor was highly intelligent. His passion for the course was inspiring.

- Ramesh Deonaraine was GREAT! He allowed adequate time for questions throughout and I think everyone felt very comfortable with him. The topics were extremely relevant and useful.

- The teacher—extremely smart. What we were taught is something you will RARELY find in a book.

- Most entertaining macro class I've had. Ramesh was able to keep me focused during the entire time he was teaching.

- I thought Ramesh was incredibly clear, thorough, and insightful. I really enjoyed the two days learning from him. I majored in Economics at Harvard and still found his session extremely helpful.

- Couldn't have been better. I don't think there were any questions asked that the instructor did not answer flawlessly.

- I left saying this was one of the best teaching experiences I have ever had in my life. Really excellent.

- One of the most knowledgeable and eloquent lecturers to ever come by. Truly impressed with the breadth of his knowledge. Also, extremely kind and enthusiastic with the lecture. Responds to high or low quality questions with generosity and enthusiasm.

- One of the best lecturers I had in my life. I was deeply interested in the lectures thanks to the teacher's outstanding capabilities and experience.

- Phenomenal style, lots of interesting examples from the past which made this course one of the best I have attended

- The professor was outstanding and in two days gave me more hands-on knowledge than a year on my MSc.

Many more reviews are available at gmsinc.us, including how to access original sources of these comments.

MACROECONOMICS—
A PRACTICAL FOUNDATION

Essential Knowledge for Everyone

Ramesh Deonaraine, Ph.D.

ISBN-13: 978-1484857021
ISBN-10: 148485702X

CONTENTS

PREFACE

SCOPE AND PURPOSE

This book offers a foundation in the study of macroeconomics.

When we examine the level of production, prices, unemployment, etc. in a country, we are studying its **"economy"**. When we study the US economy, for example, we are concerned with issues such as how much is being produced, at what price levels, how many people are unemployed, what are the factors influencing the exchange rate of the dollar relative to other currencies….

Microeconomics versus macroeconomics

When we study an individual unit of an economy such as a firm or an industry, we are studying **microeconomics**, economics at the "micro" level. Microeconomics answers questions like: How much of a commodity would be bought or sold? What's the price at which a commodity is bought or sold? How much output would a firm produce? When we study the whole economy, as will be our primary concern in this book, we are studying **macroeconomics**. Macroeconomics answers questions such as: What is the total amount of output of the whole society? What is the average price of this whole output combination? This is in contrast to the focus of microeconomics, which is mainly on the output or price, or other pertinent issues, of individual units of the economy.

Macroeconomics enables us to attempt to answer intelligently some of the most important questions we will confront in life: What will affect the employment prospects of our generation? What will influence how much we pay for the items we purchase? What determines the interest we pay on loans? What is a budget deficit? How can it be reduced? What are the consequences of reducing a budget deficit? Which Presidential candidate has policies that will reduce the budget deficit the most? What is a trade deficit? What causes currency exchange rates to fluctuate? These are only some of the questions that fall within the purview of macroeconomics.

FOR EVERYONE; ESPECIALLY SUITED FOR BUSINESSPERSONS AND POLICY MAKERS

Every day of your life you are influenced by macroeconomic events. Every day the news is full of discussions of macroeconomic events. **You cannot live as an informed person unless you know macroeconomics.** This book provides a conceptual foundation to enable you to better understand many macroeconomic issues you will encounter in your daily life. As you acquire this knowledge, you will become better informed than some "analysts" who appear on television to make pronouncements on macroeconomic questions. These will be achievements of which you can justifiably be proud.

I have encountered businesspersons and policy makers who have told me of their attempts to learn college economics to better understand the constant media coverage of economics/business and what economists say on the state of the economy and its future. These businesspersons and policy makers have frequently lamented that they found college instruction in economics to be very cumbersome. They would end a macroeconomic course feeling they had a lot of undigested information and unable to do substantial intelligent analysis of the economy.

Brief
This book seeks to resolve this problem. It is deliberately kept brief so that you can find the time to read it. Yet, it provides insights on a broad array of macroeconomic issues you will often hear about in the news. By the time you reach the end of Chapter 2, you will have the knowledge to intelligently discuss some of the great macroeconomic challenges that the human race has faced or is facing. This becomes obvious to you when these challenges are discussed in Chapter 3.

Easy to read
The chapters ahead are easy to read and rapidly give you deep insights into economic issues and a clear conceptual foundation on which you can build if you want to delve further into macroeconomics. While easy to read, they are written in the *lingua franca* of college, using college-type diagrams, some mathematics (provided as an alternative that can be avoided if you do not care for math) and theoretical foundations. This will enable you to communicate with your buddies

who have done economics in college and will equip you to better understand economists when they use jargon.

Key benefits

You will get several key benefits from reading this book. You will:

- Be better able to understand what economists have to say about topical issues like inflation, unemployment, recession, economic growth, trade deficits, exchange rates, etc.

- Acquire a sound understanding of the contexts in which economic theories are properly used. Far too often those who study economics are given voluminous information but not clear guidance on the circumstances in which a particular theory is relevant. As a result, they are confused about what theory is applicable in a particular situation.

- Get a clear grasp of why economists (classical economists, Keynesians, monetarists, new classical macroeconomists, new Keynesians, real business cycle theorists, supply-side economists, etc.) differ with each other over what policies are appropriate.

PRACTICAL

This book focuses on enabling us to better understand our world, so the theory presented is related to the real world. As you study it, you will acquire a much deeper understanding of the world and of the forces shaping your existence.

Many Presidents and Prime Ministers would have been better at their jobs and would have avoided horrible mistakes in economic management if they had learned the macroeconomics you are about to study. So often I have met adults who complain that they live beleaguered by ignorance because they never acquired knowledge of macroeconomics. On several occasions, I have encountered prominent diplomats and political leaders, including one Prime Minister, who regretted they had not studied economics when they were undergraduates. The

Prime Minister, a lawyer by training, told an international gathering that if he had to live his life over he would study economics rather than law. He said so often when his advisers spoke to him of economic policy options he had insufficient insight into what they told him because of his ignorance of economics.

NOTHING TO FEAR

We usually experience fear when we begin a task that seems intellectually demanding. Often this fear is unnecessary. In the case of reading this book, you have no real grounds for feeling fear:

- **All the presentations are developed step-by-step.**

- **There are no sudden jumps in the analysis to leave you feeling lost.**

- **Everything is written in language a thoughtful high school student can follow.**

As an economist, I am deeply concerned about the production and consumption of human happiness. I really wish that people should live to their best. One way I manifest this is by trying to present material clearly so that students can be happy while learning. I hope you will see this in the pages ahead and that you will enjoy the journey.

INSIGHT AND PERSISTENCE

If in your studies you encounter material that you don't fully grasp, persist in going through the material step-by-step, clearly identifying what you know and what you don't know. This systematic effort enables your mind to make intellectual breakthroughs in which you get insights that give clarity on what was bothering you, or on what other sources of information you need to advance your learning.

This is how you acquire a higher level of understanding. If only superficial, sporadic thinking is done, it is unlikely that these flashes of insight will occur.

Also, if at first you are slow in going through the steps of an analysis, or you feel unsure, persevere and you will become more adept. If you have tried learning to type, you should understand this process well. At first, you can barely get a few letters correctly typed per minute. As you continue your systematic learning, your fingers begin to move expertly without you even having to look at the keyboard. Many then go on to type at very high speeds. The same phenomenon occurs in the learning of any subject. If you methodically persist, you will improve.

NEW TERMS, EXERCISES, ANSWERS, HAND-DRAWN DIAGRAMS

- When a **new term** is introduced and defined in the chapters ahead, it is underlined. This helps you to keep track of new terms.

- In most of the chapters, after a suitable amount of material has been introduced on which your understanding should be tested, there are **exercises**. **Answers** to the exercises are at the end of the chapter.

- In everyday communication, you may have to quickly draw macroeconomic diagrams to convey your thoughts in academic style. You must also be readily able to understand other people's hand-drawn diagrams. (It slows down communication considerably if you have to use a computer to draw every time you need a diagram.) To get you comfortable with do-it-yourself drawings, **both computer- and hand-drawn diagrams are used in this book.**

Bon voyage! Let the good times roll!

CHAPTER 1
INTRODUCTION

NOTE: Please read the Preface. It contains valuable information to help you get the most from your study. It discusses the scope and purpose and the benefits you will get, and it offers advice on how to acquire expertise on the topics you study.

ECONOMICS

Economics studies the <u>optimal allocation</u> of <u>scarce resources</u> among <u>competing ends</u>. We are faced with competing ends because we typically have a variety of desires but lack the resources to satisfy all of them. We face a problem of choice: how to allocate the limited resources we have to get the best for ourselves, to get an optimal allocation of resources, one that lets us best meet our objectives.

Your money, for example, is a scarce resource. You (if you are typical!) do not have as much of it as you want and must constantly apportion it among the different things you want to buy (the competing ends) to maximize your well-being (attain an optimal allocation).

Governments face a similar problem—they have only so much to spend and they must apportion it among competing ends to best attain their objectives. They face questions such as: Should more be spent on education? If more is to be spent on education, do we cut defense spending to get the needed funds? Businesses must also allocate their scarce resources—money, time, labor, materials—optimally or they will be inefficient and are likely to be out-competed.

Thinking along these lines, you will readily realize that every moment of your life you are confronted with economic issues, in making choices or in thinking of the choices people or society confront. It is not surprising that many who are interested in the problems of society, the forces that shape society, how to achieve societal changes and similar questions, frequently end up studying economics.

Anne Kreuger, a well-known economist who has served as First Deputy Managing Director of the International Monetary Fund, said she started out studying political science. But she found most of the issues she wanted to understand required knowledge of economics, so she turned to economics.[1] Abba Lerner, one of the great economists of 20th century, was a tailor and typesetter among other things and then founded his own printing shop. When this went bankrupt, he enrolled as an evening student at the London School of Economics hoping to learn why his shop had failed. His outstanding mental abilities won him all the available prizes and fellowships and he was on his way to becoming a prominent economist.

Robert Lucas said he was always interested in social problems and initially studied history. However, he concluded that the main forces in history were economic and decided to specialize in economics. Robert Lucas received the Nobel Prize for economics in 1995. James Tobin said he studied economics because he realized many of the world's problems were economic in origin. To make the world better, it was necessary to know economics.[2] Tobin received the Nobel Prize for economics in 1981.

If you check why others turned to studying economics you will readily find many who did so because they were confronted with important societal issues that they could not adequately understand unless they knew economics. Economics provides us with a most important set of tools for understanding the world without which we are likely to flounder in ignorance, totally unaware of how limited is our view. That's why I always say to students: "If you are interested in politics, study economics. If you are interested in history, study economics…. If you are interested in the world, study economics."

---

[1] Stated in a conversation with Michael Parkin. See Parkin, M. (1990). *Macroeconomics*. Addison-Wesley.

[2] These comments from Lucas and Tobin are cited in Klamer, A. (1984). *Conversations with economists*. Rowman and Allanheld.

HOW WE LEARN ECONOMICS—THE USE OF THEORY

Theory

We learn economics through the use of **theory**. A theory is a set of propositions explaining the causes of a phenomenon. The word "**model**" is generally used as a synonym for theory.

There is a distinct difference between theory and mere description. A theory identifies causal links between phenomena in a logically integrated structure. A description merely offers information but does not identify causal connections. As a frequently cited quote from Poincaré states: "Science is built of facts the way a house is built of bricks; but an accumulation of facts is no more science than a pile of bricks is a house." This remark is just as apt if "theory" is substituted for "science" in it. Theory goes beyond a mere accumulation of facts to explain the causes of a phenomenon.

Let's say students had to write a paper on "Spending in America." One student writes a paper full of details on what people buy, when and how they buy, what various age groups purchase, and so on. Another student writes a paper on what factors affect the level of spending, identifying people's income and expected income as causal factors. The first student is merely describing, presenting a pile of facts. The facts presented by the first student may be very important and could be the basis of new insights on people's spending behavior. The point is, however, that the mere presentation of facts alone is not theory. The second student is building theory, attempting to explain the causes of a phenomenon.

Theory building involves: identifying a phenomenon the cause of which needs to be explained; definitions; abstraction; identification of causal connections; empirical evidence; theory reformulation.

A phenomenon to be explained

Anyone who wants to build a theory must first find a phenomenon the cause of which needs to be explained. In a famous story on Sir Isaac Newton, we are told he was sitting under a tree when an apple fell on his nose. This caused him to ponder what made unsupported objects fall to the ground and led him to develop his theory of gravity.

Definitions

Terms used in a theory must be defined so people will understand exactly to what the theory refers. In the theory on spending mentioned earlier, the student developing it would have to tell us what she means by spending, income, expected income, and so on.

Abstraction

In developing a theory we must **abstract** from, meaning we ignore, details not relevant to the specification of the causal link(s) our theory seeks to establish. **Abstraction** is used in many areas of life. For example, a map is drawn by focusing on the location of places and ignoring the architecture of buildings, their decorative features, etc. not relevant to showing how to get from one place to another. A theory is not a total replication of reality just as a map does not show all features of a locality. A theory is a generalization that enables us to focus on aspects of reality in which we are interested without getting encumbered with unnecessary detail.

For example, to develop a theory of what influences the total amount people spend we may ignore details such as what clothing they wear when making purchases and what kind of hairstyles they have if we view these details as irrelevant to what influences spending. People's incomes, however, will not be ignored because in all likelihood a sensible theory of spending will involve a causal connection between income and spending.

Abstractions are often explicitly stated in a theory as <u>assumptions</u>. An assumption in this context is whatever is held to be true for the purpose of theory construction. For example, to develop a theory to explain what quantity of a commodity people will buy and the price they will pay for it, we may, for the purposes of our theory, assume people know how much they want to buy at each price level. That is, we abstract from the detail that people may not necessarily know this information precisely. Nevertheless, once we develop such a theory (as is actually done in the study of **micro**economics) we will find it gives an appropriate guide to what happens in the real world. If, however, we attempt to incorporate all details when developing the theory, it would be rather difficult for our minds to focus on the key causal links and these would probably drown in the sea of excess detail.

Specification of causal links

The purpose of building a theory is to establish the cause of a phenomenon. The heart of the theory is the specification of what causes the phenomenon. Definitions and abstraction are all geared toward the attainment of this objective.

Empirical evidence

For a theory to be viewed as appropriate the causal links it specifies must approximate those that are observed in the real world. If what is claimed by a theory is supported by empirical evidence, the theory holds. If valid evidence contradicts a theory, the theory has to be altered, or discarded, or cannot be viewed as a guide to what happens in the real world.

Obtaining evidence may not be easy. One major challenge is that in the real world many occurrences often happen at the same time, making it difficult to ascertain which one or more of several possible factors may have caused the event. The same problem is faced in many areas of human life. For example, if your grades improve, is it because the examinations are easier, you have become better at taking tests, you have acquired better study skills, you are eating better so you are healthier and more capable at doing mental work, you are emotionally more stable because your family members are getting along better, you have stopped seeing someone who wasted a lot of your time…? It can be hard to determine which one or more of these factors were the real causes. In spite of the difficulty of obtaining proof, however, supportive empirical evidence is the only indicator that confirms a theory.

Theory reformulation

If evidence suggests a theory is inaccurate, it may be necessary to reformulate the theory to make it a better predictor of real world events. If the theory is so way off in its predictions that it cannot be salvaged, it must be discarded and a new theory should be developed.

THE *CERETIS PARIBUS* ASSUMPTION

Suppose there are various factors, A, B, C, which can cause a change in D, and we want to discuss the impact on D of a change in B alone. This means we have to examine the impact on D of the change in B with all other factors that can affect D held constant. The shorthand for saying "B changes with all other factors that can affect D held constant" is "B changes, *ceteris paribus*." *Ceteris paribus* (pronounced as "keteris paribus" or "seteris paribus") is a Latin expression meaning "other things held constant." The other things held constant are indicated by the context. In the example just cited, the other things held constant are the factors other than B—A and C—that affect D.

In economics, because there are often several factors affecting an outcome at the same time, the *ceteris paribus* assumption is frequently used when we want to study the impact of one of these factors on the outcome. When it is understood that this assumption is being used, we don't have to mention it. In the next chapter, we will see examples of how this assumption is used as we study our first theory, the AD-AS model.

My record at the University of California as an undergraduate was mediocre to say the best. I had only slightly better than a "C" average.... I had hoped to go to law school, but the war started....

What the war did was give me the opportunity of three years of continuous reading, and it was in the course of reading that I became convinced that I should become an economist.

I went back to graduate school with the clear intention that what I wanted to do with my life was to improve societies, and the way to do that was to find out what made economies work the way they did or fail to work. I believed that once we had an understanding of what determined the performance of economies through time, we could then improve their performance. I have never lost sight of that objective.

—Douglas North, Nobel Prize, Economics, 1993

CHAPTER 2
FACTORS THAT INFLUENCE AN ECONOMY'S OUTPUT AND PRICE LEVELS (THE AD-AS MODEL)
Part 1

INTRODUCTION

Here we want to present a macroeconomic theory to determine how the total output of all goods and services[3] in an economy, and the average price of all these goods and services, will be affected by various factors. This theory is called the aggregate demand–aggregate supply model, or AD-AS model for short. In describing this model, our focus will be on quickly getting insights into how the real world works. We will avoid complications that are inappropriate at this level and that do not contribute to our purpose.

We will take it that all the goods and services produced in the economy can be aggregated into an amount represented by the symbol Y and that the average price of all the goods and services in this aggregate is P. **(In Chapters 4 and 5 we get insights on how Y and P are measured.)**

Throughout the world, increasing the output of goods and services (Y) and keeping the price level (P) from escalating are major concerns, as is evident in the very frequent references to these in the daily news. A higher output level can mean more people will be employed, decreasing unemployment. A higher price level means a higher cost of living. If you think of your own life, you will see how relevant these concerns are: Don't you worry over whether there will be jobs easily available in the years ahead? Don't you worry over how much it costs you to live? If you don't worry about these questions either you are not really alive or you have attained Heavenly Bliss! Nearly all of us worry over what affects the economy's

---

[3] A good has physical characteristics. It is tangible, e.g., food, clothing. A service is intangible, e.g., medical advice, travel, hairstyling. The result of a service may be physically noticeable, but the service itself does not have physical characteristics.

output and price levels and we can become far more sophisticated in our view of the world by learning about these. This chapter begins to give us this knowledge.

AGGREGATE DEMAND

The higher the price level P, the lower will be the total amount of goods and services that people want to buy. We refer to the quantity of goods and services that people want to buy as the <u>quantity of demand,</u> or <u>quantity demanded</u>. A higher price level means people are able to buy less goods and services with the money they have available. Their <u>purchasing power</u>—the amount of goods and services a given amount of money can buy—declines when P rises. So we get an inverse relation between the quantity of goods and services demanded and the price level. This relationship represented graphically is called the **<u>aggregate demand (AD)</u>** **<u>curve.</u>**

FIGURE 1

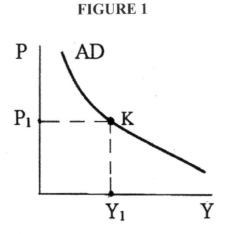

THE AD CURVE

In this diagram, P, the price level, is measured on the vertical axis. The total output of goods and services, Y, is measured on the horizontal axis. The precise shape of the AD curve, whether it is a negatively sloped straight line or negatively sloped curve, doesn't matter now since all we want to portray is a negative relationship between P and Y.

A point on the AD curve shows total amount of output demanded at the price level corresponding to that point. The point K, for example, shows that at the price level P_1 the quantity of output demanded is Y_1. In real life, P_1 and Y_1 would be numbers measuring the price level and an amount of output of goods and services respectively. As we have mentioned, in Chapters 4 and 5 we will learn how Y and P are measured.

The notion that a higher price level will mean reduced purchasing power is sometimes referred to as the <u>Pigou effect</u>, in honor of the British economist A.C. Pigou who discussed it. The Pigou effect offers an explanation of the negative slope of the aggregate demand curve. The Pigou effect is also called the <u>real balances effect</u>. "Balances" means money, "real balances" means the purchasing power of money. The real balances effect refers to the decline in purchasing power of money as the price level rises.[4]

AGGREGATE SUPPLY

In general, the higher is the price level, P, the higher will be the total amount of output producers in the economy want to make available for sale, i.e., want to supply. Greater output means more inputs such as labor have to be used to produce that output. This greater use of labor and other inputs pushes up their costs per unit of output produced—producers competing to get the amount of inputs they need

---

[4] If you continue your study of theoretical economics to levels more advanced than that of this book, you will get more complex explanations of the slope of the AD curve and of the AS curve which we discuss next. These more complicated explanations are not necessary for our purpose. They would distract us from quickly developing the AD-AS model and seeing its great power to give valuable practical insights on how the economy works.

will bid up the unit cost of these inputs. This makes it necessary for producers to get a higher price to produce a higher level of output.[5]

If we draw a diagram with P on the vertical axis and Y on the horizontal axis, we get a positively sloped curve called the **aggregate supply (AS) curve** showing the amount of output producers are willing to offer for sale at each price level (Figure 2). For AS, what we want to portray is a positive relationship between P and Y, so it doesn't matter whether we do this with a positively sloped line or curve.

FIGURE 2

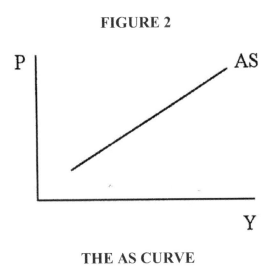

THE AS CURVE

THE ECONOMY'S EQUILIBRIUM PRICE AND OUTPUT LEVELS

Now if we draw an AD and an AS curve in the same diagram, we get a diagram like Figure 3. For the price and output combination P* and Y* in Figure 3, the quantity of output demanded (measured by the distance KL) is exactly the same as the quantity of output supplied (also measured by the distance KL).

The term equilibrium is used in this analysis to refer to situations in which quantity of output demanded equals quantity of output supplied. As you can surmise, the price and output combination associated with this equilibrium are called the

---

[5] See the previous footnote on why the explanation for the slope of the AS curve is kept relatively simple here.

equilibrium price and equilibrium output. In Figure 3, P* are Y* are equilibrium price and equilibrium output respectively.

FIGURE 3

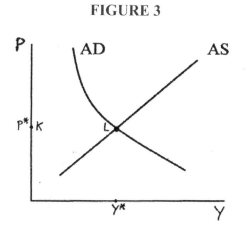

Equilibrium Price and Output are P*and Y*

EXERCISE 1

1. Say whether each of the following is true or false and offer the arguments necessary to justify your answer:
    a. The point A in the figure below shows that at the price level P_1 total output demanded is Y_1.
    b. For point B, the price level P_2 is lower than for A, and output demanded is Y_2.
    c. At point R, the price level is P_3 and the total output supplied is Y_3.

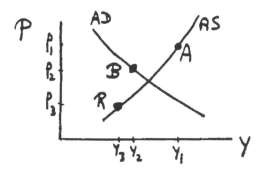

2. Can an AD curve be positively sloped? Explain.

3. In the figure in #1, why can't the economy's price level remain at P_1?

FACTORS THAT CHANGE AGGREGATE DEMAND (AD)

Any factor that causes more output to be demanded at any given price level shifts the AD curve to the right. If at the price level P_1 (Figure 4a) total output demanded is AB, at price level P_2 it is CE, at price level P_3 it is GF, etc., but then people want to purchase more at any given price level, total output demanded at price levels P_1, P_2 and P_3 would now be greater than AB, CE and GF. The new aggregate demand curve that results is AD', which is to the right of AD—there is an <u>increase in aggregate demand</u>. A shift of the AD curve to the right is called an increase in aggregate demand (Figure 4a). Any factor that causes less output to be demanded at any given price level shifts the AD curve to the left. A shift of the AD curve to the left is called a <u>decrease in aggregate demand</u> (Figure 4b).

FIGURE 4

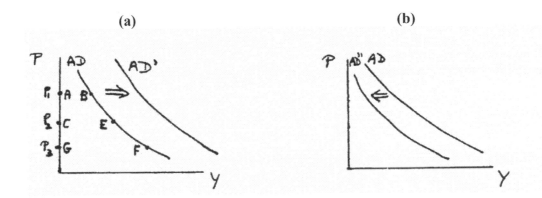

(a)   **(b)**

**An increase in aggregate
demand means a shift of
the AD curve to the right**

**A decrease in aggregate
demand means a shift of
the AD curve to the left**

A **change in aggregate demand** means a shift of the AD curve, for example, as shown in Figure 4a, in which the AD curve shifts from AD to AD', or in Figure 4b, in which the AD curve shifts from AD to AD''. A change in the **quantity** of aggregate demand is a movement along an AD curve. In Figure 4a, moving from B to E, or E to F, on the aggregate demand curve AD is a change in **quantity** demanded. Whenever you see the term "change in AD" you will know this means a shift of the AD curve; "change in the quantity of AD" means a movement along an AD curve.

The total demand (aggregate demand) for all the goods and services produced in an economy will consist of what people and entities within that country demand and also the amount of these goods and services that other countries want to buy. The goods and services demanded by the people and entities of a country can be put into three categories: for consumption, for investment, and by the government.

Consumption consists of goods and services bought by households.[6] Investment consists of goods and services bought by businesses and spending on new housing.[7] (The definitions of consumption and investment here and in the footnotes below ignore minor technical details.) Government—federal, state and local— purchases many goods and services such as paper, pens, office equipment, military

---

[6] Consumption can be put into three categories: durable goods, non-durable goods, and services. Durable goods provide services over time and generally endure a long time. Examples of durable goods bought by consumers are washing machines, TV sets, and cars. Items like food and clothing are referred to as non-durable goods because they are used up relatively quickly.

[7] Investment can be divided into three categories: non-residential fixed investment, inventory investment, and residential fixed investment. Non-residential fixed investment refers to the factory buildings, plant, equipment and software businesses buy for use in the production process. Inventory investment consists of the stocks of raw materials, goods in the process of production and completed goods held by firms. Residential fixed investment is creation of new housing. Investment, as used in this context, should not be confused with financial investments such as the purchasing of bonds (discussed in Chapter 6) or stocks (buying shares in a company) in the hope of getting a financial gain from the bonds or stocks appreciating in value or earning you interest or dividends.

equipment, and the services of a variety of workers. A country's <u>exports</u> are its goods and services bought by other countries.[8]

Any factor that causes an increase in any one or more of these components of aggregate demand at any given price level will, *ceteris paribus*, cause the AD curve to shift to the right, an increase in aggregate demand.[9] Any factor that causes a decrease in any one of these components of aggregate demand at any given price level will, *ceteris paribus*, cause the AD curve to shift to the left, a decrease in aggregate demand.

If consumers become more optimistic about the economic future, <u>consumer optimism</u> is said to rise, and consumers are likely to want to purchase more at any given price level, so the AD curve shifts to the right. If consumer optimism falls, this will shift the AD curve to the left.

Aggregate demand increases (the AD curve shifts to the right) if, for any given level of P, <u>business optimism</u> increases causing businesses to want to buy more machinery and equipment to expand business operations. Aggregate demand also increases (the AD curve shifts to the right) if for any given level of P, government increases its purchases, or if foreigners increase their preference for our goods and services leading to higher levels of exports. A decrease in any one of business optimism, government purchases and exports, for any given price level, decreases aggregate demand and shifts the AD curve to the left.

---

[8] Goods and services bought from other countries—<u>imports</u>—will be among the goods and services demanded by the consumers, businesses and government in a country. These do not count as part of aggregate demand for goods and services **produced in that country**.

[9] Typically, if any one or more of consumption, investment or government purchases in a country increase, this increases aggregate demand for that country's goods and services as some of the increased spending is very likely to be on that country's goods and services. It is unlikely that all the increased spending will be on imports.

If the government reduces taxes (or increases <u>transfer payments</u>[10]) and this increases consumer and business spending at any given price level, this increases aggregate demand. An increase in taxes or a decrease in transfer payments that decreases consumer and business spending at any given price level decreases aggregate demand.

If the <u>money supply</u> is increased, this increases aggregate demand. We have not discussed as yet what is <u>money</u>, the money supply or how the money supply can be changed. But for now we will take it on faith[11] that an increase in the money supply increases aggregate demand, and a decrease in the money supply decreases aggregate demand. In chapters ahead, we learn how money is defined in macroeconomics, about the money supply process, and how changes in the money supply cause shifts in the AD curve.[12] One way the money supply can be increased is through the governing authorities lowering interest rates—a process explained in Chapter 7. Lower interest rates make it cheaper to borrow and spend and encourage businesses and consumers to spend more, increasing aggregate demand. One way in which the money supply can be decreased is through the governing authorities raising interest rates—also explained in Chapter 7. Higher interest rates make it more expensive to borrow and spend and make businesses and consumers want to spend less. This decreases aggregate demand.

Factors we have stated here that cause a change in aggregate demand are changes in: consumer optimism, business optimism, government purchases, exports, taxes,

---

[10] Transfer payments are those for which no goods or services have to be given in exchange for the payment. Examples are welfare payments, given by government to people to help them cope with poverty, and pensions paid to retirees.

[11] As the great 19th century poet Emily Dickinson noted:
Faith—is the Pierless Bridge
Supporting what we see
Unto the scene that
we do not.

[12] Later in this book we will learn that if money supply changes are "excessive", this can harm the economy. We will get a notion of what is meant by "excessive" and we will see what the harmful effects can be.

transfers and the money supply. The governing authorities can directly change government purchases, taxes, transfers, and the money supply. They can indirectly increase consumer and business optimism by persuading the nation that better times are coming, and can attempt to increase exports by efforts to find markets abroad.

AD increases if:	AD decreases if:
Consumer optimism ↑	Consumer optimism ↓
Business optimism ↑	Business optimism ↓
Government purchases ↑	Government purchases ↓
Exports ↑	Exports ↓
Taxes ↓	Taxes ↑
Transfers ↑	Transfers ↓
Money supply ↑	Money supply ↓

FACTORS THAT CHANGE AGGREGATE SUPPLY (AS)

You have learned that a change in aggregate demand means a shift of the AD curve. Similarly, a **change in aggregate supply** means a shift of the AS curve. An increase in aggregate supply means a shift of the AS curve to the right (Figure 5a). A decrease in aggregate supply means a shift of the AS curve to the left (Figure 5b).

If, for any level of output, the price of an input widely used in producing the economy's goods and services becomes cheaper (e.g., a fall in the price of oil for a country that has to import oil, or a fall in the price of labor), any level of output can now be produced at lower unit costs and can be offered for sale at a lower price. The AS curve shifts to the right—an increase in AS. If, for any level of output, the price of such an input increases, any level of output will now cost more to produce, so producers will require a higher price for it. The AS curve shifts to the left—a decrease in AS.

FIGURE 5

(a)   **(b)**

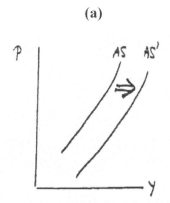

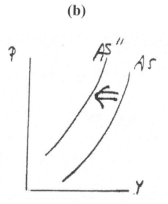

**An increase in aggregate
supply means a shift of
the AS curve to the right**

**A decrease in aggregate
supply means a shift of
the AS curve to the left**

Improvements in technology that make production more efficient, a decrease in taxes on businesses, or a decrease in oppressive government regulations[13] that makes possible increased business profitability, will each lower unit costs of production for every level of output and increase AS. Technological deterioration (e.g., through lack of proper maintenance of technology), increases in taxes on businesses, and an increase in oppressive government regulations will each decrease AS.

AS increases if: **AS decreases if:**

Price of a widely used input ↓   Price of a widely used input ↑

Technology becomes more efficient   Technology deteriorates

Taxes affecting unit profits ↓   Taxes affecting unit profits ↑

Oppressive government regulations ↓   Oppressive government regulations ↑

---

[13] Government regulations are very important for the health and safety of workers, protecting the environment, the maintenance of law and order, etc. Governments, regrettably, often become obsessed with control, and force businesses to go through unnecessary procedures that increase business costs without benefiting society. This raises unit costs of production and stifles business.

So main factors that cause a change in aggregate supply are changes in: the price of inputs (such as oil or labor) widely used in production, technological efficiency, taxes on businesses, and government regulations affecting business profitability.

The governing authorities have direct control over taxes and regulations. They can indirectly influence technological innovation by measures like encouraging research (e.g., through increased funding) and improving educational systems. They may have control over the price of widely used inputs in circumstances such as if the wages workers receive can be determined by the government, and/or if the price of widely used material inputs (e.g., oil) is under their control.[14]

Supply shocks

Factors that cause a sudden change in aggregate supply are called **supply shocks**. If a sudden change occurs that causes a decrease in aggregate supply, this is often referred to as an adverse supply shock. Because oil is so widely used in the production process, dramatic changes in the price of oil have often been a cause of adverse supply shocks to countries around the world that have to import oil.

A change that causes a quick increase in aggregate supply is often referred to as a beneficial supply shock, which I like to refer to as a supply blessing. A sharp fall in the price of oil would be a supply blessing for a country that imports a lot of oil.

IMPACT OF CHANGES IN AD AND AS ON THE ECONOMY'S PRICE AND OUTPUT LEVELS

An increase in AD pushes up the economy's price and output levels (Figure 6a). Using symbols, we can write this as: AD→ => P↑ , Y↑. (We will use horizontal arrows to represent shifts in curves and vertical arrows to represent changes in quantities.)

---

[14] If the governing authorities make it easier and less costly for businesses to borrow, this can also lower the cost businesses incur to fund the production of goods and services and can increase aggregate supply. Of course, the reverse happens if the authorities make it more costly for businesses to borrow.

If AD falls, this decreases the economy's price and output levels:
AD← => P↓ , Y↓ (Figure 6b).

If AS increases, this decreases the economy's price level and increases its output
level: AS→ => P↓ , Y↑ (Figure 7a).

If AS decreases, this increases the economy's price level and decreases its output
level: AS← => P↑ , Y↓ (Figure 7b).

FIGURE 6

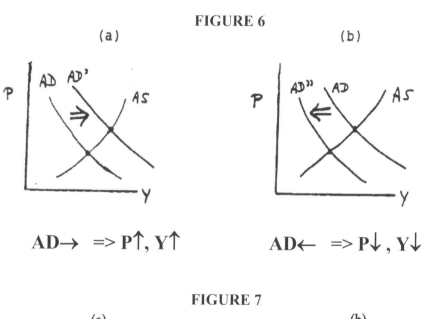

AD→ => P↑, Y↑   **AD← => P↓ , Y↓**

FIGURE 7

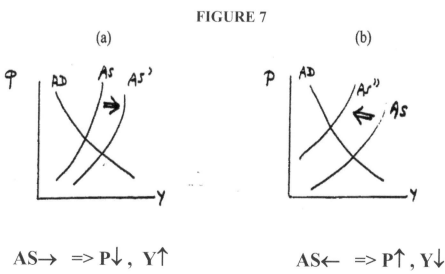

AS→ => P↓ , Y↑   **AS← => P↑ , Y↓**

If AD and AS shift simultaneously and we only know the direction of the shifts but not by how much each has shifted, we will not be able to determine what happens to one of P or Y when such a simultaneous shift occurs. For example, if AD and AS each increase but we don't know by how much each has increased, we have:

$$AD\rightarrow \quad => P\uparrow, Y\uparrow$$
$$AS\rightarrow \quad => P\downarrow, Y\uparrow$$
$$AD\rightarrow + AS\rightarrow \quad => P?, Y\uparrow$$

AD increasing pushes up P; AS increasing pushes down P. But we don't know by how much P is pushed up or down. So we cannot determine what happens to P unless we are given more information on how much each of AD and AS has shifted.

Employment

Typically, rising/falling output will be associated with more/less employment because if businesses have to produce more/less they will need more/less workers. Therefore, in the AD-AS model we have learned so far, factors that increase AD or AS are likely to increase employment (decrease unemployment), factors that decrease AD or AS are likely to decrease employment (increase unemployment).[15]

EXERCISE 2

1. For each of the following (a to h), say whether it increases or decreases AD or AS:
   a. A rise in government purchases
   b. A fall in the price of oil
   c. A rise in consumer optimism
   d. Technological improvements that make production more profitable
   e. A fall in business optimism

---

[15] Often, it takes time for the changes in employment to occur. For example, a business seeing increased demand for its products might let its current employees work longer hours to meet the increased demand. It may hesitate to hire new employees until it is sure that the increased demand is long term.

    f. A sharp increase in other countries' demand for our goods

    g. New taxes that decrease consumer spending

    h. An increase in government regulations that diminish business profitability

2. Explain how a rise in consumer optimism leads to higher output and a higher price level in the economy. Do it first using only words and then illustrate what happens in terms of an AD-AS diagram.

3. An increase in the money supply is likely to be associated with which one of the following:

    a. Aggregate demand falling because of the money supply increase

    b. A lower price level as the increase in the money supply takes effect

    c. Lower interest rates

    d. Decreased employment as the increase in the money supply increases aggregate supply

4. Suppose there is a crisis in the Middle East that causes the price of oil to increase dramatically. Use the AD-AS model to explain how this can cause unemployment to rise in the US.

5. When output is stagnant or falling and the price level is rising the economy is said to be experiencing **stagflation** ("stagnation plus inflation"—inflation means the price level is increasing; we discuss inflation later in this book). In 1974-75 and 1979-80, the US economy experienced stagflation caused by dramatic increases in the price of oil. Explain, using the AD-AS model, how sharp increases in the price of oil caused those episodes of stagflation.

6. Can stagflation be caused by falling aggregate demand?

7. Use the AD-AS model to explain why a massive cut in US government spending could reduce US output and employment. If a politician claims she will reduce government spending drastically and also create more jobs, but does not say how she will do this, would you be skeptical of her claim?

WHAT LIES AHEAD

After learning the economics in this chapter alone, you have the knowledge to prevent some great economic catastrophes, as you will see in Chapter 3, where we look at some very important practical examples of how you can apply this knowledge.

Much of the rest of this book is devoted to extending your knowledge of the AD-AS model. Chapter 3 elaborates on this model. Chapters 4 and 5 provide details on the economy's output and price levels. Chapters 6 and 7 discuss money and the money supply, how the money supply can be changed, and how changes in the money supply affect aggregate demand. Chapter 8 deals with issues pertaining to changes in the price level and to unemployment. Chapters 9 and 10 teach more precise notions on exports and imports, the interconnections between the various types of economic transactions a country has with the rest of the world, and on the exchange rates between currencies. Chapters 5–10 fulfill the important purpose of expanding on notions introduced in the schematic presentation of the AD-AS model in this chapter.

Chapter 11 presents different versions of the AD-AS model, each of which has a specific situation for which it is appropriate. Chapter 12 discusses various schools of thought in macroeconomics. This discussion is closely related to the various versions of the AD-AS model presented in Chapter 11. Chapter 13 provides a framework for thinking about government spending, budget deficits and debt, and Chapter 14 concludes with thoughts on paths you could follow after finishing this book.

ANSWERS

EXERCISE 1

1.
   a. False. The point A shows that total output supplied is Y_1.

b. True. B is a point on the aggregate demand curve corresponding to price level P_2 (which is less than P_1) and to a level of output demanded of Y_2

c. True. R is a point on the aggregate supply curve corresponding to price level P_3 and a level of output supplied of Y_3.

2. No. An AD curve cannot be positively sloped because a higher price level implies decreased purchasing power and a lower quantity of aggregate demand. This implies the AD curve is negatively sloped.

3. See the figure below. At price level P_1, the quantity of output supplied (measured by the distance XA) is greater than the quantity demanded (measured by the distance XY). This will put downward pressure on the price level as producers find people don't want to buy the quantity of goods and services they are offering for sale at the price level P_1. This will continue until equilibrium is reached, corresponding to where the AD and AS curves intersect.

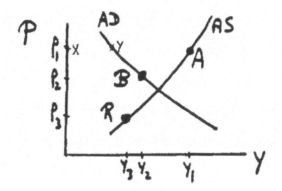

EXERCISE 2

1.   a, c, and f increase AD.
      e and g reduce AD.
      b and d increase AS.
      h decreases AS.

2. When consumer optimism rises, consumers become more confident about their financial condition. This causes them to shop more. (Not everyone will shop more, but, on the average, consumers will shop more.) Businesses, noticing greater demand for their goods and services, will increase production to meet the increased demand. As businesses increase their production, they will need more labor and other inputs. This increased demand for these inputs pushes up their prices, increasing unit costs of production, and, to make up for these higher costs, businesses charge a higher price for their goods and services. The result of all this is a higher level of output and a higher price level in the economy.

   In terms of an AD-AS diagram, the output and price levels are Y_1 and P_1, represented by the point A in the diagram below. Then the increase in consumer optimism causes AD to increase to AD'. Businesses see this increased demand,

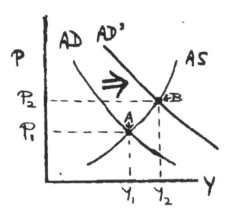

   and they increase output from Y_1 to Y_2, so there is movement from point A to point B along the AS curve. At point B, the unit input costs are higher because the increased demand for inputs to produce the higher level of output Y_2 will have pushed up the cost of labor and other inputs. So for the level of output Y_2, businesses charge a higher price P_2. The new level of output is Y_2 and the new price level is P_2, as compared to Y_1 and P_1, which were the levels before consumer optimism increased.

3. An increase in the money supply is likely to cause an increase in aggregate demand, a higher price level and higher output and employment. It is likely to be associated with lower interest rates. So c is the correct answer. Later in this book we will learn more about money, how the money supply can be changed, and the effects on the economy of these changes.

4. $P_{oil} \uparrow \Rightarrow AS\leftarrow \Rightarrow Y\downarrow \Rightarrow$ unemployment $\uparrow$

5. $P_{oil} \uparrow \Rightarrow AS\leftarrow \Rightarrow P\uparrow, Y\downarrow \Rightarrow$ a rising price level and unemployment $\uparrow$, which is stagflation.

6. Stagflation means output remaining the same or falling while the price level is rising. Changes in AD cannot cause this because if AD increases both the price and output levels increase. If AD decreases both the price and output levels decrease.

7. Government spending $\downarrow$ (G $\downarrow$) $\Rightarrow AD\leftarrow \Rightarrow$ output $\downarrow$ and employment $\downarrow$. So you should be skeptical of the politician's claim because a decrease in government spending is likely to decrease employment. The politician would have to clearly spell out what other means she will use to create enough jobs to both offset the loss of jobs due to the decreased government spending and to create additional jobs.

The complicated analysis which economists...carry through are not mere gymnastic. They are instruments for bettering human life.

—A. C. Pigou, who made important contributions to economics and was based mainly at the University of Cambridge

CHAPTER 3
FACTORS THAT INFLUENCE AN ECONOMY'S OUTPUT AND PRICE LEVELS (THE AD-AS MODEL)
Part 2

In this chapter, we deepen our knowledge of the AD-AS model, learning important terms and looking at very instructive practical applications.

IMPORTANT TERMS

Fiscal and monetary policy

Fiscal policy is a government's decisions on its spending and the taxes it collects. **Monetary policy** is policy to change the money supply.

A fiscal or monetary policy is called **expansionary** if it will increase output and employment and **contractionary** if it will decrease output and employment. For example, in the AD-AS model learned in Chapter 2, increases in government spending or decreases in taxes will increase output and employment. So these are expansionary fiscal policies. A contractionary fiscal policy is one that decreases government spending or increases taxes.

We learned in Chapter 2 that increases in the money supply will increase output and employment. So an expansionary monetary policy seeks to increase the money supply. A contractionary monetary policy aims at decreasing the money supply.

If the authorities in a country want output and employment to be higher, they can use expansionary policies. If they want to bring down an escalating price level, they can use contractionary policies, such as tighter monetary policies, to reduce aggregate demand and get the price level to more acceptable levels. Because contractionary policies decrease output and employment, lower output and employment is typically the cost that a country has to pay to get its price level under control.

The term <u>easy</u> (or <u>loose</u>) is often used to refer to policies that are quite expansionary, and <u>tight</u> is used to refer to strongly contractionary policies.

When expansionary/contractionary policies are discussed, the focus is typically on policies that increase/decrease aggregate demand. This results from the way knowledge about the economy has developed. Until the 1930s, the dominant theory in economics stated that an economy if left to itself will self-correct to keep output and employment at appropriately high levels. However, prolonged periods of high unemployment and falling output that occurred in the 1930s were associated with the development of Keynesian economic theory, proposed by John Maynard Keynes, which showed how government action to increase aggregate demand can be used to increase output and employment, rather than just leave an economy floundering with high levels of unemployment and falling output. (These theories are discussed in Chapter 11.)

So the focus shifted to the use of expansionary policies that increase aggregate demand as ways of increasing output and employment and on contractionary policies to bring down aggregate demand if the objective was to restrain the price level. As a result, discussions of expansionary/contractionary policies tend to focus on policies that increase/decrease aggregate demand.

Of course, we know from the AD-AS model, that increases in AS are expansionary and will increase output and employment while contributing to bringing down the price level. Policies like the reduction of burdensome business taxes and excessive regulations on businesses can cause increases in AS, and so be expansionary while at the same time curbing price level growth. In spite of the traditional focus on AD in discussions of fiscal and monetary policies, we should not forget the role that AS can play.

Business cycles; recessions
Business cycles are the recurrent fluctuations in economic activity an economy experiences. There are times when economic activity rises, and at other times it falls, due to fluctuations in AD and/or AS. These expansions and contractions of economic activity vary in length and intensity, so they do not occur in any kind of regular pattern.

A popular view is that a **<u>recession</u>** has occurred if an economy's output falls over 2 consecutive calendar quarters. In many countries, this is how a recession is determined. However, in the United States, the Business Cycle Dating Committee of the National Bureau of Economic Research (NBER) determines when recessions have occurred. The NBER is a private, nonprofit, nonpartisan research organization whose views on the dating of recessions for the United States are accepted as "official" in the economics profession. The NBER defines a recession as a significant decline in economic activity spread across the economy and lasting more than a few months. In assessing economic activity, the NBER looks not just at output but also a variety of other variables in the economy such as employment, income earned by the population, level of sales in the economy, etc.

Recessions cause much concern and are widely viewed as needing special policy responses. But policy makers do not want every brief downward blip in economic activity to be viewed as a recession and to cause undue concern and inappropriate policy reactions. This is why, for a decline in economic activity to be viewed as a recession, it has to be sustained ("more than a few months", according to the NBER).

The Business Cycle Dating Committee of the NBER is only able to determine that a recession has started or ended months after these events have occurred because it takes a lot of time to get and to study the wide range of data necessary to determine if a recession has occurred according to the NBER standards. For example, the US economy was in decline from 2007, but it was not until Dec. 2008 that the NBER was able to conclude its study of the economic data and announce that a recession had started in the US in Dec. 2007.

FURTHER PRACTICAL APPLICATIONS OF THE AD-AS MODEL

Bush versus Greenspan on increasing the money supply

During his Presidency, George H.W. Bush (41st President of the US, 1988–92) wanted an expansionary monetary policy to increase aggregate demand, output and employment in the US (Figure 1). Rising employment increases a President's popularity, influence in getting policies implemented, and chances of being re-elected.

FIGURE 1

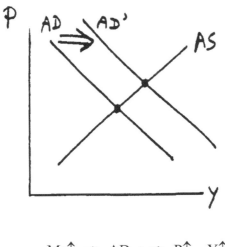

$$Ms\uparrow \Rightarrow AD\rightarrow \Rightarrow P\uparrow , Y\uparrow$$

Bush wanted $M_S\uparrow$ enough to ensure $Y\uparrow$ to cause much higher employment. Greenspan, however, wanted to constrain the growth in M_S to restrain AD and keep increases in P under tight control.
This was the conflict of opinion between Greenspan and Bush on what should be done with monetary policy.

But Alan Greenspan, Chairperson of the Federal Reserve (which is called the Fed for short), the US institution responsible for control of the US money supply, was obsessed with strictly containing increases in the price level. In the face of rising unemployment, he only reluctantly increased the US money supply because of his fear that this would stimulate aggregate demand and push up the US price level.

This caused a persistent conflict of opinion between Bush and Greenspan on what should have been done with the monetary policy. Under the rules of US government, the President does not have the authority to direct the Chairperson of the Federal Reserve on what to do with monetary policy. The President can only persuade. Bush had quite a time trying to persuade Greenspan!

Some economists believe that if Greenspan had been less hesitant in increasing the money supply, output would have been higher and less people would have been out of jobs in the US as the economy weakened during the George H. W. Bush Presidency. James Tobin, a distinguished economist (mentioned in Chapter 1), has noted that the Fed's action in increasing the money supply were "too little and too late." While Tobin was a prominent supporter of Bill Clinton (versus George Bush) in the 1992 Presidential Election, he noted that "George Bush had the misfortune of taking office" when an economic downturn was on its way largely because of a tight monetary policy by the Fed.[16] Bush faced the major problem of unemployment rising from 5.2 % in June 1990 to 6.3 % in Dec. 1990 and on to 7.4 % in Nov. 1992, when he lost his re-election bid to Bill Clinton.

Reducing the US budget deficit

A government runs a **budget deficit** when its expenditures exceed its revenue.[17] It has a **budget surplus** if revenue exceeds expenditures. If expenditures exceed revenue, and the government doesn't have funds from previous budget surpluses to finance its expenditures, it has to borrow to fund its spending. As it borrows more, it faces the challenge that interest payments on its debt could become so high that not enough is left to spend on other needed government programs.

In the US, Europe, and in many other countries, growing budget deficits have led to widespread concern over getting budget deficits down by reducing government purchases and/or raising tax rates to increase revenue. The AD-AS model tells us immediately that: decreasing government purchases => AD← => Y↓, which,

---

[16] Tobin, J. (1992). Voodoo Curse: Exorcising the legacy of Reaganomics. *Harvard International Review*, *14*(4), 10-13.

[17] Government expenditures consist of items such as government purchases of goods and services, payment of interest on its debt and government transfer payments, e.g., welfare payments given by government to help people cope with poverty. The roles of government purchases and of transfer payments in the AD-AS model were mentioned in Chapter 2.

ceteris paribus, will mean higher unemployment; increasing taxes => AD← and/or AS← => Y↓, which will mean higher unemployment.

Politicians who tell us they will reduce a country's budget deficit and increase employment at the same time may have plans for doing so that are ultimately in the best interests of the overall economy, but they should be asked to explain how they plan to overcome the loss of jobs that would result from decreasing government spending or increasing taxes to reduce the deficit.

Policies a government should pursue to get a country out of recession

From the AD-AS model, we know policies to get an economy out of recession must focus on increasing AD and/or increasing AS. Expansionary fiscal and monetary policies can increase output and employment. The government can also attempt to increase consumer and business optimism by giving the clear impression that it has policies to improve the economy and by fostering a feeling that better times are ahead. Policies to increase AS, such as eliminating government bureaucracy and overregulation that stifle business, not only help to increase output and employment but also help to curb the price level.

Cuts in government spending,[18] tightening the money supply, and tax increases, are among policies that risk worsening a recession—as you can readily verify using the AD-AS model. Politicians who advocate policies like these must tell us what they will do to offset the rise in unemployment these policies are likely to cause.

The Great Depression

If a recession is very severe, it is referred to as a depression. There is no definite rule for determining when a recession becomes a depression. In the US, of the severe recessions that have occurred, the worst of these was during 1929–1933. It has appropriately been called the **Great Depression**—output fell by about 30 % and the unemployment rate rose from around 3 % to about 25 % over 1929–1933.

---

[18] However, if a government is widely perceived to have been spending irresponsibly, its attempts to get government spending under control may increase confidence in its economic management and boost business confidence and this can have a positive effect on output and employment.

In the most recent period of economic difficulty in the US, associated with a recession that began in Dec. 2007, unemployment did not go above 10 %, and yet there has been so much concern over this economic downturn. So you can imagine how much more traumatic was the Great Depression. The price level also fell sharply during the Great Depression, suggesting that falling aggregate demand was a dominant cause.[19]

If you were alive then and were a policy maker with knowledge of the AD-AS model, as you noticed output had started falling and unemployment rising, you would have wanted fiscal and/or monetary policies and other policies to increase output and employment. Unfortunately, the prevailing economic ideas at the time encouraged the view that the economy should be left to work itself out of the slump. The knowledge embodied by the AD-AS model we have just learned was not prevalent then, so the policies this model suggests for increasing AD and employment were not vigorously pursued. Instead, the leaders at the time were reluctant to engage in government spending, and they allowed the money supply to fall sharply. These policy failures exacerbated the Great Depression.

This is a powerful illustration of the importance of knowledge and reminds us that ideas that seem relatively straightforward to us now have often only been arrived at after decades or centuries of evolution in knowledge.

EXERCISE

1. If you had the power to make economic policy in the US in the 1920s and 30s, as you noticed output falling from 1929, what policies would you have advocated?

---

[19] Among the factors that have been cited as responsible for the fall in AD in the Great Depression are: mismanagement of the US money supply that caused the money supply to drop sharply; declining business confidence as gloom about the economy developed; and political pressure in the US to exclude foreign goods that caused other countries to react by cutting back on the purchases of US goods and services, resulting in a decline in US exports.

2. Suppose Americans force their politicians to adopt legislation to exclude most foreign goods and services currently bought in the US.

  a. What will this do to AD and output in the countries whose goods and services are being excluded from the US?
  b. If output abroad were less, would foreigners be likely to have less income?
  c. If foreigners have less income, are they likely to buy less or more American products?
  d. What effect will this have on American exports and on AD in the US?
  e. Do you think politicians abroad would be forced to adopt measures like those adopted by the US?
  f. If such measures are adopted abroad, what will they do to AD for American goods and services?

3. A recession can be caused by increasing AS. True or false? Explain.

4. Cite two situations in which a government might want to use contractionary policies.

5. What is the policy dilemma a government could face when it increases aggregate demand to increase output and employment in the economy?

TERMS ASSOCIATED WITH BUSINESS CYCLES

When economic activity reaches its lowest level in a recession, that level is called a trough (point B in Figure 2). As economic activity increases, the economy (or the business cycle) is said to be in an expansion or upturn, as in the move from B to C in Figure 2. If the economy is in expansion after a recession, it is said to be in recovery. The level at which economic activity peaks, before decreasing again, is called a peak, e.g., points A and C. As economic activity declines, the economy (or business cycle) is in a contraction or downturn, as in the move from A to B, which may be a recession if it meets the definitional requirements. If one recession is quickly followed by another short one, before the economy resumes expansion, this is called a **double-dip recession**.

FIGURE 2

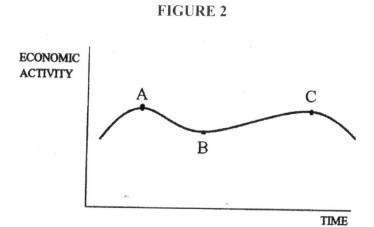

W, U, V, L shaped recoveries

If you draw a chart of the level of economic activity over time as an economy falls into recession and then recovers, what letter of the alphabet does the chart remind you of? If the economy experiences a double dip recession, the movement in the level of economic activity reminds one of the shape of a W. In the media, you will see this referred to as a **W shaped recovery**. In a **U shaped recovery**, the economy declines, remains at the trough level for a substantial time, and then rises again. In a **V shaped recovery**, economic activity declines, there is a brief recession, and the economy rapidly recovers. An **L shaped recovery** is one in which economic activity declines sharply and then meanders along at that lower level for a long period of time—so this is not really a recovery. Describing recoveries in terms of letters of the alphabet is popular in the news media because it is catchy, and suited to the quick sound bites the news media thrive on.

ANSWERS

1. Policies to increase AD and AS would have been appropriate, for example, increases in government spending, increases in the money supply, decreases in tax rates.

2.

    a. AD and output abroad will decline, *ceteris paribus*.

    b. Yes.

    c. Less. When peoples' incomes decline, *ceteris paribus*, they tend to buy less, including less imported goods.

    d. It will reduce American exports and AD for American products.

    e. Yes, retaliation is likely.

    f. This will decrease AD for American products.

3. False. Increasing AS causes increases in output. A recession, however, is associated with falling output.

4. Two situations in which a government might want to use contractionary policies: to curb price level growth; or if it needed to reduce its budget deficit, it could reduce government spending or raise taxes—which are contractionary policies.

5. The possible policy dilemma is that increasing aggregate demand increases not just output and employment but also the price level; if the price level gets too high, the rising cost of living will burden the people and make the government unpopular.

CHAPTER 4
MEASURING OUTPUT

INTRODUCTION

In Chapters 2 and 3 we referred to the economy's total output and to its price level as Y and P respectively without going into details on what these are. In this chapter, we go into details on what is meant by Y.

The accounts that total an economy's output are called <u>national income and product accounts</u> (or <u>GDP accounts</u>). The process of putting together these accounts is called <u>national income accounting</u> (or <u>GDP accounting</u>).

GROSS DOMESTIC PRODUCT

A country's **gross domestic product** is the value of all <u>final</u> goods and services produced in the country in a specified time period. Gross domestic product is called GDP for short.

Final goods and services are those not bought for use as inputs in the production of other goods and services. An <u>intermediate</u> good or service, however, is one that is bought for use as an input in the production of other goods or services. Bread that people purchase to eat is a final good. This bread is not viewed as being used in the production of other goods and services. Wheat used for making bread, however, is an intermediate good because it is used as an input in the production process. We count only final goods and services when finding GDP because if we counted intermediate goods and services we would be double counting—counting the intermediate goods twice. If $50 of flour were used to make $80 of bread, the value of output produced by this occurrence is $80, which is the value of the final good, the bread. If we counted the $50 wheat and the $80 bread, we would be counting the flour, the intermediate good, twice—once by itself and again when it is a part of the bread. To sum up, then, only the value of final goods and services are counted when GDP is calculated.[20] This avoids <u>double counting</u>—the counting of the same goods and services twice.

"Specified period of time" in the GDP definition means that the measure of GDP for a time period only takes account of goods and services produced in that time. For example, US GDP for 2012 will only consist of the value of final goods and services produced in 2012. Any goods or services produced before or after 2012 will not count in 2012's GDP. Similarly, GDP for the fourth quarter of 2012 will take account only of goods and services produced in the fourth quarter of 2012.

You only have to look around you to realize the diversity of the goods and services that comprise GDP—clothing, watches, pens, chairs, tables, paintings, cars, houses, washing machines, wine, haircuts, teaching, medical services, banking services…. It is the painful task of those who work in the government agency responsible for computing GDP (the Department of Commerce, in the US) to put together the value of all these goods and services and tell us the total.

To contribute to GDP an activity must result in the production of a good or service. If a barber gives me a haircut, this is a service and is a part of GDP.[21] If you give a gift of money to a friend, this payment does not represent the creation of a good or

---

[20] Suppose at the end of the time period for which GDP is being measured there are raw materials produced in that time and held in store by businesses for use as inputs in the production of goods and services to be made in the future. These raw materials are not counted as intermediate goods. The end of the time period for which GDP is being found finds them in a final state as raw materials rather than as having being used as inputs in the production of other goods and services. For practical purposes, for the time period for which GDP is being computed, they are like final goods and are counted as such. For example, let's say at the end of 2012 businesses have in store $2 million worth of flour produced in 2012, which they plan to use in making bread in 2013. This flour would be counted as if it were a final good in the GDP calculation for 2012 because the end of 2012, the period for which GDP is being found, finds it in a final state as flour.

[21] Because of the difficulty of getting records of all goods and services created, not everything that should be counted in GDP actually gets counted. If the barber mentioned above does not report as income the payment I give him, this payment does not get recorded as a part of GDP.

service and will not count as GDP. If I buy a car (that has already been counted in GDP) and then I resell it, the price of the car when I buy it or when I resell it does not count in GDP because the car is no longer a newly created good—it has already been counted in GDP. If I sell you shares of Coca-Cola Company, this is an exchange between us and the value of the shares does not represent the creation of any new good or service and will not count in GDP. However, if broker's fees had to be paid to facilitate this transaction, the broker's service counts in GDP.

The aim here is not at all to ensure you can determine how every item is treated in GDP accounting but to give you a sense of what is included in GDP. If you ever have to work in a government agency putting together a country's GDP, you will be given lengthy guidelines on the relevant practices. Now there is not much to be gained from worrying over how all kinds of complicated situations are dealt with; the details we have gone into here should be enough.

EXERCISE 1

1. Which of the following will count as part of 2012's GDP?
    i.   The value of a house constructed in 2012
    ii. The amount paid in Jan. 2012 for a car which was produced in 2008
    iii. The price of a ten year old house sold in Aug. 2012
    iv. The broker's fee for the selling of the house mentioned in iii

2. Which of the following will count in GDP?
    i.   The price of a used motor cycle you bought from your frolicking grandma
    ii. $5,000 robbed from a bank
    iii. The broker's fee paid to buy 1000 shares of Pepsi Corporation
    iv. Unemployment insurance received by a laid off worker

NOMINAL AND REAL GDP; ECONOMIC GROWTH; GDP PER CAPITA

Nominal GDP is the value of the output obtained by using the prices of the time period for which GDP is being found. US nominal GDP for 2012 is obtained by valuing the relevant US output using 2012 prices; US nominal GDP for 1999 is output valued using 1999 prices. Nominal GDP is often referred to as <u>GDP in current dollars</u>.

Real GDP, however, is the output in GDP valued with the prices of a time period called the <u>base period</u>. Real GDP for 2012 with base period 2005 is 2012 output valued using 2005 prices; real GDP for 1998 with base period 1985 is 1998 output valued using 1985 prices. These could be referred to as GDP in 2005 dollars and GDP in 1985 dollars respectively. <u>GDP in Year A dollars</u> means real GDP with base period Year A. GDP in 1982 dollars is real GDP with base period 1982. Real GDP is often referred to as <u>GDP in constant dollars</u>.

Real GDP for 2005 with base period 2005 is 2005 output valued using 2005 prices. So it will be the same as nominal GDP for 2005. Nominal GDP and real GDP for the base period are always the same. In the simple example in Table 1 (next page), nominal GDP and real GDP for 2007 with base period 2007 are each obtained using the 2007 price. Each equals the same, $16.50.[22]

Nominal GDP is found by taking the various amounts of output and multiplying each amount by the relevant price in the time period for which nominal GDP is being found. The quantity of output and/or the prices used for valuing the output could change from one time period to another. If a country's nominal GDP rises from one year to another, from this information alone we cannot conclude that the country's output has increased. Output could even have declined and yet nominal GDP could have risen if the prices used for valuing the output increased by enough to cause a rise in output multiplied by prices. In Table 1, output fell in 2006 from

---

[22] Here the purpose is to give you an understanding of concepts without getting into complications that most of us are unlikely to ever need. You can see the appendix at the end of this chapter **for more complex notions involved in calculating real GDP**, such as <u>chained dollars</u>.

the 2005 level. Yet nominal GDP was $12 in 2006 compared to $10 in 2005 all because the price ($1.50) in 2006 was much higher than the price ($1) in 2005.

However, for real GDP, the output of different time periods are all valued using constant prices, those of a base period. In Table 1, the output of each year is valued in terms of the 2007 price of $1.10. So if real GDP rises/falls it must be because output has risen/fallen. In Table 1, real GDP declined in 2006 because output (see the data under QUANTITY in the table) fell. Real GDP rose in each year after 2006 because output increased each year.

TABLE 1
A Simple Example of Nominal and Real GDP Calculations
(for a mythical economy producing only oranges!)

YEAR	QUANTITY	PRICE ($)	NOMINAL GDP ($)	REAL GDP (base 2007)
2005	10	1	10 X 1 = 10	10 X 1.1 = 11
2006	8	1.50	8 X 1.5 = 12	8 X 1.1 = 8.80
2007	15	1.10	15 X 1.1 = 16.50	15 X 1.1 = 16.50
2008	20	2	20 X 2 = 40	20 X 1.1 = 22
2009	22	2.20	22 X 2.2 = 48.40	22 X 1.1 = 24.20

Economic growth

Economic growth is measured by the growth in real GDP. If real GDP declines from one time to another, economic growth is negative. The **economic growth rate** is the growth of real GDP expressed as a percentage. For the data in Table 1, the economic growth rate from 2007 to 2008 is {(22 – 16.50)/16.50} x 100 = 33.3 %. The growth rate from 2005 to 2006 is {(8.8 – 11)/11} x 100 = –20 %. It is negative because output in 2006 was less than in 2005. Please see the appendix at the end of this chapter **for more complicated notions involved in calculating economic growth.**

GDP per capita

The GDP of a country divided by the country's population is called **GDP per capita**. This figure gives the average per person of the value of final goods and services produced in that country in a specified time period. US nominal GDP for

2011 was $15,094 billion; its population was about 311.946 million. Its <u>nominal GDP per capita</u> for 2011 was $15094 billion/311.946 million = $48,387. US real GDP for 2011 was $13,315 billion.[23] So US <u>real GDP per capita</u> for 2011 was $13315 billion/311.946 million = $42,684.

TABLE 2
Top fifteen countries in the world in nominal GDP per capita, 2011, in International Monetary Fund (IMF) database

	Country	Nominal GDP per capita (US $)
1	Luxembourg	113,533
2	Qatar	98,329
3	Norway	97,255
4	Switzerland	81,161
5	United Arab Emirates	67,008
6	Australia	65,477
7	Denmark	59,928
8	Sweden	56,956
9	Canada	50,436
10	Netherlands	50,355
11	Austria	49,809
12	Finland	49,350
13	Singapore	49,271
14	United States	48,387
15	Kuwait	47,982

Source: IMF, *World Economic Outlook*, April 2012

OBSERVATIONS ON GDP ACCOUNTING

Not every good or service created in the economy has a money payment associated with it. For example, parents do not receive a monetary payment for their service

---

[23] These data get revised over time as the agencies that put them together seek to correct inaccuracies in the data collection and calculation processes. So if you check data sources later on, you may see US GDP numbers for 2011, etc. somewhat different from those cited here.

of raising children. For some goods and services that do not have money payments associated with them, GDP accountants have found ways of estimating their value. Others, however, which constitute important economic activities, continue to be excluded from GDP measurement largely because of the difficulties of estimating their value.[24]

For owner-occupied housing, the GDP accountants in the US estimate the rent the owners would pay if, instead of owning the homes they lived in, they were renting the homes. This estimated rent is included in GDP as payment for the service of housing.[25] It is called <u>imputed rent</u>. (Imputed means attributed.)

When people produce food for their own consumption, e.g., growing crops that they consume, they are said to be engaged in <u>subsistence</u> activities. Because of the difficulties of becoming aware of these activities, GDP accountants face a challenge incorporating subsistence output into GDP.

Parents who remain at home to take care of home-making chores such as raising children do not receive a monetary payment for this and this activity is not counted in GDP. However, if people work as paid domestics, this work is counted in GDP because the definite money payment made for it makes it easy to value it for inclusion in GDP.

Illegal activities very often have money payments associated with them that do not get officially recorded and are not included in the GDP accounts. Illegal economic activities are said to constitute the <u>underground economy</u>, or the <u>second</u> or <u>parallel economy</u>. Among these activities are the taking of cash payments to avoid paying taxes on them and the underreporting of tips.

---

[24] If you are interested in the details of GDP accounting methods, check with the organization that computes GDP for the country of your interest to get information on the latest practices.

[25] When a new house is built, the value of the house is counted in GDP. After this, the service of housing provided by the house is counted as part of the output produced in each time period GDP is measured.

International comparisons of GDP

If we are told Switzerland's real GDP per capita is $67,000 and Barbados's is $2,000, does this mean the "standard of living" in Switzerland is nearly thirty four times that in Barbados? Definitely not!

GDP per capita tells us nothing about the distribution of income in a country. If you have done statistics you know that an average tells nothing about the relative size of the values for which the average is computed. Three persons with incomes of $100,000, $10,000 and $1,000, have an average income of $37,000. But three persons with income of $40,000, $35,000 and $36,000 also have an average income of $37,000. The first three persons have a much more unequal distribution of income than the second three. Yet both groups have the same average income.

A GDP figure offers no details on the types of goods and services that constitute GDP. Two countries that have the same GDP per capita could have very different goods and services being produced. If one country focuses on goods and services relating to education, health, and the environment, what it produces is likely to be quite different from a country focused on military goods.

Further, each country's GDP per capita has to be expressed in the same currency (usually the US $) to facilitate comparison. An exchange rate—how much of one currency has to be paid for another—has to be used to get each country's GDP into the currency unit in which the comparison is being done. This poses a major problem because exchange rates fluctuate a great deal. A foreign country's GDP expressed in US dollars can change sharply not because that country's output has changed but merely because the exchange rate of its currency for the US dollar is changing. In Chapter 10, we discuss a method of calculating GDP that tries to overcome this problem.

The cost of living also differs sharply between countries. In some countries, $3 US per day could ensure you are well fed; in the US, it would be very challenging to eat enough with that. This makes it very difficult to reach conclusions about the relative standards of living between countries by comparing their GDP per capita figures.

These cautions should be kept in mind when one is tempted to make inferences about the quality of life in a country on the basis of its GDP figure.

THREE APPROACHES TO MEASURING GDP

We have talked about GDP in terms of the value of final goods and services produced, i.e., what final users would spend to buy what is produced. This approach to measuring GDP is call the <u>expenditures approach</u>—GDP in terms of how much would have to be spent to purchase the final goods and services produced.

The value of a firm's output minus the intermediate goods it purchased from other firms is called the firm's <u>value added</u>. A country's GDP can be obtained by summing the value added for all the productive activities that occur. This approach to measuring GDP is called the <u>value added approach</u>. To illustrate this, let's consider a simple example (Table 3) in which a farmer just tills the soil and produces $30 of wheat. He sells this to a miller, who labors on it and turns it into $50 of flour. She sells this to a baker, who labors on it and produces $80 of bread, which is sold to people for them to eat.

From the expenditures approach, the value of GDP in this case would be $80—the value of the final good produced. The value added by the farmer, the miller and the baker are $30, $20 and $30 respectively. The total value added is therefore $80, which is the same as the value of the final good.

TABLE 3
A very simple example of the three approaches to measuring GDP

	Intermediate inputs used	Value of product produced and sold	Value added	Income
Farmer	0	30	30	30
Miller	30	50	20	20
Baker	50	80	30	30

Another approach to measuring GDP, called the <u>income approach</u>, gives what is called <u>Gross Domestic Income, GDI.</u> This is a sum of all the income generated in the process of producing GDP. The last column of Table 3 shows the income each of the three producers in our very simple economy earns. The total income is $80.

The aim here is just to give you a sense of what each approach is about. So it is not necessary to go into the statistical challenges of measuring GDP by each of these three approaches.

GROSS DOMESTIC PRODUCT versus GROSS NATIONAL PRODUCT

Earlier, gross domestic product was defined as the value of all final goods and services produced in a country in a specified time period. As long as a final good or service is produced in a country, it is counted as part of that country's GDP regardless of which country owns the labor and property that produced the good or service.

<u>Gross national product (GNP)</u>, however, is the value of all final goods and services produced by a country's labor and property in a specified time period regardless of whether or not the labor and property is being used in the country itself or is operating abroad.[26] If there is a Japanese owned firm operating in the US that employs both Japanese and US labor, the output due to the Japanese labor (as measured by the wages paid to that labor) would not count as part of US GNP, but would count as part of Japan's GNP. Output due to an American working at J. P. Morgan in Brazil counts as part of US GNP but not as part of US GDP. This person's output would, of course, count as part of Brazil's GDP because it is produced within Brazil.

If the output due to US labor and property in use in the US equals A, the output due to US labor and property in use abroad equals B, and the output due to foreign-

---

[26] The US Department of Commerce October 2009 publication *Concepts and Methods of the US National Income and Product Accounts* gives details on relationships between GDP, GNP, etc., discussed here and in the pages ahead.

owned labor and property in the US equals C, then US GDP = A + C and US GNP = A + B (Figure 1).

Net income payments from abroad, which we will refer to for short as <u>net income payments,</u> equal the value of output attributable to a country's labor and property in use abroad minus the value of output attributable to foreign-owned labor and property in the country. It equals B minus C for the US in the example just cited.

GDP = A + C, and net income payments = B – C. So GDP + net income payments = A + C + B – C = A + B = GNP.

In summary, **GDP plus net income payments equals GNP.**

FIGURE 1

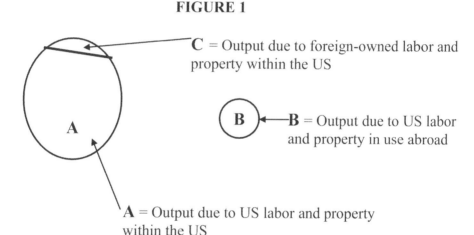

C = Output due to foreign-owned labor and property within the US

B = Output due to US labor and property in use abroad

A = Output due to US labor and property within the US

US GDP = A + C
US GNP = A + B

EXERCISE 2

1. Say whether each of the following statements is true or false and offer the argument(s) to justify your response.
   a. A country's GNP measures the total value of all final goods and services produced in that country in a specified time period.

   b. While GNP is defined as the value of all the final goods and services attributable to a country's labor and property in a specified period of time, because of the difficulties of accurately measuring this value some of the goods and services that should be counted in GNP may not get counted.

2. For 2011, the output due to Ruritania's labor and property operating in Ruritania = $400 m, the output of Ruritania's labor and property abroad = $100 m, and the output of foreign labor and property in Ruritania = $50 m. What were Ruritania's net income payments, GDP and GNP in 2011?

NATIONAL INCOME; PERSONAL DISPOSABLE INCOME; SAVING RATE

As you read this section, do not be too concerned with memorizing the relationships stated. The agencies that have to compute these relationships have to worry about exactly what they are. Instead, grasp the reasoning that takes us from a measure of GDP to measures such as **personal disposable income** and the **personal saving rate**, which are defined toward the end of this section. The aim is that when you hear these terms mentioned in the news, you will have a good sense of their meaning.

In the previous section, we saw that:

$$GNP = GDP + \text{net income payments}$$

In the process of production, machinery and factories get worn down. Depreciation (also called capital depreciation, or the capital consumption allowance) is a measure of the amount of this wear and tear that occurs in the course of producing the GNP. When it is subtracted from GNP, we get net national product (NNP):

$$NNP = GNP - \text{depreciation}$$

For some items, part of what is paid for them goes to the government as a tax. These taxes are called indirect taxes because they are not levied directly on businesses themselves but on the items produced by the businesses. For example, if when you purchase items you have to pay an 8 % tax in addition to the price, this tax (usually called a <u>sales tax</u>) is an indirect tax. The value of NNP minus the total amount of indirect taxes paid to the government equals the amount received (called <u>national income, NI for short</u>) by those who own the labor and property that produce the GNP:

$$NI = NNP - \text{indirect taxes}^{27}$$

National income consists of items such as the wages and profits people and businesses in the economy receive as output is produced. To get the amount of income people actually have available for spending, called <u>personal disposable income</u>, various amounts must be added to, or subtracted from, national income. Taxes such as personal and corporate income taxes and Social Security taxes (all of which we will refer to as income taxes) have to be subtracted because these reduce the amount of national income actually available for people to spend. Also, some profits are not paid out to the owners of the corporations but are retained by the corporations to meet future financial needs. So this amount, called <u>retained corporate profits</u>, also has to be subtracted from national income to get personal disposable income. Transfers such as pensions and unemployment compensation have to be added to national income to get personal disposable income because these increase the amount people have for spending. Personal disposable income (PDI) therefore equals national income minus income taxes minus retained corporate profits plus transfers:

$$PDI = NI - \text{income taxes} - \text{retained corporate profits} + \text{transfers.}^{28}$$

---

[27] Sometimes governments pay subsidies. A <u>subsidy</u> to the producer of a good or service is a payment from the government in addition to the price the producer receives from the sale of the good. If you produce a good which receives a $0.10 subsidy and which sells for $1, you will actually be getting $1.10 for it—$1 from the purchaser and $.10 from the government. Subsidies are often paid by governments to ensure producers make adequate profits or to keep the price to consumers low. If there are subsidies, then NI = NNP − indirect taxes + subsidies. The amount of indirect taxes minus subsidies is called <u>net indirect taxes</u>.

[28] Economics textbooks differ in their specification of what is subtracted from or added to NI to get PDI. Categories like taxes and transfers cover a variety of items and can be separated in various ways. For example, the distinction can be made

Personal disposable income is called PDI for short and sometimes also referred to as <u>disposable personal income</u> or <u>disposable income</u>.

Personal disposable income is income people have available for them to use as they wish. It can be spent on consumption or it can be saved[29]:

$$PDI = Consumption + Personal\ Saving$$

The term <u>personal saving</u> is the amount saved by individuals, i.e., PDI minus consumption. The <u>personal saving rate</u> is the percentage of PDI saved:

$$Personal\ saving\ rate\ (as\ a\ \%) = \frac{Amount\ of\ PDI\ saved}{PDI}\ X\ 100$$

GDP = DOMESTIC ABSORPTION + NET EXPORTS

In Chapter 2, we defined consumption, investment, government purchases, imports and exports. Here we will refer to these as C, I, G, Z, and X. Total spending on goods and services by the households, businesses and government of a country will be C + I + G. This total C + I + G is called <u>domestic absorption</u>. It measures the total purchases of goods and services by consumers, businesses and government in our economy, which is the total amount of goods and services "absorbed" by all the entities of our economy.

Parts of C, I and G will be goods and services bought from foreign countries. For example, American spending on consumption, C, includes spending on American produced goods and services and also on many items produced abroad—Chinese silk, English hats, French shoes, Italian sweaters, Japanese cars.... Similarly,

---

between personal taxes and corporate taxes. Here our purpose is to provide concepts without getting bogged down in unnecessary details.

[29] Other uses to which PDI is put are ignored here because they constitute very small amounts of PDI. For example, a small amount of PDI is sent abroad as gifts to foreigners.

businesses and government also buy some foreign produced items. The total amount of our GDP utilized by our residents is therefore C + I + G – Z.

Part of our GDP goes to foreigners as exports, X. So if we add X to C + I + G – Z, we get: GDP = C + I + G – Z + X. The total of X – Z is called <u>net exports</u>,[30] which we shall represent here as NX. So:

$$GDP = C + I + G + NX = domestic\ absorption + net\ exports[31]$$

EXERCISE 3

1. Use the following data to find NNP, NI, PDI and the personal saving rate:

	$ million
Capital consumption allowance	40
GNP	850
Indirect taxes	10
Income taxes (income, Social Security etc.)	100
Transfers	50
Retained corporate profits	50
Personal saving	70

---

[30] For example, if our imports = $20 million but our exports = $50 million, net exports = $30 million. Net exports will be negative if imports exceed exports, implying we are buying more goods and services from foreign countries than we are selling to them.

[31] In other sources, you may see this formula written as GNP = C + I + G + NX because such sources ignore the difference between GNP and GDP. You, however, should only ignore this difference if you have suitable justification for doing so. As was explained earlier in this chapter, as long as net income payments from abroad do not equal zero, the value of GNP and GDP will differ.

2. Use the following data to find NX, G, GNP and NNP:

	$ million
GDP	400
C	200
I	100
Z	20
X	10
Depreciation	5
Net income payments from abroad	10

SEASONAL ADJUSTMENT

When you look at GDP and other economic data, you will often see tables that are titled as "**seasonally adjusted**". To get a sense of what is seasonal adjustment, consider an example. Suppose we are measuring retail sales, which is the sales made by department stores, auto dealers, restaurants, and so on. We know that the stronger is the economy, the more people are likely to shop, as they feel financially better off and more optimistic about their prospects. We also know that every year in the December holiday season in the United States these sales are likely to increase as people make purchases for the holiday celebrations. So if we look at December retail sales data and see that sales have increased, how much of this increase is due to just the holiday shopping spree, and how much of it is due to changes in the strength of the economy?

From previous years' data the statisticians can make an estimate of how much of the increased sales in December is due to the holiday shopping spree. If they subtract this amount from the December sales, they get a better estimate of how much of the retail sales is due to the condition of the economy.

When this adjustment is made, the data are said to be seasonally adjusted. So when you look at seasonally adjusted retail sales data and you see an increase in December sales, if the seasonal adjustment was done accurately, you don't have to wonder if the increase in sales was due to just the December shopping spree. You can be sure that the shopping spree's influence on the data has been removed to the extent that is possible given the current state of statistical knowledge.

Seasonally adjusted data seek to eliminate the impact of events that recur every year due to holiday seasons, weather, schools closing for holidays, auto plants closing down for annual retooling, etc. This adjustment makes it easier to determine how much of the change in data is due to changes in underlying economic conditions.

As is typical with statistical procedures, seasonal adjustment is not a perfect process. There is no way of knowing with absolute precision what the amounts used in making seasonal adjustments should be. The statisticians can only make estimates of what these adjustments should be, and they do it based on past experiences with data. To the extent that seasonal occurrences do not quite fit past patterns, seasonal adjusted data will be reduced in accuracy.

In countries where statistical data gathering and assessment capabilities are not well developed, seasonally adjusted data will not be available.

EXERCISE 4

1. Which of the following are likely to be taken account of when seasonal adjustments are made in the compilation of economic data?
    a. The increase in shopping that consumers engage in prior to and during holiday seasons
    b. A blizzard that damages crops
    c. A labor strike that causes production to shut down in the auto industry
    d. The changes in the size of the workforce that result from students being off school and available to work in the summer and then leaving the workforce to go back to school when the summer ends
    e. The annual closure of auto plants as they retool assembly lines for the next year's models

2. Do economic fluctuations due to seasonal occurrences affect an economy's underlying strength/weakness?

UNDERSTANDING GROWTH RATES AND ANNUALIZATION

The term **% change on a year ago** means the amount at a certain time minus the amount a year ago and expressed as a percentage. If a country's GDP was $10.1 billion at the end of Q4 (the fourth quarter) of 2011, and was $10 billion at the end of Q4 of 2010, then growth in Q4 2011 on a year ago would be

$$\frac{10.1 - 10}{10} \text{ X } 100 \% = 1 \%$$

The media has traditionally cited GDP growth rates for China as % change on a year ago. The data for Q2 2011 was 9.6 %. This means that from the end of Q2 2010 to the end of Q2 2011, GDP in China grew by 9.6 %. (The authorities that issue these data usually revise them. So if later on you check the figure for Q2 2011 and see it is different from what is stated here, this just means it has been updated.)

When we discussed seasonal adjustment earlier, we mentioned that in countries where statistical data gathering and assessment capabilities are not well developed, seasonally adjusted data would not be available. In these countries, growth rates will typically be expressed as % change on a year ago, e.g., Q3 2012 compared to Q3 2011. This way, a period in one year is compared to a similar period a year earlier, ensuring that a quarter in which there is a seasonal occurrence will be compared to a quarter a year earlier in which there was the same kind of seasonal occurrence. This comparison cancels out the effect of the seasonal occurrence and gives information on the impact of underlying economic conditions.

Percentage change on a previous quarter expressed at an annual rate means the growth in a quarter is compared to the previous quarter **and expressed as if it continued for four quarters, i.e., a whole year**. Let's use some simple numbers to see what this means. If an amount is 100 at the end of Q4 2009 and 110 at the end of Q1 2010, this is a 10 % growth in the Q1 2010. To express this at an annual rate, we calculate what would be the percent increase over the four quarters from the end of 2009 if growth continued at 10 % for every one of those quarters. Table 4 shows that if this 10 % growth continued through four quarters, the amount would be 146.41. Since the amount started with at the end of 2009 was 100, the growth over four quarters would be 46.41 %.

The percent growth for Q1 2010 expressed at an annual rate would be 46.41 %. So, to reiterate, the amount at the end of Q1 2010 is 10 % higher compared to what it was at the end of the previous quarter. But the growth in Q1 2010 **expressed at an annual rate** is the percent growth that would result if this 10 % growth continued for four quarters, as illustrated in Table 4.[32]

TABLE 4
Amount at end of 2010 if 10 % growth continued
through every quarter of 2010

Amount at end of Q1 2010	110
Amount at end of Q2 2010	110 + 10 % of 110 = 110 + 11 = 121
Amount at end of Q3 2010	121 + 10 % of 121 = 121 + 12.1 = 133.1
Amount at end of Q4 2010	133.1 + 10 % of 133.1 = 133.1 + 13.31 = 146.41
Amount change over the 4 quarters	46.41

A common mistake is to think that the growth for Q1 2010 expressed at an annual rate should be 4 times 10 %. This is incorrect because it is not only the amount that

---

[32] It's like if you put $100 in a bank account that is earning 10 % interest per quarter compounded. This means that after the first quarter you will be earning interest not just on the $100 but on the interest in previous quarter(s). For those of you familiar with it, the compound growth rate formula for expressing quarterly growth at an annual rate is $r = [(GDP_q/GDP_{q-1})^4 - 1] \times 100$, where r is the % change expressed at an annual rate, GDP_q is the amount of GDP in the quarter for which the growth rate is being annualized, and GDP_{q-1} is the amount of GDP in the previous quarter. So if GDP grows from 100 at the end of one quarter to 110 at the end of the next quarter, the % growth of GDP at an annual rate for the latter quarter is $[(110/100)^4 - 1] \times 100 = 46.41$ %.

Q1 2010 started with that is growing at 10 %. The increment due to growth in each quarter is also growing at 10 % in subsequent quarters. In the example depicted in Table 4, in the second quarter it is 110 (not just 100) growing at 10 %; during the third quarter it is 121 (not just 100) growing at 10 %, and so on.

The US authorities give quarterly GDP growth rates as percent change from the previous quarter expressed at an annual rate. As noted earlier, GDP growth rates for China are typically cited as percent change from the year ago period. When you come across GDP growth rates for countries, if you want to compare them, you have to make sure they are being measured in the same way, e.g., percent change from a year ago, or percent change from the previous quarter expressed at an annual rate.

When data is expressed at an annual rate it is said to be **annualized**. We have just seen how to annualize a growth rate.

If just an amount, not a growth rate, is to be annualized, this means it is measured for a period that is less than a year and then calculated for what it would be for a single year. A person's salary is a common example. If you are earning $4,000 per month, this is $48,000 at an annual level. Multiply the monthly level by 12 to get the annual level. If a quarterly level is to be expressed at an annual level, just multiply it by 4 to get the annual level.

If you check US Department of Commerce data for the amount of US GDP, you will see US quarterly GDP data annualized. For example, Q2 2011 real GDP data is listed at a $13260.5 billion **annual rate**. This means the amount of real GDP produced in Q2 2011 was a quarter of $13260.5 billion and this amount when annualized (multiplied by 4) gives $13260.5 billion.

Notice how easy it is to annualize an amount that is not a growth rate. If it is an amount for a quarter, you simply multiply it by 4. (If it is an amount for a month, you multiply it by 12.) If a growth rate is to be annualized, however, **compounding has to be done**, and you cannot simply multiply a quarterly growth rate by 4 to express it at an annual growth rate—as was demonstrated in the discussion on "percentage change on a previous quarter expressed at an annual rate".

EXERCISE 5

1. As we have said, data for China's GDP growth is typically cited as % change on a year ago. Suppose the data for Q1 2011 is 9.7 %. Does this tell you by how much GDP grew from the end of Q4 2010 to the end of Q1 2011?

2. In *The Economist* magazine, in the table "Output, prices and jobs", the following data is given for the US GDP for Q2 2011:

% change on a year ago	% change on previous quarter, annual rate
1.5	1.0

Explain what these two numbers mean.

3. If output in an economy in Q1 2012 is valued at $3 billion, what is it expressed at an annual rate?

4. An economy grew at 2 % in Q3 2012 when compared to Q2 2012. Which one of the following is the economy's growth rate for Q3 2012 compared to the previous quarter expressed at an annual rate?
   a. 2 %
   b. 8 %
   c. Less than 8 %
   d. More than 8 %

ANSWERS

EXERCISE 1

1. i, iv

2. iii

EXERCISE 2

1. a. False—this is the definition of GDP, not GNP.
   b. True. This statement contains an accurate definition of GNP and an accurate statement of why some goods and services may not get counted in GNP.

2. Net income payments = 100 – 50 = $50 m.
   GDP = 400 + 50 = $450 m.
   GNP = 400 + 100 = $500 m.

EXERCISE 3

1. NNP = GNP – capital consumption allowance = 850 – 40 = 810

   NI = NNP – indirect taxes = 810 – 10 = 800

   PDI = NI – income taxes – retained corporate profits + transfers = 800 – 100 – 50 + 50 = 700

   Personal saving rate (%) = [Personal saving / PDI] X 100 = 70/700 X 100 = 10

2. NX = X – Z = 10 – 20 = –10.

   GDP = C + I + G + NX, so G = GDP – C – I – NX = 400 – 200 – 100 – (–10) = 110.

   GNP = GDP + Net factor income from abroad = 400 + 10 = 410.

   NNP = GNP – Depreciation = 410 – 5 = 405

EXERCISE 4

1. a, d, and e are events that occur every year and will be taken account of if seasonal adjustments are made to economic data.

2. Seasonal occurrences do not affect an economy's underlying strength or weakness.

EXERCISE 5

1. No, it does not—this data alone gives us no information on how GDP grew from the end of Q4 2010 to the end of Q1 2011. It tells us how much GDP grew from the end of Q1 2010 to the end of Q1 2011.

2. The % change on a year ago of 1.5 for Q2 2011 means that in the year preceding the end of Q2 2011, i.e., from the end of Q2 2010 to the end of Q2 2011, GDP in the US grew by 1.5 %.

   The % change on previous quarter, annual rate, of 1.0 for Q2 2011 means that from the end of Q1 2011 to the end of Q2 2011 GDP growth occurred, which, when expressed at an annual rate, amounted to 1.0 %. It does not mean that the actual amount of GDP by which GDP grew in Q2 2011 was 1.0 % but only that amount by which GDP grew **when expressed at an annual rate** was 1.0 %.

3. To get the annual rate for this quarterly amount simply multiply by 4, which gives $12 billion. (As this amount is not a growth rate, no compounding is involved, so multiplying by 4 is all that is necessary to get the annual rate.)

4. d—as the discussion of percentage change on a previous quarter expressed at an annual rate illustrated.

APPENDIX
CALCULATING ECONOMIC GROWTH; CHAINED DOLLARS

Here are details on a more sophisticated method of measuring real GDP than the simple notion of using a base year's prices that was described in this chapter. The notion of **chained dollars** will be introduced.

- Prices and quantities in a GDP computation change from one year to another. For example, some laptop prices have fallen substantially from last year, but dairy and vegetable prices have increased. The measure we get for real GDP therefore varies depending on which year we are using as a base year.

- Let's say we are calculating economic growth (real GDP growth) from Year 1 to Year 2. First we use Year 1 as a base, so we use Year 1's prices to calculate real GDP for Year 1 and Year 2, and we then find economic growth from Year 1 to Year 2 by calculating the percentage change in real GDP from Year 1 to Year 2. (When we use Year 1's prices as base, we are calculating what is called a Laspeyres index.)

- Next we use Year 2 as a base, so we use Year 2's prices to calculate real GDP for Year 1 and for Year 2, and we then find economic growth from Year 1 to Year 2 by calculating the percentage change in real GDP from Year 1 to Year 2. (When we use Year 2's prices as base, we are calculating what is called a Paasche index.)

- The economic growth rates we get from these two calculations would be different because of the changes in prices and quantities from one year to the next.

- The GDP statisticians have concluded that the best way to deal with this problem is to take these two growth rates, multiply them and then take their square root (what is called the geometric mean of these two numbers). This then becomes the growth rate from Year 1 to Year 2, and with this calculation we don't have to worry that we will get a different growth rate depending on whether we use Year 1 or Year 2 as a base. (This geometric mean of the Laspeyres and Paasche indexes is called a Fisher index.)

- The Bureau of Economic Analysis (BEA) of the US Department of Commerce, which is responsible for compiling GDP statistics for the US, began using the Fisher Index to calculate real GDP and economic growth in 1996. This was aimed at overcoming the problem that different real GDP numbers and growth rates can result if one uses Laspeyres versus Paasche indexes.

- If we use the Fisher Index to find growth from Year 2 to Year 3, Year 2 now becomes the first year in our calculation, the way Year 1 was when we were finding growth from Year 1 to Year 2. For the growth from Year 3 to Year 4, Year 3 becomes the first year in our calculations. The last year in a pair of years, becomes the first year in the next pair of years. So these years are **linked as in a chain** in these GDP and economic growth calculations.

- If we are using Year 1 as our base year in finding real GDP for a set of years, we know that real GDP in Year 1 equals nominal GDP in Year 1 (as we learned in this chapter). Let's say we get $1000 for this real GDP, using a simple number to help to illustrate key ideas. If we calculate the Fisher index for economic growth from Year 1 to Year 2, and find this is 3 %, then real GDP in Year 2 would be $1000 plus 3 % of $1000, which equals $1030. These $1030 are called <u>chained Year 1 dollars</u> because they are determined using the chained-type index described in the previous bullet and with Year 1 as the starting year, which is usually referred to as the <u>reference</u> year. Currently, US real GDP is expressed in terms of <u>chained 2005 dollars</u> by the BEA of the US Department of Commerce.

- Most of us will never need these details. For those who require more technical insight, however, the BEA website offers information.

CHAPTER 5
MEASURING THE PRICE LEVEL AND INFLATION

INTRODUCTION

In Chapters 2 and 3, we referred to the economy's total output and to its price level as Y and P respectively without going into details on what these are. In Chapter 4, we got details on what is meant by Y. Now we get more insights into what is meant by P.

MEASURES OF THE PRICE LEVEL

Three popular measures of the price level are the **consumer price index (CPI)**, **the producer price index (PPI)**, and the **GDP deflator**. In the US, the Bureau of Labor Statistics is responsible for obtaining the CPI and the PPI and the Department of Commerce obtains the GDP deflator.

Consumer Price Index (CPI)

There are various measures of the CPI in the US. We will focus mainly on the one that gets the most coverage in the news and will refer to it simply as the CPI. It measures the price level of a combination (basket) of goods and services purchased by the "typical" urban consumer. "Typical" is put in quotes because the basket of goods and services used to compute the CPI is not one purchased by a real consumer. It is an estimate of what a hypothetical consumer, with buying habits averaging those of urban consumers, would purchase.

Among the goods and services included are food and beverages, apparel, housing, transportation, entertainment, education, communication, and medical care. The combination of these currently (2012) in the US CPI basket is based on surveys of spending patterns in 2007-2008. After a number of years, the basket is re-estimated to take account of changes in spending patterns that have occurred. This fixed basket of goods and services is priced every month in the US[33] to get an indication of how the cost of living for the typical urban consumer is changing. The price of this fixed basket is then expressed as an index to make it convenient to interpret changes in the price level.

HOW TO CREATE AN INDEX

Here is how a simple index can be obtained for a set of numbers: Take one of the numbers, give it a value of 100 and then express all the other numbers in terms of this 100. For example, suppose the cost of the CPI basket over three years is: 2005—$20000, 2006—$25000, 2007—$28000. Let us call the 2005 figure 100. Then the 2006 figure will have to be 100 multiplied by (25000/20000) = 125; and the 2007 figure will be 100 multiplied by (28000/20000) = 140.

The time period with the value we expressed as 100 is called the <u>base period</u> (because all the other values are then based on the 100). The convenience of having the numbers expressed this way is that we can readily discern by what percentage they have changed since the base period. 2006's figure of 125 immediately tells us the CPI in 2006 rose 25 % from 2005. The 140 figure immediately tells us that the 2007 figure rose 40 % from the 2005 level. Tables stating indexes always say what is the base period.

To determine the composition of the market basket used for the CPI, the US Bureau of Labor Statistics (BLS) conducts an extensive Consumer Expenditure Survey. During each of 2007 and 2008, the US Bureau of Labor Statistics collected

---

[33] In some countries, these statistics are calculated less often because of factors like lack of resources, ineptitude, unconcern, or an attempt to suppress information that may show a rapidly rising cost of living and embarrass a government.

information from 28,000 weekly diaries kept by families selected by the BLS from around the USA to list their purchases. The BLS also conducted 60,000 quarterly interviews. The information gleaned from this research determined the composition and weighting of the current CPI basket.

Every month, BLS data collectors call or visit thousands of retail stores, service establishments, rental units, doctors' offices, etc. throughout the United States, to record the prices of about 80,000 items, representing a scientific sample of the prices paid by consumers. This data goes into calculating the CPI each month.

These details on how the market basket for the CPI and the monthly CPI are determined make us aware of the complexity of compiling price indexes for a country.

HARMONIZED INDEX OF CONSUMER PRICES (HICP)

The **harmonized index of consumer prices (HICP)** is the most widely used consumer price index in the European Union (EU). It is called "harmonized" because a consistent methodology for calculating it is used across these countries. Eurostat, the statistical agency of the EU, and the member states' statistical agencies are responsible for the compilation of the HICP.

The term Eurozone refers to the EU countries that have the euro as their currency and the European Central Bank as responsible for their monetary policy. To get the HICP for the Eurozone as a whole, a weighted average of the euro area member countries' HICPs is calculated. The weights used are the countries' share of household consumption expenditure in the euro area total. The weights are determined from national accounts data and are updated annually.

Chained CPI

The CPI we have discussed so far prices a fixed basket of goods and services every month. If item X is becoming more expensive and consumers shift to purchasing item Y, a cheaper substitute for X, the CPI would still price a basket of goods and services that has the same amount of X in it. It would therefore overstate the costs consumers are actually experiencing.

To get a more accurate measure of the cost of living, the US Bureau of Labor Statistics (BLS) in 2002 began calculating another type of CPI, called the **Chained CPI,** in which the basket of goods and services changes from month to month as consumers spending patterns change. The Chained CPI is so called because its calculation involves linking (as in a chain) what consumers purchase each month to what they purchased the month before to take account of changes in quantities of various items they buy.

The BLS feels the Chained CPI better reflects the cost of living consumers experience as prices change because it takes account of how consumers' purchases shift from items that are getting expensive to cheaper substitutes. To give you an idea of how the Chained CPI compares to the CPI we discussed earlier, for Sep. 2012, the change in the CPI over the previous 12 months was 2 %; for the Chained CPI, however, it was 1.6 %. Policy makers and the news media often mention the Chained CPI as giving a more accurate measure of the cost of living than the CPI does.

Producer Price Index (PPI)

The producer price index (PPI) was called the wholesale price index (WPI) in the US up to 1978. It is still called the wholesale price index in some countries. It measures the prices received by producers for the goods and services they sell. The producers typically sell these items to intermediate dealers and distributors who then sell them to consumers. The prices consumers pay for these items will usually be higher than what the producers got—the dealers and distributors will add a percentage to the price to cover their costs and to make a profit, and taxes (e.g., sales taxes) are sometimes added to the price the consumer has to pay.

The PPI in the US actually consists of a family of indexes. For example, there is the PPI for finished goods.[34] This is the one that is widely reported on in the media. But there are also many other PPIs for various products and product groups, covering the entire marketed output of US producers. The goods and services covered by the PPI come from agriculture, forestry, fisheries, mining, manufacturing, transportation, retail trade, insurance, real estate, health, legal, and professional services, utilities, finance, business services, and construction sectors of the economy, etc. If you are interested in the details of the components of the PPI family of indexes for the US, just check the US Bureau of Labor Statistics website.

A fixed set of goods and services is priced at regular intervals to obtain the PPI. While the CPI includes imports, the PPI **does not**. It covers only domestically produced goods and services.

GDP deflator

The GDP deflator is an index that measures the average price of all domestically produced goods and services that comprise GDP. By the end of this subsection, you will understand why it is called a "deflator".

Of the three measures of the price level, it covers the broadest array of goods and services. Also, unlike the CPI and PPI which are obtained by the pricing of a fixed set of items at regular intervals, the items covered by the GDP deflator are all those produced in the time period for which the deflator is being measured. So they are likely to vary from one time period to another.

The GDP deflator is calculated in terms of the prices of a base year, currently 2005 in the US. So the GDP deflator for the US for 2005 would be 100. For Q4 of 2011,

---

[34] These are goods that will not undergo further processing and are ready for sale to the final user—consumers or businesses. Examples of finished goods are unprocessed foods such as eggs and fresh vegetables, processed foods like bakery products, durable goods such as household furniture and appliances, automobiles, trucks, tractors, machine tools, and non-durable goods like apparel and home-heating oil. (The terms durable goods and non-durable goods were defined in Chapter 2.)

it was 114.077, indicating that since 2005 the price level as measured by the GDP deflator has gone up 14.077 %.

In Chapter 4, we saw that nominal GDP takes account of both changes in quantities and changes in prices. But to get real GDP, we hold prices constant. So if we remove the amount contributed to nominal GDP by price changes, what we are left with is real GDP. For Q4 2011, the US GDP deflator was 114.077 (2005 = 100), indicating that since 2005 the price level as measured by the GDP deflator has gone up 14.077 %. This means prices have changed by a proportion of 114.077/100 since 2005. If we divide the Q4 nominal GDP (which was $15319.4 billion) by this amount, we will get real GDP: $15319.4 billion divided by 114.077/100 = $ 13,429 billion:

Real GDP = Nominal GDP/ [GDP deflator/100]

This is why the index measuring the prices of all the goods and services in GDP is called the GDP deflator—it gives the amount by which nominal GDP has to be deflated (reduced) to get real GDP. The GDP deflator is sometimes called the implicit GDP deflator, or the implicit price deflator, because it is implied by the ratio of nominal to real GDP.

INFLATION

Inflation is a rise in the average price level. We measure inflation in an economy using a price index. When inflation is occurring, it doesn't mean that the price of every good or service is increasing. Some goods or services could even be going down in price. But if other goods or services are increasing in price so that overall the price index we are looking at is increasing, then there is inflation according to that index.

The inflation rate is the percentage change in the price level. The US CPI for 2010 and 2011 (with 1982-1984 as 100) were 218.056 and 224.939 respectively. The CPI inflation rate (meaning the inflation rate found by using the CPI) for the US for 2011 was [(224.939 – 218.056)/ 218.056] x 100 = 3.2 %.

Which price index to use?

We just learned 3 main measures of the average price level: the consumer price index (CPI), the producer price index (PPI) and the GDP deflator. There are also other measures of the price level that are less well known and which we do not delve into here.

Which of these price indexes we use to get our measure of inflation depends on our purpose. If a measure of the changes in the cost of living—the money costs the typical person experiences in daily life—is required, the CPI is most appropriate because it measures the prices of the goods and services purchased by the typical consumer. Or we could use the Chained CPI, which is a variant of the CPI that the US Bureau of Labor Statistics feels is a more accurate measure of the cost of living than the CPI, as we discussed earlier.

The PPI measures the prices of products when producers sell them, so sales and purchasing contracts usually specify price adjustment based on the PPI. If a measure of the change in the average price of all the goods and services produced in the economy was required, then of the three main indexes we have discussed, the GDP deflator would be the most appropriate.

Relation between PPI and CPI

One cannot assume that a change in the PPI will lead to a similar change in the CPI. Many products covered by the PPI reach the consumer through traders who buy the goods after they are produced, selling them to others, who sell them to supermarkets and other retail outlets. By the time these products reach the consumer, distribution costs would be added to their price. The price the consumer pays might also include taxes, such as sales taxes. Also, the PPI and the CPI measure the prices of different items. The PPI contains goods that will not all be purchased by consumers, e.g., factory equipment bought by businesses. The CPI cover imports, while the PPI does not. These are all factors that may cause inflation as measured by the CPI not to necessarily track that measured by the PPI.

Escalator clause

An <u>escalator clause</u>[35] is a stipulation that money payments will be raised automatically and periodically to keep pace with changes in a price index. If you are a laborer and you have a wage contract that includes an escalator clause that ties your annual change in wages to the change in the CPI, you are entitled to periodic wage increases as the CPI rises. (Workers do not like wage cuts and generally will not accept them in response to a declining CPI, unless such declines are sustained and substantial.) Escalator clauses are also used in determining social security benefits, some welfare payments, alimony payments, insurance contracts, etc.

If the components of the basket of goods and services used for measuring the CPI do not accurately reflect consumer purchases, the CPI will give a misleading measure of inflation. This can lead to exaggerated increases in payments governed by escalator clauses. In 1979–81, for example, the CPI in the US gave an exaggerated measure of inflation because the basket of goods and services used for computing it gave too great a weight to housing costs. An exceptionally high CPI inflation rate of over 18 % reported in the first quarter of 1980 caused a degree of concern in the administration of President Jimmy Carter which would have been much less if the CPI measure had been more accurate, in which case it would have shown inflation as measured by the CPI to be several percentage points lower.

One indicator of a government's performance is the inflation rate. The higher is this rate, the more likely it is that opponents of the government will argue the latter has been inept at keeping down the cost of living. The Carter administration was severely criticized for the high inflation during its time in office. The fact that an inaccurately measured CPI was overstating inflation made it worse for President Carter and his supporters. The incorrectly calculated CPI figures caused unwarranted increases in wage rates, social security, and other payments governed by escalator clauses.

---

[35] An escalator clause is called a <u>cost of living adjustment clause</u> or <u>COLA</u> when it is used to adjust payments such as wages or transfers to make these payments keep up with rising prices.

CORE INFLATION

In the US, **CPI core inflation** is measured by the overall CPI index excepting food and energy prices. Food and energy prices are volatile, so a price index calculated excluding them gives a better measure of "core" inflation, the more enduring elements of inflation. When the US authorities concentrate on keeping inflation under control, this core inflation is what they need to focus on. This way, they don't get misled by inflation due to volatile food and energy prices that may just be a quickly passing phenomenon. In the US, **core PPI inflation** and **core GDP deflator inflation** are also measured by excluding food and energy prices. In other places, such as the Eurozone and the UK, core inflation is also looked at by the governmental authorities to get a sense of the more enduring elements of inflation.

SEASONAL ADJUSTMENT

As was discussed in the previous chapter, **seasonally adjusted data** eliminates the effects of occurrences that take place at about the same time and in the same magnitude every year. Examples are annually recurring climatic conditions, holidays, the annual closure of various plants for retooling, the summer driving season, etc.

If the price index this month is sharply up compared to last month, is it because inflation is ratcheting up? Or is there a seasonal factor causing this increase? If there is a seasonal factor, we need to eliminate its effects to know how much of the change in the price level is due to underlying economic conditions, so we have to look at seasonally adjusted data.

Let's say you are looking at details on the seasonally adjusted CPI data for a month and they show gasoline prices fell by 2 percent from the previous month. But when you check the actual data on gasoline prices, you see these prices have increased 6 percent from the previous month. You check further and you learn that the seasonal adjustment took account of the start of the driving season. As the weather gets warmer, people go out driving more and this increases the demand for gasoline, pushing up gasoline prices. To seasonally adjust the data for this annual occurrence of the driving season pushing up gasoline prices, the statisticians reduce the actual prices by a certain amount. This adjustment led to gasoline prices showing a decline of 2 percent even though the actual prices went up 6 percent. This means that while increased demand due to the driving season would have pushed up gasoline prices, underlying economic conditions would have caused gasoline prices to fall.

Sometimes people look at this kind of data, and they get upset. They claim the seasonally adjusted data is lying. In truth, the seasonally adjusted data just does what it is intended for—showing us what the data would be if the seasonal factors were eliminated (to give a better measure, in this case, of the impact on gasoline prices of underlying economic conditions).

As noted in the last chapter, seasonal adjustment is not a perfect process. There is no way of knowing with absolute precision what the amounts used in making seasonal adjustments should be. The statisticians can only make estimates of what these adjustments should be, and they do it based on past experiences with data. To the extent that seasonal occurrences do not quite fit past patterns, seasonal adjusted data will be reduced in accuracy.

To get the impact on prices of underlying economic conditions, one should look at seasonally adjusted data. If the concern is with prices actually paid, then unadjusted data should be looked at. Labor union wage contracts and pension plans are usually tied to the unadjusted CPI.

CONCLUDING OBSERVATION

In this chapter, we got a better understanding of what is meant by the price level. We are on our way to a deeper understanding of the terms referred to in the presentation of the AD-AS model in Chapters 2 and 3. Next we turn to learning about money and bonds in Chapters 6 and 7. You ain't seen nothing yet!

EXERCISE

1. Of the CPI, the PPI and the GDP deflator, which
   a. Do not cover imports?
   b. Covers the widest array of items?
   c. Does not cover a fixed basket of goods?

2. What is the purpose of having core inflation measures? Give two examples of core inflation measures in the US.

3. Why does the BLS argue that the Chained CPI gives a better measure of the cost of living than the CPI for the typical urban consumer?

4. If seasonally adjusted prices are rising, actual prices (prices before seasonal adjustment is done) could be falling. True or false? Explain.

1

ANSWERS

1. a. PPI, GDP deflator
   b. GDP deflator
   c. GDP deflator

2. The purpose of having core measures of inflation is to exclude items that have volatile prices so a core measure could give a better assessment of how the sustained elements of inflation are changing. Two examples of core inflation measures in the US are the core CPI and the core PPI.

3. The CPI for the typical urban consumer is based on a fixed basket of goods and services. The Chained CPI, however, takes account of how consumers adjust this basket as prices change. For example, if item A becomes more expensive, consumers may shift to buying more of item B (which is a substitute for A) and less of A. So the BLS argues that the Chained CPI will show the consumer's basket as costing less than the unchanged basket of the regular CPI, and will more accurately reflect the costs the consumer faces.

4. True. If actual prices are falling and this is due to a seasonal factor, then the seasonally adjusted prices (obtained when the seasonal adjustment factor is added to the actual prices) could show prices rising.

CHAPTER 6
MONEY AND BONDS

In Chapter 2, we took it mainly on faith that changes in the money supply can affect aggregate demand and the economy's price and output levels. Now we begin learning about money and will later go on to see how changes in the money supply have these effects.

MONEY AND ITS FUNCTIONS

Money is a generally accepted means of exchange. For an item to function as money, it must be readily exchangeable for goods and services. Coins and currency notes have this property and are obviously money. Coins and notes make up what is called <u>currency</u>.

An economy with no money would be very inconvenient, as people would have to spend much time running around finding others who want to engage in barter (the exchange of goods and services for other goods and services) with them. Money enhances the development of an economy's productive capabilities, reducing the time, effort and resources needed to obtain what is required for production and facilitating sales of what is produced.

Money can have four functions:

- Medium of exchange—readily exchangeable for goods and services

- Store of value—embodies value

- Unit of account—unit in which the prices of goods and services are expressed

- Standard of deferred payment—unit in which payments to be made in the future (e.g., loan repayments) are expressed

A country's money must be a medium of exchange and a store of value because to qualify as money it has to be readily exchangeable for goods and services, and this means it has to also embody value or no one will want to accept it. Medium of exchange and the store of value are two functions a country's money must have.

However, the unit of account and standard of deferred payment functions are ones a country's money may not always have. If you live where prices in terms of your country's currency are rising persistently and rapidly (we will learn why prices can rise like this in Chapter 8), you might find it more convenient to set prices for what you sell in terms of another country's currency that is readily acceptable in your country. The US dollar is usually the foreign currency used because it is well known and widely accepted internationally. In various parts of the world, sellers prefer to be paid for their goods and services in US dollars rather than local currency because they feel the purchasing power of the local currency will decline while that of the US dollar will remain stable.

After euro coins and notes came into existence in 2002, the euro also became a foreign currency in which prices are set in countries where there is a loss of confidence in the local currency. (Why this loss of confidence in the local money occurs will be discussed in Chapter 8.)

Here is a more specific example of prices set in a foreign currency. Let's say you live in a country where the peso is the currency, and the price of an apartment you are offering for rental rises over a few months from 1000 to 2000 to 3000 pesos. But it remains at $US100 because the amount of pesos which have to be paid for a US dollar increases from 10 to 20 to 30. You will find it more convenient to set your rent in terms of US dollars at $100. Then you will not have to frequently change the rent you are asking for, as would be the case if you set the rent in pesos. Setting the rent in US dollars is especially convenient if you have to specify in a lease a rent that must remain fixed for the time covered by the lease. (A lease is a contract that specifies the rental time and payment for something—land, an apartment, a house, a car ....)

A dollarized economy is one in which a currency of another country (typically the

US dollar or the euro) becomes widely used.[36] In dollarized economies, confidence in their own currency falls to the point where people prefer to quote prices in other countries' currencies and to specify payments to be made in the future (e.g., loan repayments) in terms of a foreign currency.

Asset, liability, liquidity

An item that is owned is called an <u>asset</u>. Anything owed is a <u>liability</u>. Money is an asset to those who possess it. Assets can be a variety of items—houses, cars, furniture, jewelry, and so on. What distinguishes money from all other assets is that money is a generally accepted medium of exchange, other assets are not.

<u>Liquidity</u> refers to the ease with which an asset can be converted into currency. The more liquid is an asset, the more easily it can be converted into currency. A house no one wants to buy is not a liquid asset. A gold watch for which there is a ready market is quite liquid. Currency is said to be fully liquid—because it is already money! Currency is the most liquid of all assets.

MONEY, INCOME, WEALTH

The terms money, <u>income</u> and <u>wealth</u> do not have the same meaning even though in everyday conversation they are sometimes erroneously used as synonyms:

- Income is a <u>flow</u>. A flow is a quantity that has to be specified in terms of time, for example, income of $5000 per month or $60000 per year. Income is a flow because, for any mention of income to make sense, it must specify time over which the income is earned. If you said your income was $5000, your meaning would be unclear. Is it $5000 per week, per month or per year? A flow must have this time dimension associated with it.

---

[36] The term "dollarized" became the name of this occurrence because the US dollar has traditionally been widely used as an alternative to the local currency in many countries. So even when a currency other than the US dollar is being used in place of the local currency, often this would be described as "dollarization".

- Money and wealth are <u>stocks</u>.[37] A stock just has a magnitude. A time period does not have to be specified with it for it to make sense. For example, if you said you had $100, your meaning would be clear. Money is a stock. Wealth is another example of a stock. Wealth is the difference, measured in terms of money, between what a person owns and what the person owes. Wealth is specified without reference to per unit of time. For example, if you said your wealth was valued at $10,000, your meaning would be clear.

Commonly experienced examples of a flow and a stock should help to make the distinction between the two clear to you. So let us consider the everyday example of water flowing from a tap. If I asked you to specify how much water is coming from a tap, your answer would have to include a time dimension to make sense, e.g., ten gallons per minute. If you only told me "ten gallons" and did not mention the time dimension, to make sense of your response, I would then have to ask you for the time it takes to get the ten gallons. The water flowing from a tap is an example of a flow. If this water is flowing into a tub, and I asked you how much water was in the tub, and you told me "50 gallons," your meaning would be clear. For the amount of water in a tub, there is no reference to per unit of time. The amount of water in a tub is an example of a stock.

The differences between money, income and wealth are implicit in what has been said about them so far. Money is a generally accepted means of exchange. Income may be paid using money and is generally measured in terms of money per time period. Wealth is measured in terms of money and may include money but does not necessarily consist of money alone. Money an individual owns is a part of that person's wealth, but so are all other items possessed by the individual that have money value—houses, paintings, gold, jewelry, and so on.

---

[37] "Stock" as used here means a quantity that does not have a time dimension. The word "stock" can also mean a share in a corporation, which is an entirely different meaning from what stock means here.

TYPES OF MONEY

In the course of human history, a variety of items have served as money—beads, gold, silver, etc. It is good to know this because this awareness sensitizes us to the forms money can take and to **the notion that money as we know it is an evolving medium that may ultimately take forms quite different to what we are accustomed to now.** Here are a few examples of forms of money over the centuries:

- The word "pecuniary" meaning "pertaining to, or consisting of, money" comes from *pecus*, a Latin word for cattle, a byproduct of a time when cattle was used for making large payments.

- The Chinese are said to have used paper money since the 9th century.

- Paper money developed in Europe in the 17th century when jewelers began accepting the then prevalent gold and silver coins for safekeeping and issuing receipts for coins deposited with them. Soon people began using these receipts to make payments, similar to the way checks are used in our time. A form of paper money developed.

- The American colonies initially used English and Spanish coins, wampum[38], beaver skins, corn, rice and tobacco as money.

The various items that have served as money can be put into three categories:

- <u>Commodity money</u> is an item that is also bought and sold as a good. We mentioned earlier a number of goods such as gold and silver that have also served as money. If a commodity is used as money, its value as a commodity

---

[38] Wampum is an anglicized version of a Native American word meaning "string of white shells." According to a legend, in 1626, the Dutch bought Manhattan from the Native Americans for wampum and other items said to have been worth $24. (It's interesting to calculate what the $24 would be worth in 2012. Compounded annually from then to 2012, at 3 %, it would be $2.2 million; at 4 %, $90.2 million; at 5 %, it would be $3.6 billion.)

and its value as money have to be equal. Otherwise, people will put it to its most valuable use. For example, if gold functioned as money and happened to be more valuable in jewelry than when used as money, people will avoid using it as coins and convert it into jewels.

- Token money is money that represents purchasing power based, not on the intrinsic value of the materials constituting the money, but on its general acceptability as representing that purchasing power. For example, dollar notes represent purchasing power far in excess of the value of the materials constituting the notes. Token money, which is generally accepted because government has made it so by law, is called legal tender or fiat money. "Tender" means "offer in payment." "Legal tender" means currency that cannot legally be refused in payment of a debt. "Fiat" means "decree." Fiat money is money because it has been decreed as such by the governing authority.

- IOU ("I owe you") money. When you write a check to someone, your check indicates you owe the amount of the check. Checks are IOUs that serve as money—a generally accepted means of payment.

THE COMPONENTS OF THE MONEY STOCK (MONEY SUPPLY)

If coins and notes were the only generally accepted means of payment in our economy, the total amount of money in the economy—called the **money supply or money stock**—would consist of only coins and notes. However, there are other generally accepted means of making payments. For example, you can readily make payments based on deposits you have in a bank against which you can write checks. Not surprisingly, there is controversy over what best measures all the components of money in an economy.

One definition of money is called M1. In the US, M1 consists of all currency in circulation, various types of checkable deposits and traveler's checks.

- Currency in circulation means coins and notes held by the public—people like you and me.

- Checkable deposits are deposits in banks against which people can write checks. One kind of checkable deposits, called <u>demand deposits</u>, refers to checking accounts from which withdrawals can be made as the holder of the account demands (hence the term demand deposits), without any restrictions on the number or timing of checks.

- Traveler's checks are bought by paying the face value plus a fee, and you can use them to make payments or convert them to cash. They are safer to carry around than cash as they can usually be replaced if lost or stolen and are popular with travelers.[39]

- For reference, the appendix at the end of this chapter cites other definitions of money—M2, M3—the existence of which you should be aware. M2 consists of M1 plus various other components, so it is a broader definition of the money supply than M1. M3 is broader than M2. You don't have to remember precise definitions of these measures of the money stock. It is enough for you to know that there are different measures with names M1, M2, M3, etc. Every country has its own preferred measure(s) of the money supply. In the US, for example, in Mar. 2006, the authorities stopped collecting data on M3 because they concluded that M3 data do not give them any information about economic activity that is not already given by M2. In the Eurozone countries, however, what the Eurozone authorities define as M3 is very carefully monitored.

- Little would be gained here from going into a debate on what should be the components of the money supply. **Instead, for the purpose of developing the theories in this book we shall abstract[40] from some details of what**

---

[39] The definition of M1 is more specific than is stated here. For example, only traveler's checks issued by non-bank institutions are counted in M1. But we have no need here to concern ourselves with these additional details.

[40] The role of abstraction in theory building was discussed in Chapter 1.

constitutes the money supply and simply view the general term money supply or money stock as meaning currency in circulation and deposits in banks. If, however, a specific definition of money, for example M1, is referred to this will, of course, refer to exactly what the specific definition means.

In Chapters 2 and 3 we studied the aggregate demand-aggregate supply model and learned that the money supply has an important role in affecting the economy's price and output levels. Because the money supply is so important, each country has a central authority, called a **central bank**, responsible for controlling the size of the money supply and usually also for regulating the behavior of the banks in the country. In the US, this central bank is the Federal Reserve, or Fed for short. In the UK, it is the Bank of England; in the Eurozone countries, it is the European Central Bank (ECB); and in Japan, it is the Bank of Japan.

When funds are deposited into banks, the banks can use these for making loans to earn interest income rather than just keep them idle in the banks. They will generally not loan out all the deposits they receive. For some types of deposits, the Fed determines a minimum amount that must be kept by banks. One reason for this is to ensure that banks do not overextend themselves in making loans. Banks must also keep some funds for meeting requests of depositors for withdrawals. To meet such requests, banks keep cash in their vaults—called vault cash, and also keep deposits at the Fed to facilitate payments of checks. If your bank is Citibank and my bank is Chase, and I write you a Chase check, when you deposit this check into your Citibank account, to facilitate the check clearing, funds will shift from the deposits Chase has at the Fed to those Citibank has.

When we stated what M1, M2, and M3 were, we noted that **currency held by the public, called currency in circulation, is counted as part of the money supply. Currency that is in a central bank is not considered as currency held by the public and is not part of the money supply.**

Suppose you deposited $1000 in your bank. Your deposit counts as part of the money supply, and it counts as long as you continue to have that deposit. If the bank kept this $1000 in its vault, this $1000 of vault cash would not also be counted in the money supply. **As the bank's vault cash, it is not cash held by a** member of the public, so it is not currency in circulation and does not count as part of the money supply. If the bank deposits this $1000 at the Fed, that deposit at the Fed would not be part of the money supply, since what is in the Fed does not count as part of the money supply. **Deposits in a central bank are not part of the money supply.**

We shall use the symbols M, C and D to refer to the money supply, currency in circulation and deposits in banks respectively. As was noted a few paragraphs above, **we shall abstract from some details of what constitutes the money supply and simply view the general term money supply or money stock as meaning currency in circulation and deposits in banks. So, M = C + D.** By currency in circulation, we mean currency outside of the Fed and owned by the public. By deposits in banks, we mean deposits in banks other than the Fed.

EXERCISE 1

1. Which of the following is part of the money supply?
    a. Currency held by the public
    b. Deposits of the public in banks
    c. Currency of banks kept in their vaults (vault cash)
    d. Currency in the Fed
    e. Bank deposits in the Fed

2. Which of the following is part of the money supply?
    a. $500 cash in your wallet
    b. A deposit you make into your checking account
    c. $50 million of currency in the Fed
    d. Your $10,000 bank account
    e. $20,000 kept in a Citibank vault from deposits made by customers
    f. $1000 you keep in a safety deposit box in a bank

BONDS

In the chapters ahead, there are several references to bonds. The details below give a sense of what is a bond.

Governments (federal, state and local) and businesses frequently need to borrow money to fund their expenditures. One way to borrow is by issuing <u>bonds</u>. A **bond** is essentially a loan made by the person buying the bond to the issuer of the bond. Let's say AXY Corporation wants to borrow 5 million dollars and issues 5000 bonds of $1000 each, and you buy one of these bonds. You would pay $1000 to AXY Corp., in effect lending this $1000 to AXY. Suppose these bonds are to be repaid in ten years and pay 9 % annual interest. Then each year over the next ten years you would receive $90 in interest (9 % of $1000) and at the end of the tenth year you will also receive repayment of the $1000 you had lent to AXY when you bought its bond.

A bond is a certificate of indebtedness issued to a lender by a borrower to indicate a sum of money has been borrowed. There are various types of bonds, some of which are listed in the section TYPES OF BONDS later in this chapter. In order to teach you the fundamentals, however, we have to focus on the key ideas underlying bonds. We will do so by focusing on one type of bond that is popular and which has traditionally had a certificate specifying the amount to be repaid by the borrower (called the **par value**), the date when repayment has to be made (the **maturity date)**, and the interest rate (the **coupon interest rate**) the borrower has to pay the lender each year for the privilege of using the lender's funds.

The coupon interest rate is often referred to as the <u>coupon interest</u> or just <u>coupon</u>. This coupon interest is the percent of the par value of the bond the borrower has to pay the lender in interest each year. For example, for a bond with a par value of $1000 and a coupon interest of 10 %, the borrower has to pay the lender 10 % of $1000 = $100 in interest each year. Some bonds have detachable coupons, each of which represents a scheduled interest payment, which is sent to the issuer when the interest is to be paid. This is why this interest rate came to be referred to as coupon interest rate. (Nowadays, with so much done electronically, names like "coupon interest" continue to be used but the transactions, record keeping and payments are often done electronically.) The dollar amount of the coupon interest each year is called the <u>coupon interest payment</u> or <u>coupon payment</u>. In the example just cited, the coupon interest rate is 10 % and the coupon interest payment (or coupon payment) is $100.

A person who buys a bond becomes a <u>bondholder</u>. One reason people buy bonds is to earn income from the interest paid by the issuer of the bonds. Bonds have traditionally been called **fixed-income securities** because the amount of income you get from a bond (e.g., the coupon interest) is fixed. The term fixed-income securities has continued to be used to refer to bonds even though there are some bonds that are issued with **floating interest rates**, meaning that the interest they pay changes over time as interest rates in the economy change.

If you hold a bond until maturity, you are entitled to be repaid the full amount of the par value. Bonds are therefore appealing to those who want to receive the full amount of their principal when the bond matures.

PRIMARY MARKET, SECONDARY MARKET

The market in which newly issued bonds are bought and sold is called the **primary market**. After bonds are issued, they can be traded in the **secondary market**. When you buy the bond from the AXY Corporation that is a transaction in the primary market. If you then decide to sell the bond to me, this will be a transaction in the secondary market because the bond you are selling to me has already been sold in the primary market.

The market price at which I buy this bond from you need not be $1000. The price I pay may be more than, equal to, or less than the par value of $1000 and depends on the interest rate at which new bonds are being issued in the primary market when I want to buy your bond. For example, if bonds are being issued at 5 % coupon interest when you want to sell your bond (that has a 10 % coupon interest) to me, you would want more than $1000 for your bond. Why? If you keep your bond, you are guaranteed 10 % of $1000 = $100 in interest payment each year. However, if I have to buy a newly issued bond with a par value of $1000, I would only get 5 % of $1000 = $50 interest payment each year. Your bond is now worth more than $1000 because of the $100 interest payment associated with it. If you were a sensible seller, you would want more than $1000 for it. I would also be willing to pay more than $1000 for it because it pays much more interest than newly issued bonds.[41]

If interest rates went above 10 percent, say to 12 %, I would want to pay less than $1000 for your bond because newly issued bonds would earn me more interest than your bond.

Therefore, if you have a bond and you sell it, the price you get could be less than, equal to, or more than its face value depending on what is the level of interest rates at the time when you are selling the bond. **If interest rates rise/fall, the prices of existing bonds will fall/rise.**

Of course, if you keep the bond to its maturity date, you are then entitled to get its face value when it matures. **When a bond is bought for less/more than its face value, it is said to be bought at a discount/premium.**

THE YIELD ON A BOND

The price at which a bond sells in the secondary market is the current price of the bond. The **current yield** of the bond in percent is the annual coupon interest payment divided by the current price of the bond and multiplied by 100 to get it as a percentage:

% Current Yield = [Coupon interest payment ÷ Current price of bond] X 100

---

[41] If you study bond math, you will learn formulas for determining the current price of a bond. The discussion here is just to convey the notion that the current price of a bond can differ from its par value and will rise/fall as interest rates go down/up.

More generally, the <u>yield</u> on any asset is the annual payment received by the owner of the asset divided by the current price of the asset and expressed as a percentage. (Note that in the case of bonds, this yield is referred to as "current yield".) For example, if you have an asset with a current price of $1000 that earns a payment of $40 per year, the yield on this asset presently would be (40/1000) X 100 percent = 4 %. As the price is in the denominator of the formula for calculating yield, if the price of the asset increases/decreases, the yield decreases/increases—**the price of the asset and its yield are inversely related.**

There are other concepts of yield such as <u>yield to maturity (YTM)</u>, which are more complex than current yield. Adding all the gains expected from the bond, dividing this by the current price of the bond and expressing this as percentage annual return gives the YTM. To find all the gains, you add all the interest payments to be expected, including what you would obtain from reinvesting interest payments received over the life of the bond, and you also include the gain/loss you would get when the bond matures depending on whether you bought it at a discount or premium. Obviously, the calculation of YTM is much more complex than that of current yield. The purpose here is to give you a sense of what is meant by YTM and not to take up time with its precise math calculation, which is not at all necessary for our purpose. Whatever the measure of yield used, the higher/lower the price of a bond, the lower/higher will be its yield—**the price of a bond and its yield are inversely related.**

EXERCISE 2

1. You bought a $1000 bond from ABC Corporation when that corporation issued bonds in May 2011. You are to be paid $150 in interest each year and the bond matures in ten years. What are the following: a. Par value of the bond; b. Coupon interest rate; c. Year when the bond matures; d. Stream of payments you will receive from ABC?

   Did you purchase this bond in the primary or the secondary market?

2. (Assume here that all the bonds are being issued by borrowers that are equally creditworthy, so you don't have to worry that one may be riskier than another.)

   You have a bond with a par value of $1000 that earns a coupon interest of $100 each year. New bonds of par value $1000 are currently being issued with a coupon interest of 6 %. Would you sell your bond to me for a $1000, less than $1000 or more than $1000? Explain.

   Suppose a year from now bonds of $1000 par value are being issued with 15 % coupon interest. Do you think I will pay $1000 for your bond then? Explain.

3. Use the formula relating current yield, coupon interest payment and current price of a bond to find the missing values in each of the following:

	Current yield	Coupon interest payment	Current price
a.	---	$ 100	$1000
b.	5 %	----	$2000
c.	5 %	$ 100	-----
d.	15 %	$ 75	-----

   What is the coupon interest rate for each of the bonds in a, b, c and d if the current price of each bond is equal to its par value?

TYPES OF BONDS

Here are brief descriptions of some types of bonds.

US Treasury bills, notes and bonds—issued by the US Government. Treasury **bills** mature in a year or less. They are sold below their par value and pay no interest. When a treasury bill matures, the gain the bondholder gets is the difference between the par value and what was paid for it. Treasury **notes** mature in 2 to 10 years, and treasury **bonds** mature in over ten years. **Bills, notes and bonds are all usually referred to as just bonds, or as treasuries, or as US**

Treasury <u>**securities**</u>.[42] US Treasury bonds are of great importance to world financial markets. They are key components in financial portfolios not just in the US but throughout the world, and movements in their yields are a major influence on US and world interest rates.

Municipal bonds, called "munis"—issued by state and local governments. If the government of a country has a long record of always meeting its payment obligations (e.g., the US government), its bonds will typically be considered less risky than state and local government bonds. This is because state and local governments often have less pristine financial status than that of governments like the US and are more prone to not being able to repay their obligations.

Corporate bonds—issued by corporations. Generally, corporate bonds will have higher interest rates than bonds issued by a very creditworthy government, because there is greater likelihood that a corporation will not make payments due on a bond. The lower the risk associated with a corporation, the lower the interest rate the investor receives.

Zero-coupon bond—bought from the issuer at a price below the par value and pays no interest. When the bond matures, the bondholder receives the par value and so gains the difference between the par value and what was paid for the bond.

Callable bond—the issuer can pay off the buyer of the bond and take back (call) the bond. The calling of bonds is also known as <u>redemption</u>. If interest rates fall, for example, the issuer may want to call existing bonds and issue new bonds at lower coupon interest.

Convertible bond—is convertible into stock. The time when this can be done and the amount of stock the bond can be exchanged for are specified at the time the bond is issued.

Debenture—backed only by the good faith of the organization issuing it.

---

[42] A security is a document specifying ownership of property or a claim to a flow of income. A bond is a security.

Junk bond—issued by a company viewed as having high risk of not being able to repay what it borrows. To induce people to buy its bond, it offers the bond at a coupon interest substantially higher than that of safer bonds. Some junk bonds have been very profitable investments, while others have been real junk! See the section further ahead on bond ratings for the grade assigned to junk bonds by credit rating agencies.

TYPES OF RISK

There are a variety of terms associated with the financial risk of holding bonds, a few of which overlap in their meaning. Some of the main ones are:

- **Credit risk**—the likelihood that the interest and/or principal[43] will not be repaid. The more likely this is, the higher the credit risk. US Treasury securities (bills, notes and bonds) are viewed as having zero credit risk because the US government is perceived as firmly committed to meeting its legal obligations. This is one reason US Treasury securities are so widely held by investors around the world.

- **Default risk**—risk that the interest and/or principal will not be repaid.

- **Risk of principal**—risk that the principal will not be repaid.

- **Interest rate risk**—risk of the price of a bond declining as interest rates rise.

- **Inflation risk**—risk of the decline in the purchasing power of the value of a bond if inflation occurs. If inflation is rising, issuers of bonds will have to

---

[43] Principal is the amount of the loan apart from interest. If you lend $1000, this amount is the principal.

offer higher interest rates to compensate potential bondholders for the inflation risk.

BOND RATINGS

In the US, three main credit rating agencies are Standard and Poor's (S&P), Moody's and Fitch. The table below provides a summary of their bond rating scales.[44] A bond's **credit rating** is an assessment of the likelihood of its issuer repaying the debt to bondholders.

Bonds from companies in top financial condition have the highest ratings. Those that have considerable risk associated with them are ranked as "speculative." When bonds fall to ratings of Ba or BB and lower, they are classified as junk bonds (which were defined in an earlier section of this chapter).

RISK	GRADE	BOND RATING	
		Moody's	S&P/Fitch
Highest Quality	Investment	Aaa	AAA
High Quality	Investment	Aa	AA
Upper Medium Grade	Investment	A	A
Medium Grade	Investment	Baa	BBB
Speculative	Junk	Ba,B	BB,B
Highly Speculative	Junk	Caa,Ca,C	CCC,CC,C
In Default	Junk	C	D

WHAT'S AHEAD

The next chapter teaches more about money in the economy. It shows how the behavior of the banks, the public and the central bank affects the amount of money

---

[44] For additional details and updates, check with the rating agencies.

and the level of interest rates in the economy, and it gives deeper insights into the connection between the money supply and the level of aggregate demand. It provides details on some very important interest rates and discusses a key relationship called the Fisher relation. It ends with an examination of the connection between the money stock and variables called the monetary base and the money multiplier.

ANSWERS

EXERCISE 1

1. a and b count as part of the money supply.

2. a, b, d, and f—a and f are part of currency in circulation because they are your holdings of currency. They are part of the money supply. So are b and d, which count as deposits.

EXERCISE 2

1.
   a. $1000

   b. $150/1000 \times 100 = 15\%$

   c. 2021

   d. $150 each year from 2012 to 2020, then $150 plus the par value of $1000 in 2021

   Your purchase occurred in the primary market.

2. Your bond with a par value of $1000 earns you $100 per year. Currently issued bonds, however, only earn 6 % = $60 for a bond of $1000 par value. Your $1000 bond earns more than currently issued $1000 bonds, so you should ask for more than $1000 for it.

If a year from now bonds are being issued at 15 % coupon interest (= $150 coupon payment on a bond of $1000 par value), I would want to pay less than $1000 for your bond because it only has a $100 interest payment.

3. For brevity here we will use cy, cip and cp to mean current yield, coupon interest payment and current price respectively.

    a. $cy = 100/1000 \times 100 = 10\ \%$

    b. $5 = cip/2000 \times 100 => cip = \$100$

    c. $5 = 100/cp \times 100 => cp = \$2000$

    d. $15 = 75/cp \times 100 => cp = \$500$

Coupon interest rate = coupon interest payment ÷ par value X 100, so:

    a. $100/1000 \times 100\ \% = 10\ \%$

    b. 5 %

    c. 5 %

    d. 15 %

Notice that these numbers for the coupon interest are the same as those for current yield. This is because the current price of each bond is exactly equal to its par value.

APPENDIX
DEFINITIONS OF THE MONEY SUPPLY

These are included here for reference if you need an awareness of what constitutes some measures of the money supply in the US. These are general definitions and do not include all the specifics for some of the components.

M1 =
currency in circulation (Currency held outside of banks.)

+ **demand deposits** (Deposits in banks, excluding those of other banks, the government, and foreign governments, against which checks can be written without restriction as to how many, size or timing of the checks—except that the account cannot be overdrawn without penalty.)

+ **some other checkable deposits** (In addition to demand deposits, there are other deposits against which checks may be written. Among those counted in this category of M1 are ATS and NOW. ATS—automatic transfers from savings accounts—are deposits kept in a savings account but transferred to a checking account when a payment for a check has to be made. NOW — negotiable order of withdrawal—accounts are interest-earning accounts against which a limited number of checks may be written.)

+ **traveler's checks** (These are bought by paying the amount the check represents plus a purchasing fee. You can then cash this check or use it to make payments. It is considered safer to carry around than cash, so it is popular with travelers. Only traveler's checks sold by non-banks count as part of M1.)

M2 = **M1**

+ **savings deposits** (Interest earning deposits against which checks cannot be written.)

+ **small-denomination time deposits**, also called CDs—certificates of deposits (Interest earning deposits of less than $100,000 made for a fixed term, from which withdrawals can only be made with prior notification to the bank and with penalties for early withdrawal.)

+ **money market mutual funds balances managed by investment companies** (A mutual fund consists of funds raised from shareholders by an investment company and put into various types of financial investments. The money market refers to the market for interest bearing assets of short time maturity. A money market mutual fund is a mutual fund used to buy interest-bearing assets—such as bonds—of short time maturity.)

+ **money market deposit accounts** (Banks also manage mutual funds consisting of interest bearing assets of short time maturity. The deposits used for this purpose are called money market deposit accounts, against which a limited number of checks can be written.)

M3 = **M2**

+ **large denomination time deposits** ($100,000 or more)

+ **overnight and term repurchase agreements** (A repurchase agreement, RP, involves a bank borrowing from a nonbank customer by selling a security to the customer with the agreement to buy it back at a set price at a set date.)

+ **overnight and term Eurodollar deposits** (Eurodollar deposits are bank accounts consisting of US dollars held in overseas banks and used for international transactions. Accounts consisting of such currency originated in Europe; this is how they came to be called "Eurodollar.")

+ **money market mutual funds owned by institutions**

In Mar. 2006, the US authorities stopped collecting data on M3 because they concluded that the information about economic activity conveyed by M3 is already obtained from the data on M2.

If you became a political leader and you were inclined to have your government borrow from the central bank to finance very large increases in spending, bear in mind that the central bank by issuing money this way increases the money stock. If these increases in the money stock occur in very large and rising amounts, this will cause high levels of inflation, even hyperinflation. If, after reading this book, you know this lesson alone you will be wiser than many political leaders the world has very painfully endured.

—Stated by the author in Chapter 8 of this book

CHAPTER 7
THE MONEY SUPPLY, INTEREST RATES
AND AGGREGATE DEMAND

In the last chapter, we acquired fundamental notions on money and bonds. Here we learn about the role of banks, the public and the central bank in determining the money supply.

We first look at the role banks (other than the central bank) and the public play in determining the money supply. Then we examine the critical role of the central bank in the money supply process. The central bank we will focus on is the Federal Reserve (Fed), the US central bank. The main processes used by the Fed to manage the US money supply are similar to those used around the world.

HOW BANKS AFFECT THE MONEY SUPPLY

Banks are in business to earn income. If they held idle the deposits made into them they would earn nothing.[45] They make loans with these deposits to earn interest income.

Banks, however, cannot lend out all the deposits they receive. They are generally required by central bank regulations to hold a percentage of deposits as reserves. This amount is called <u>required reserves</u> or <u>reserve requirements,</u> and the ratio of required reserves to deposits expressed as a percentage is called the <u>required reserve ratio</u> or <u>reserve requirements ratio</u>. Reserves held in excess of the required amount are called <u>excess reserves</u>.

---

[45] Some central banks pay interest on the reserves that banks keep at the central bank. But this is a relatively small amount, currently 0.25 percent annual interest in the US. If banks just held the deposits of their customers as reserves at the Fed, they would earn this 0.25 percent interest. If they made loans, however, they would earn a much higher return.

Even if banks in a country are not required to hold a specific level of reserves, they will still hold some reserves to meet depositors' demand for funds. The total amount of reserves banks hold (referred to here with the symbol R) divided by the total amount of deposits (D) is called the **reserve-deposit ratio** or **reserve ratio** (rr). So rr = R / D.

We shall now show that when banks make loans they increase the quantity of money supplied.

- Suppose the money stock in the economy is $1 million—$200,000 in currency in circulation and $800,000 in deposits.

- Then you go to your bank and deposit into a checking account $10,000 you had in your safe at home. You have merely shifted $10,000 from one component of the money stock into another component—from currency in circulation into a deposit. So the money stock is still $1 million after your action—$190,000 in currency in circulation plus $810,000 in deposits.

- The bank will not just keep the $10,000 you have deposited in it. It will loan some of this to earn income from the interest payments it receives on the loans it makes. Let's say the bank decides to use the funds you deposited into it to make a $8,000 loan to me. If it makes this loan by giving me cash, currency in circulation—currency outside of banks—increases by $8,000, and you still have your $10,000 checking account.

- So now currency in circulation equals $198,000 and deposits equal $810,000. **The money stock has increased** by $8,000 to $1 million plus $8,000.

- If instead of lending me cash, the bank loans me the $8,000 by letting me open a checking account into which the bank places $8,000, then the deposits component of the money stock increases by $8,000. So the money stock would now be $190,000 of currency in circulation plus $818,000 in deposits. **The money stock has increased** by $8,000 to $1 million plus $8,000.

HOW THE PUBLIC AFFECTS THE MONEY SUPPLY

The total amount of currency in circulation (C) divided by the total amount of deposits (D) is called the **currency-deposit ratio**, which we represent here with the symbol cd. So cd = C / D.

Every dollar held as currency in circulation counts as a dollar in the money stock. If that same dollar, however, is deposited in a bank, the deposit counts as a dollar in the money stock. But the bank can now lend a part of that dollar, and what it lends will also count as part of the money stock. So when money moves from currency in circulation into bank deposits, it can lead to the money stock increasing.

In the example given earlier of how banks can increase the money stock, we saw how $10,000 in currency in circulation counted as $10,000 of the money stock. But when put into a bank deposit, it counted as $10,000 of the money stock (in the form of deposits) and also became the source of funds from which the bank made a loan of $8,000, so further increasing the money stock by $8,000.

If people become more optimistic about the banking system and want to keep less currency in circulation and hold more deposits, banks will have more funds to use for making loans. This facilitates expansion of the money supply and enhances possibilities for the growth of output and employment in the economy.

But if people become very fearful about the safety of banks and rush to withdraw their funds, this decreases the deposits on the basis of which banks make loans, impedes growth of the money stock and inhibits economic growth. For example, as the Eurozone has experienced the ongoing economic crisis, massive withdrawals of deposits from banks in Greece, Ireland, Italy, Portugal and Spain have further constrained money supply growth in those countries and worsened their economic prospects.

We have therefore seen how the behavior of banks and the public can affect the money stock.

EXERCISE 1

1. The banking system in Ruritania has $100 million in deposits. Currency in circulation equals $80 million. The reserve requirement is 10 % of deposits, but banks have a total of $15 million in reserves at the central bank. What are: a. the money stock; b. required reserves; c. excess reserves; d. the reserve ratio; e. the currency-deposit ratio?

2.

   a. If currency in circulation = $50 million, and bank deposits = $100 million, what is the size of the money stock?

   b. If I now take $5000 I was keeping at home and deposit it into my bank, what is the size of the money stock after my action?

   c. If the bank loans $3000 of the funds I deposited to another customer, what happens to the size of the money stock?

   d. Can we conclude that the action of a bank in making loans increases the money stock?

3. During the Great Depression, banks began to fail because the deteriorating economy made borrowers unable to pay back loans. The public, fearing they would lose their deposits if banks failed, withdrew their funds from banks. Banks cut back on loans and also began to keep higher reserves to be able to meet the increased requests from depositors for funds. In these circumstances, what do you think happened to the reserve ratio, the currency-deposit ratio and the money supply? From the AD-AS model, what can you conclude happened to aggregate demand as a result of the situation just described? Do you see how these developments contributed to a worsening of the Great Depression?

HOW THE CENTRAL BANK CHANGES THE MONEY SUPPLY AND INTEREST RATES

It was stated in Chapter 2 that changes in the money supply affect the economy's output, employment and price levels. Central banks seek to control the money supply to keep the price level and inflation under control and to ensure the economy's output can grow at an appropriate pace.[46] They constantly monitor economic conditions in order to implement policies to meet these objectives.

The most important role of the central bank in any economy is managing the money supply. The central bank in the US, the Federal Reserve, changes the money supply mainly in three ways:

- Open market operations (aimed at affecting the federal funds rate)
- Changes in the discount rate
- Changes in reserve requirements

Methods similar to these are used by central banks around the world.

Open market operations, the federal funds rate and the discount rate are new terms that are explained in the pages ahead. Reserve requirements were encountered in a previous section of this chapter.

In response to the subprime/credit crunch crisis, the Fed has developed new additional methods. Some of these are discussed later. No doubt you have heard much about the subprime/credit crunch crisis in the news. **APPENDIX I at the end of this chapter provides a brief explanation of this crisis.**

---

[46] The European Central Bank (ECB) states that its primary objective is to maintain price stability. This is referred to as a **single mandate** and so sometimes media pundits and others make the mistake of thinking that the ECB is just concerned with price stability. They overlook the word "primary" in the statement of the objective of the ECB. **Every central bank is typically concerned with doing what it can to foster conditions for optimal economic growth.** In the case of the Fed, its objectives are to implement policies to get maximum employment, stable prices and moderate long-term interest rates. These objectives are often called a **dual mandate**, referring to the maximum employment and stable prices objectives.

Open market operations

Open market operations, called OMOs for short, are the purchase or sale of government securities[47] by the Fed. Open market operations are so called because the Fed conducts these purchases or sales in a market in which securities dealers compete on the basis of price to do business with the Fed. In conducting OMOs, the Fed buys or sells Federal government bonds. If it bought or sold corporate bonds, or state or local government bonds, it could be accused of favoring one business over another, or one state or city over another.

Suppose the Fed bought $1 million in bonds from you and paid you with an electronic deposit to your bank account. The amount of deposits in the banking system, which count as part of the money stock, increases by $1 million, which means the money stock immediately increases by $1 million. Your bank will now use some of these deposits to make loans further expanding the money stock, as we learned in the discussion of how banks affect the money supply.

So we see that an open market operation in which the Fed buys bonds causes an increase in the money stock. We see also that the money stock can increase by more than just the amount of the purchase by the Fed. We will learn later in this chapter how to estimate by how much the money stock can increase. **Now the key point to grasp is that a purchase of securities by the Fed causes the money stock to increase. One can think of the purchase of securities by the Fed as the Fed taking in securities and giving out money in return, so increasing the money stock.**

Sales of bonds by the Fed does the opposite, decreasing the money stock. If Ms. Jones buys securities from the Fed, funds shift from her deposits in her bank (where they are a part of the money stock) to the Fed, where they are no longer part of the money stock. The money stock decreases. **One can think of a sale of securities by the Fed as the Fed giving out securities and taking in money, so decreasing the money stock.**

---

[47] As was mentioned in Chapter 6, a security is a document specifying ownership of property or a claim to a flow of income. A bond is a security. Recall from what was said in Chapter 6 (in the discussion of treasury bills, notes and bonds) that bills, notes and bonds are all frequently referred to simply as "bonds."

To sum up, when the Fed engages in OMOs, it buys or sells securities. When it buys securities, it increases the money stock. When it sells securities, it decreases the money stock.

The fed funds rate

One type of lending in which banks engage is the lending of reserves to each other. If Bank A is running short of reserves (to meet reserve requirements and/or customer demand for funds) it can borrow from a bank that has excess reserves. The interest rate that banks charge when they lend their excess reserves to each other is called the **fed funds rate** (or the federal funds rate), and the arrangements in which banks borrow and lend these funds is called the <u>fed funds market</u>.

As we have discussed, when the Fed engages in OMOs, it affects the amount of reserves that banks have. When the Fed engages in an OMO buying bonds, the amount it pays the dealers gets deposited in banks. As these funds are deposited into banks, this increases their reserves and they now have more excess reserves to lend. As banks get more excess reserves, this encourages them to lower the interest they charge for lending those reserves, i.e., the fed funds rate.

The reverse of this happens if the Fed is engaging in OMOs selling bonds. As it sells bonds, it has to be paid. So funds move from banks to the Fed. This decreases the amount of reserves banks have, decreasing the amount of excess reserves they have for lending. As the amount they have for lending is decreased by the Fed's OMOs selling bonds, this causes the interest rate banks charge for lending their excess reserves to go up—with less funds available for lending, the price of these funds (the fed funds rate) goes up.

Each business day, the Fed engages in OMOs (typically short term transactions) to affect the amount of reserves in the banking system and keep the fed funds rate at a desired level, or change it to a new level. The Fed sets a target for the federal funds rate and then uses OMOs to help the federal funds rate reach and stay around the target level. In this way, the Fed is able to use OMOs to alter not just the money supply but also interest rates.

To give you a sense of how the fed funds target rate has been changed by the Fed, here is information on it for recent years. From January 3 to December 11 of 2001, the FOMC (Federal Open Market Committee), the arm of the Fed that makes decisions on what the federal funds rate should be, lowered the target federal funds rate 11 times from 6.50 percent to 1.75 percent—the lowest target federal funds rate in forty years. On November 6, 2002, the FOMC lowered the federal funds target rate further to 1.25 percent, and on June 25, 2003, it lowered the rate to 1 percent.

On June 30, 2004, the FOMC raised this rate to 1.25 % and increased it sixteen times (a quarter point each time) from then to 5.25 % (on June 29, 2006).

The Fed lowered this rate to 4.75 % on Sep. 18, 2007 and decreased it further several times, so that by Oct. 29, 2008, it was lowered to 1 %. On Dec. 16, 2008, the Fed established the target range of 0 to 0.25 % for the fed funds rate, a target that still exists as 2012 ends.

Changes in the discount rate

Banks that are temporarily short of reserves may be permitted by the Fed to borrow from it. The **discount rate** is the rate of interest the Fed charges when it makes these loans to banks. When banks borrow from the Fed at the discount rate they are said to be borrowing at the <u>discount window</u>.

A decrease in the discount rate makes it cheaper for banks to borrow from the Fed to meet temporary shortfalls in reserves. This encourages banks to keep less excess reserves and to make more loans, so increasing the money supply.

An increase in the discount rate makes it more expensive to borrow from the Fed, encouraging banks to keep more reserves to avoid borrowing from the Fed. The more reserves banks keep, the less loans they make, and the smaller is the money supply. An increase in the discount rate reduces the money supply.

Changes in reserve requirements

A decrease in reserve requirements means that banks can keep less reserves and make more loans, increasing the money supply.

An increase in reserve requirements means banks have to keep more reserves and make less loans. This decreases the money supply.

The prime rate

The **prime rate** is the interest rate banks in the US use as a base rate in determining what to charge their customers. For example, if the prime rate is 5 % and Business XYZ is a creditworthy customer of Bank of America, Bank of America might charge this 5 % rate for a loan to XYZ. If ABC is a less creditworthy business it may be charged the prime rate of 5 % plus a premium that takes account of the risk Bank of America faces in lending to ABC. The prime rate is a benchmark rate, a rate used in determining the level of rates charged on loans. Credit card issuers widely use the prime rate in determining the interest rate they charge customers.

Whenever the Fed announces a new target for the fed funds rate, banks in the US announce new levels for the prime rate. Typically, the prime rate is 3 % above the fed funds target announced by the Fed.

In the media, when you see a number quoted as the "prime rate," without reference to it being the prime rate charged by a specific bank, this typically means this number is an average of the prime rates charged by major banks.

Expansionary/contractionary monetary policy

We learned in Chapter 3 that an expansionary monetary policy is one aimed at increasing the money supply. The purchase of securities by the Fed associated with the lowering of the fed funds rate, the lowering of the discount rate and the lowering of reserve requirements are all expansionary monetary policies. A contractionary monetary policy is one aimed at decreasing the money supply. The sale of securities by the Fed associated with the raising of the fed funds rate, the raising of the discount rate and the raising of reserve requirements are all contractionary monetary policies.

In APPENDIX, Part I *at the end of this book*, **there is a detailed discussion of money demand and money supply using diagrams and a model showing money demand and supply interacting to determine an equilibrium interest rate.** The more abstract presentation of this appendix is consistent with what you would typically encounter in theoretical courses in academia.

EXERCISE 2

1. Would each of the following increase or decrease the money supply? The Fed:
    a. Sells bonds
    b. Lowers the discount rate
    c. Buys bonds
    d. Raises reserve requirements

2. Say whether each of the following is true or false and explain your response:
    a. When the Fed engages in an OMO, it is always because the Fed has a new target for the fed funds rate.
    b. The Fed's target for the fed funds rate and the fed funds rate actually charged by banks as they lend reserves to each other are always the same amount.
    c. When the Fed wants to tighten monetary policy by raising its interest rate target, it announces a new target for the prime rate.

3. Distinguish between the fed funds rate and the discount rate.

SOME OF THE FED'S POLICY RESPONSES TO THE SUBPRIME/CREDIT CRUNCH CRISIS

Quantitative Easing

- When the lending rate a central bank focuses on targeting (e.g., the fed funds rate in the US) is near to zero, if the central bank wants to stimulate the economy, it can engage in **quantitative easing (QE)**.

- This occurs when the central bank buys assets (e.g., long term bonds), which enables it to inject funds into the economy, without having to rely on the mechanism of OMOs affecting the fed funds rate **(which are typically short term transactions)** described earlier in this chapter.

- Purchase of long term treasuries by the central bank increases demand for them, pushing up their price and decreasing their yield—recall from the discussion of bonds in Chapter 6 that price and yield are inversely related. When yields on long term treasuries are brought down, this encourages investors to seek higher yields elsewhere. To get a better return on their financial investments, investors become more willing to take risks and move out of safe treasuries and invest in other areas of the economy, stimulating economic activity. For example, investors might become more interested in purchasing corporate bonds, making it easier for corporations to fund their operations. Investors will also move into riskier assets like stocks, pushing up stock prices and increasing the wealth of stock holders, who are then likely to spend more based on their increased wealth.

- In executing QE, the Fed has also been buying <u>agency mortgage-backed securities</u> (described at the end of this paragraph). Buying these makes funding more readily available for mortgages (loans for purchasing property) and brings down the cost of getting a mortgage. This makes it easier for people to borrow to fund purchases of homes and so can help to revitalize the housing sector and the economy. (A <u>government sponsored enterprise, GSE</u>, also called an <u>agency</u>, is a corporation created by the US Congress to make funding more readily and cheaply available to various sectors of the US economy. For example, the Federal Home Loan Mortgage Corporation—called Freddie Mac—is a GSE created to lower mortgage costs and increase access to financing in the US housing market. Agencies like Freddie Mac buy mortgages from the financial institutions that have issued them, thus providing the institutions with funds to make more mortgages. The agency then creates bonds, the interest and principal payments on which are based on the payments made by those who have obtained mortgages—the interest and principal payments of those who have obtained mortgages are channeled through to those who acquire the bonds. Because these bonds are issued by agencies and their payments are based on those received from mortgages, they are called agency mortgage-backed securities.)

- This policy has been called <u>quantitative</u> easing because of its focus on the central bank buying a certain <u>quantity</u> of assets. Instead of the focus on targeting a key interest rate, as in typical OMOs, the central bank's focus in QE is on purchasing a certain quantity (in terms of money value) of assets in the hope that these purchases will have the desired effect of stimulating the economy.

- QE has been used in:

    o Japan from 2001 to 2006 and again since 2009.
    o The UK from Mar. 2009 to Jan. 2010, and since Oct. 2011.
    o The US from Mar. 2009 to Mar. 2010, and from Nov. 2010 to end of June 2011. This second bout of QE in the US is referred to as QE2. On 9/13/12, the Fed announced a third bout of QE, which is referred to as QE3.

Maturity Extension Program (Operation Twist)
This policy is called Operation Twist because it is very similar to a Fed policy that was used in 1961 that was given the name Twist, after a dance that was popular at the time.

The Federal Reserve announced it on Sep. 21, 2011 stating the Fed would sell $400 billion of shorter-term (maturities of up to 3 years) Treasury securities by the end of June 2012 and use the proceeds to buy longer-term (maturities of 6 to 30 years) treasuries. On June 20, 2012, the Fed announced it was extending this same buy-sell program for about $267 billion to the end of 2012.

The name Twist is related to the fact that this policy aims at increasing short term treasury yields (as the Fed sold short term treasuries) but bringing down long term treasury yields (as the Fed bought long term treasuries), so it is "twisting" yields.

The Fed felt this would:

- Reduce long term rates and stimulate the economy. (How buying long term treasuries would reduce long term rates and stimulate the economy was explained a few paragraphs above in the discussion of QE.)

- Continue what QE was meant to do in lowering longer term rates.

- Avoid the monetary expansion that QE could cause and so prevent the inflationary risks associated with QE. As the Fed sells short term securities and buys an equal amount of long term securities, it is not changing the money supply directly by this action. So the possibility of inflation, which is exacerbated by an increasing money supply, is reduced.

Paying interest on bank reserves

On Oct. 9, 2008 the Fed began paying interest on bank reserves, both required and excess.

- When banks do not receive interest on required reserves, they forego the income they could have earned by loaning the funds they have to keep as reserves. Being required to keep reserves that earn no interest is therefore like a tax on banks. Paying interest on reserves reduces this "tax," lowering the costs of banking.

- When the fed funds rate was discussed, it was noted that the Fed sets a target for this rate and then engages in OMOs to keep the rate around the target. But banks are free to lend above or below this target level. By paying interest on reserves, the Fed ensures that no bank lending in the fed funds market would want to lend at less than the rate it can get just by holding its reserves at the Fed. So by paying interest on reserves, the Fed established a lower bound for the fed funds rate *for those banks that could earn this interest by placing reserves at the Fed.* This gives the Fed more control over the fed funds rate.

- But this doesn't mean that the average rate for all lending in the fed funds market will be no less than the interest rate the Fed pays on excess reserves. If every institution could earn this interest rate, no institution would normally lend at less than it. However, institutions such as government sponsored enterprises (GSEs—described earlier in the section on quantitative easing) are not eligible to receive any interest on excess reserves. But they can lend in the fed funds market. So they lend at less than the rate the Fed pays on excess reserves rather than earn nothing. This is why the average rate for all lending in the fed funds market is below the interest rate the Fed pays on excess reserves.

- This policy of paying interest on reserves also gives the Fed an additional tool for manipulating the money supply. If the Fed wanted to encourage banks to lend, it could lower this interest rate, giving banks an incentive to get a higher return by increasing their lending. If the Fed wanted to discourage banks from lending, it could raise this interest rate, giving banks more of an incentive not to lend to people and businesses but to just put funds in the Fed and earn this interest rate on reserves.

MONEY AND AGGREGATE DEMAND

In this chapter, we have seen that increases in the money supply are associated with more availability of credit (loans) and lower interest rates; decreases in the money supply are associated with less credit availability and higher interest rates.

Think of how consumers behave if credit is more easily available to them and the interest they have to pay when they borrow is going down. This will decrease the cost of borrowing and encourage consumers to borrow and spend, increasing the total demand for goods and services. The same happens with businesses when the cost of borrowing is going down—businesses find it cheaper to borrow and spend and this increases their demand for goods and services. So increases in the money supply lead to increases in aggregate demand.

If the money supply is being decreased so credit is harder to get and interest rates are rising, this raises the cost of borrowing. Consumers and businesses find it more costly to borrow. This discourages them from borrowing and spending, which reduces the demand for goods and services. A decrease in the money supply reduces aggregate demand.

In Chapter 2, it was mentioned that increases in the money supply, *ceteris paribus*, led to increases in aggregate demand. Or that decreases in the money supply decrease aggregate demand. The links discussed in this chapter between the money supply and the availability of loans and interest rates, let us better understand how changes in the money supply cause changes in aggregate demand.

In APPENDIX, Part II *at the end of this book*, **there is a detailed discussion of how changes in the money supply affect aggregate demand.** This appendix uses diagrams and a model in which changes in the money supply lead to changes in the level of investment, which then changes aggregate demand. The more abstract presentation there is consistent with what you would typically encounter in theoretical courses in academia.

THE NOMINAL INTEREST RATE AND THE REAL INTEREST RATE

We want to go on now to further refine our concept of the interest rate. A **nominal interest rate** is the interest rate actually paid in any transaction that involves an interest payment. If you lent me $100 for a year at 10 % interest, the 10 % interest I pay you is the nominal rate of interest. If you have a savings account in a bank and you are paid a 2.5 % interest on it, the 2.5 % is the nominal interest—the actual amount that is paid.

A **real rate of interest**, however, is defined as the nominal rate of interest minus the rate of inflation during the period the interest is earned:

$$r = i - n \text{ , where } r = \text{the real rate of interest}$$
$$i = \text{the nominal rate of interest}$$
$$n = \text{the inflation rate}$$

If you lend me a $100 for a year at 10 % interest, and the inflation rate for the year is 3 %, the real rate of interest you receive is 7 % (10 % minus 3 %).[48] If there is no inflation (0 % inflation), the real rate of interest is 10 % (10 % minus 0 %). At the end of the year the $110 you are repaid would have a purchasing power 10 % higher than the amount you lent me.

---

[48] If the nominal interest rate is i % a year, $1 now will become 1+i in a year. If the inflation over this year is n %, the amount this 1+i can purchase will be (1+i) divided by (1+n). So r, the real rate of return on this dollar, is the change in the amount it can purchase at the end of the year compared to the beginning = (1+i) / (1+n) – 1. So r = [(1+i) – (1+n)] / (1+n) ➔ r = (i – n)/(1+n) ➔ r+nr = i – n ➔ r = i – n – nr, so r is approximately i – n, since nr is typically a very small amount.

However, with inflation at 3 % per year, the amount of increased purchasing power you earn from lending me $100 no longer equals 10 %. The 3 % inflation means average prices have risen by 3 % so you can now purchase less than if inflation had been 0%. Your purchasing power has increased by the 10 % nominal interest you receive minus the 3 % inflation. The real rate of interest measures the change in purchasing power of an amount earning interest. (The relation $r = i - n$ is called the Fisher relation in honor of the economist Irving Fisher. In college, I sometimes encountered students who made the mistake of writing $i = r - n$, which is, of course, an error. I call this error the fishy relation!)

The Fisher relation is also stated as $r = i - n^e$, where n^e is the expected rate of inflation. If you are a lender seeking a return of 10 % in the year ahead, and you expect inflation to be 4 %, you will ask for a 14 % real rate of interest. In this context, when the inflation that is expected is subtracted from the nominal rate of interest to get the real rate of interest, the Fisher relation will be stated with n^e, instead of n, as $r = i - n^e$

THE MONETARY BASE, THE MONEY MULTIPLIER, AND THE MONEY STOCK

The term **monetary base** refers to the total amount of currency in circulation (C) and reserves (R). R, of course, includes reserves held as vault cash and reserves held at the Fed. We will represent the monetary base as H, so $H = C + R$.

Open market operations—OMOs—are the main policy tool the Fed uses for managing the money supply on a day-to-day basis. When the Fed engages in an OMO, it buys or sells bonds. This changes the monetary base by the exact amount of the bonds bought or sold. If the Fed buys $1 million in bonds, it pays out $1 million. Bank reserves and/or currency in circulation increase by $1 million. H, the monetary base, increases by $1 million. If the Fed sells $1 million in bonds, it has to be paid $1 million, so $1 million moves from reserves and/or currency in circulation into the Fed. H decreases by $1 million.

In Chapter 6, we stated that we will view the money stock as consisting of currency in circulation plus deposits, C + D. When the monetary base (H) changes, the extent of the change in the money stock depends on how much reserves banks keep (the reserve-deposit ratio) and how much currency the public holds (the currency-deposit ratio). To manage the size of the money stock, the Fed needs to know by how much the money stock changes when the monetary base changes. For this, it relies on a formula, a simplified version of which is:

$$M = \frac{(cd + 1)H}{(cd + rr)}$$

Here cd and rr are the currency deposit ratio and reserve-deposit ratio respectively, as we learned in the previous chapter. **Elementary algebra is used to derive this formula in APPENDIX II at the end of this chapter.**

The amount (cd + 1)/(cd + rr) is called the **money multiplier**, which we will represent with the symbol mm. It tells by how much the money stock, M, changes when there is a change of $1 in H. For example, if the Fed buys $1 million in bonds, H changes by $1 million. If the money multiplier is 2.5, this means M changes by 2.5 times $1 million.

The amounts represented by cd and rr are fractions, so cd + 1 > cd + rr . The numerator of the money multiplier is therefore greater than the denominator, and the money multiplier is greater than one, in this simple formulation for the money multiplier. This means every dollar of increase in the monetary base leads to an increase of more than one dollar in the money stock. Because rr is in the denominator of the money multiplier (mm) an increase in rr increases the denominator of mm and decreases mm. For a given amount of H, a decrease in mm decreases the money stock. So, for a given amount of H, a rise in rr, decreases the money stock. For example, if H = $100 million and mm = 2.5, M = 2.5 X $100 million = $250 million. If rr now increases so that mm falls to 2, then for H = $100 million, M now equals 2 X $100 million = $200 million.

The currency-deposit ratio (cd) is in both the numerator and denominator of mm. Elementary mathematics can be used to show that a rise in cd decreases mm.[49] So, just as we learned earlier in this chapter, a rise in cd would cause a decrease in the money stock and a decrease in the money supply. A decrease in cd increases mm and increases the money supply. **APPENDIX III at the end of this chapter uses calculus to show that mm is inversely related to cd.**

EXERCISE 3

1. If the nominal interest rate is 8 % and the real interest rate projected for the year ahead is 6 %, what is the expected inflation rate?

2.
   a.   If mm = 3, and H increases by $10 million, by how much does the money stock change?
   b.   If M = $400 million, C = $100 million, and R = $100 million, what are the: i. currency-deposit ratio; ii. reserve-deposit ratio; iii. monetary base; iv. money multiplier?

3. Say whether each of the following is true or false and justify your response:
   a.   If people hold more currency relative to deposits, this increases currency in circulation and so increases the money stock.
   b.   An increase in the reserve ratio increases the money stock.
   c.   The money multiplier decreased during the Great Depression.

---

[49] The amounts represented by cd and rr are fractions, so cd + 1 > cd + rr . The numerator of mm (cd + 1) is therefore greater than the denominator of mm (cd + rr). Because the numerator is larger than the denominator, a rise in cd increases the numerator by a smaller percentage than it increases the denominator, so the whole fraction (cd + 1)/ (cd + rr) decreases. For example, suppose cd = 0.5 and rr = 0.3, then mm = (0.5 + 1)/(0.5 + 0.3) = 1.875. If cd increases to 0.6, mm now equals (0.6 + 1)/(0.6 + 0.3) = 1.778. This illustrates that an increase in cd decreases the money multiplier.

CONCLUSION

A main focus of this chapter was how the central bank changes the money supply and interest rates. The roles of banks and of the public were also discussed. Various interest rates—the fed funds, discount and prime rates—were defined, and the connection between changes in the money supply, interest rates and aggregate demand were specified. This information will be very valuable in helping you to make sense of the daily business news on central bank actions and interest rates levels.

If you would like a more theoretical treatment of the interaction between money supply and <u>money demand</u>, you can read the **END OF BOOK APPENDIX, Part I.** Money demand is defined there and you are shown how money supply and money demand interact in a theoretical model to determine the interest rate. For a more detailed discussion of how changes in the money supply and interest rates affect the level of investment and aggregate demand, see **END OF BOOK APPENDIX, Part II.**

ANSWERS

EXERCISE 1

1.

    a. $D = 100$, $C = 80$, so $M = C + D = \$180$ million.
    b. Required reserves = 10 % of $D = (10/100) \times 100 = \$10$ million.
    c. Excess reserves = actual reserves held minus required reserves = $15 - 10 = \$5$ million.
    d. Reserve ratio = $R/D = 15/100$.
    e. Currency-deposit ratio = $C/D = 80/100$.

2.

    a. $C = 50$, $D = 100$, so $M = C + D = 50 + 100 = \$150$ million.
    b. Remains at $150 million. I have merely shifted $5,000 from C to D.
    c. Increases by $3,000.
    d. Yes, as the answer to c illustrates.

3. As banks kept higher levels of reserves, the reserve ratio (rr) went up, and banks made less loans. If someone repaid a bank loan, for example, the bank would hold on to the funds, or to most of the funds, rather than seek to loan it all out. As the public withdrew funds from banks, the currency-deposit ratio (cd) went up, leaving banks with less funds with which they could make loans. Each of these occurrences reduced the money supply. From the AD-AS model, we know that the fall in the money supply would decrease AD, and decrease output and employment, worsening the Great Depression.

EXERCISE 2

1.
    a. Decrease
    b. Increase
    c. Increase
    d. Decrease

2.
    a. False. The Fed engages in OMOs daily to keep the fed funds rate at levels the Fed would like. Of course, when the Fed announces a new target for the Fed funds rate, the Fed engages in OMOs to get the rate to that level. After that, the Fed will engage in OMOs to seek to keep the fed funds rate at the desired level.

    b. False. The Fed's target for the fed funds rate is often referred to as the fed funds rate in the news media, but the context makes clear that it is the fed funds target rate that is being referred to. The rate a bank charges in lending its excess reserves to other banks is called the fed funds rate and this rate can vary from one bank to another and from one loan of excess reserves to another. For example, if Bank ABC has a lot of excess reserves and the fed funds target rate is 0.5 %, Bank ABC may choose to lend these reserves at 0.4 % to Bank K, rather than have the reserves remain idle. At the same time, Bank Q, lending its excess reserves to Bank L, might charge 0.55 % because of Bank Q's perception of the risk of lending to Bank L. The Fed's target for the fed funds rate indicates that the Fed has the official intention of trying to ensure that the average interest rate on all these loans of excess reserves by banks is around the target level. The Fed would engage in OMOs daily as it seeks to have this average fed funds rate at the level the Fed desires.

    c. False. When the Fed wants to tighten monetary policy by raising its interest rate target, it announces a new, higher target for fed funds rate. Banks then respond by increasing their prime rate, which is typically 3 % above the fed funds target rate.

3. The fed funds rate is the rate banks charge when they lend their excess reserves to other banks. The discount rate is the rate the Fed charges when it makes loans to banks at the discount window.

EXERCISE 3

1. $r = i - n^e$, so $n^e = i - r = 8\% - 6\% = 2\%$.

2.

    a. The change in M = mm times the change in H = 3 X 10 = $30 million.

    b.

        i.   M = 400 and C = 100, so D = M − C = 400 − 100 = 300. C/D = 100/300 = 1/3.

        ii.   R/D = 100/300 = 1/3.

        iii. H = C + R = 100 + 100 = $200 million.

        iv. M = mmH. mm = M/H = 400/200 = 2. [A long-winded way of finding mm is: mm = (cd + 1)/(cd + rr) = (1/3 + 1)/(1/3 + 1/3) = (4/3) / (2/3) = 2.]

3.

    a. False. If people hold more currency relative to deposits, this increases cd, which decreases mm and decreases M.

    b. False. An increase in rr decreases mm and decreases M.

    c. True. As we saw in EXERCISE 1, #3, rr and cd both increased during the Great Depression. Each of these increasing caused mm to decrease.

APPENDIX I
THE SUBPRIME/CREDIT CRUNCH CRISIS

The subprime crisis came to the fore in the US in 2007.

- Very inadequate regulation of lending enabled financial institutions to make loans to those who were far less than creditworthy, aptly described by the term **subprime**—less than prime quality.

- Financial institutions did not mind giving the loans because financial markets had developed in which these loans could be repackaged and sold. So loan givers could profit from making loans to the less than creditworthy but did not have to hold on to the loans. The financial institutions got fees from making the loans and from acting as the agent for collecting the payments due on the loans.[50]

---

[50] A financial product that became very prevalent was the **collateralized debt obligation (CDO)**. The creator of a CDO would buy loans from institutions that had issued them, and so become entitled to receive the interest and principal payments due on these loans. The creator of the CDO would then issue a set of bonds, the interest and principal payments on which would be funded with the interest and principal payments received on the loans that had been bought. Bonds that offered the lowest yield were ones whose coupon and principal payments were given priority. Bonds that paid the highest yield were the riskiest, those most closely linked to the probability of default on the loans. As creators of CDOs sold these bonds, they got more funds to buy more loans from those who had issued the loans. So they were able to create more bonds. Investors who were hungry for financial gain bought the risky bonds for their high returns. Asset managers, seeing their colleagues at other firms getting high quarterly returns from these ventures, were hard pressed to show that they could do as well, and felt impelled to get involved in buying risky bonds to get high returns. In the euphoria, these asset managers didn't think that massive loan defaults would occur that would make it impossible for them to get the payments due on the bonds they had bought. The stage had been set for a financial collapse once defaults on the loans on which the bonds were based reached a certain critical level.

- As these institutions sold loans they had made, they got funds to make more loans, and in the frenzy to make loans, kept lowering standards. People who had no income, no jobs and assets were able to get loans. (These were called <u>NINJA loans</u>!—No Income, No Jobs or Assets)

- The easy availability of credit caused a boom in real estate and prices of houses and apartments shot up. People rushed in to speculate on real estate. Flipping became common—buying a property, waiting a short while for the price to shoot up and then selling (flipping) it.

- Many who received loans soon became unable to repay and defaulted. Those who had bought bonds based on repackaged loans (see details in the earlier footnote describing CDOs) began to experience severe losses as the payments due on the bonds could not be made because of defaults.

- Investors became unwilling to buy the bonds based on repackaged loans, so the market for these dried up. Institutions that made loans with the aim of repackaging them found themselves stuck with bad loans, unable to sell these to get funds to make more loans to potential home buyers. Some of these institutions began to be viewed as failures.

- No longer fuelled by easy credit, real estate prices stalled and then began to collapse. Speculators were left stuck with properties no one wanted to buy.

- As the real estate construction industry collapsed, and financial institutions failed, the economy collapsed. The subprime crisis was in full swing and became a credit crunch crisis as lenders, doubtful about who might be a worthy credit risk, became extremely reluctant to lend. Many fine businesses that funded their daily operations on credit, as many businesses typically do, found it very hard to get credit. Central banks like the Fed had to create massive programs to make loans available to various sectors of the economy to ease the credit crunch.

APPENDIX II
HOW TO DERIVE THE RELATION M = mmH

As specified in this chapter:

M = money stock
cd = currency-deposit ratio
rr = reserve ratio
H = monetary base

We want to obtain a relation between M, cd, rr, and H. We engage in algebraic manipulation to do this:

We know $M = C + D$, $H = C + R$, $cd = C/D$, $rr = R/D$.

Since $H = C + R$, when we multiply $C + D$ by H and divide by $C + R$, we are in fact multiplying and dividing by H, so $C + D$ is unchanged. We multiply and divide by H and $C + R$ (which equals H) respectively because this is a manipulation which takes us toward getting M in terms of cd, rr and H.

So we can write: $M = C + D = (C + D)H/(C + R)$.

We will divide the numerator and denominator by D because this immediately leads us to an expression involving cd and rr:

$$M = (C + D)H/(C + R) = (C/D + D/D) H/(C/D + R/D) =$$

$$(cd + 1) H/ (cd + rr).$$

But $(cd + 1)/(cd + rr) = mm$. Therefore, $M = mmH$.

APPENDIX III
USING CALCULUS TO SHOW
mm IS INVERSELY RELATED TO cd

(If you haven't done calculus, you will still be able to live very happily without bothering with this.)

$mm = (cd + 1)/(cd + rr)$.

If mm is inversely related to cd, the derivative of mm with respect to cd, dmm/dcd, will be negative.

$dmm/dcd = [(cd + rr) - (cd + 1)] / (cd + rr)^2$.

$(cd + rr)^2$ will always be positive, being the square of a real quantity.

$(cd + rr) - (cd + 1) = rr - 1$, which is negative since rr is less than 1.

So dmm/dcd has a positive denominator but a negative numerator, so it is negative, which implies that mm is inversely related to cd—when cd increases, mm falls, and when cd decreases, mm increases.

CHAPTER 8
INFLATION AND UNEMPLOYMENT

INTRODUCTION

Inflation and unemployment are very often in the news, portrayed as fearsome phenomena that adversely affect our standard of living. In this chapter, we learn more about these phenomena and their consequences, what causes them, and what governmental authorities can do to control them. We will use the AD-AS model in several parts of the discussion. This will deepen understanding of applications of this model and let us march on with the objective—first mentioned in Chapter 2—of broadening our knowledge of the use of this model to understand the world.

INFLATION: DEFINITION AND RELATED TERMS

In Chapter 5, we learned that inflation is a rise in the average price level. When inflation occurs, this does not mean the price of every good or service is going up. What it means is that on the average prices are going up. We also learned that the inflation rate is measured by the percentage rise in a price index. For example, if the consumer price index rises from 120 to 132 in a year, the CPI inflation rate is 10 % for that year [(132 - 120)/120 multiplied by 100].

Creeping inflation, as the word "creeping" suggests, occurs when the inflation rate is inching upward. **Galloping inflation**, as the word "galloping" suggests, occurs when inflation becomes more and more rapid.

Disinflation means the inflation rate is decreasing. If the inflation rate fell from 4 % to 2 %, this is disinflation. The average price level is still rising, but at a lower rate—2 % rather than 4 %.

Deflation means the inflation rate is negative, the average price level is falling. **Reflation** is when the average price level is rising back to a previous level. [51]

HYPERINFLATION

Extremely rapid inflation is called **hyperinflation**. To make this definition more precise, economists sometimes refer to hyperinflation as inflation in excess of 1000 % per year, a number chosen because it suggests extremely rapid inflation, not because there is any more scientific basis for it. To give you a notion of what inflation of 1000 % per year means, consider that if the price of bread rose by 1000 % in one year, and a loaf of bread cost $1 at the beginning of the year, it would cost $11 at the end of the year. You can imagine the chaos it would cause you if prices rose this rapidly! Argentina, Bolivia, Bosnia Herzegovina, Brazil, Germany, Peru and Zimbabwe are just some of the countries that have experienced hyperinflation.

These cases of hyperinflation provide stunning examples of prices rising astronomically. The inflation rate in Bolivia reached an annual rate of 60,000 percent from May 1985 to Aug. 1985. If the price of bread rose at this rate, a loaf that cost a dollar would cost $601 a few months later!

In the German hyperinflation (the early 1920s), prices rose to such high levels that people walked around with wheelbarrows full of money to make their purchases. Prices increased so rapidly that beer drinkers found that by the time they had finished drinking a beer and ordered a second one, the price had gone up. What a

---

[51] The words deflation and reflation have other meanings that should not be confused with the meanings stated here. Another meaning of deflation is the fall in an economy's output, price level and employment resulting from a reduction in aggregate demand. Reflation is also used to mean an increase in aggregate demand after there has been a period of falling aggregate demand, or the increase in output, the price level and employment as aggregate demand increases from lower levels to which it had fallen.

tragedy this must have been, how unfair to these poor beer drinkers! Later in this chapter we will learn what causes inflation and hyperinflation.

THE CONSEQUENCES OF INFLATION

If inflation occurs and wages are not rising to keep pace with inflation, workers would be able to buy decreasing amounts of goods and services with their wages. They lose purchasing power as a result of inflation.

What frequently happens, however, is that workers agitate for and receive higher wages as inflation occurs. The workers would then lose purchasing power as a result of inflation only if the percentage wage increases are less than the inflation rate. Even if people are obtaining wage increases that keep pace with inflation, they may fail to recognize that were it not for the inflation they would not have been able to obtain wage increases, and they may still be bothered by the rising prices because of the thought of how much more they could have purchased if prices were not rising. This discontent could cause them to withdraw their support from the political authorities they hold responsible for the inflation.

Another possibility is that **money illusion** occurs. If your income rises and the price level also rises by the same percentage as the rise in income, but the income increase makes you feel richer and causes you to purchase more, you are suffering from money illusion. Your **real income** (income divided by the price level, which means the same as the **purchasing power of income**) has not changed, but the illusion that you are richer causes you to behave as if it has and induces you to spend more.

The elderly receiving retirement pensions that are not **indexed** to keep pace with inflation suffer a loss in the purchasing power of their pensions when inflation occurs. **Indexation** is the adjustment of payments to maintain the purchasing power of the payments when inflation occurs. For example, if inflation was 4 %, the payments would have to rise by 4 % if they are fully indexed. If there is only partial indexation, then the payments will increase by less than the inflation rate.

(Do not confuse "indexed" or "indexation" with the price *index* we learned of in Chapter 5.)

Savers could also lose from inflation. If you have money in a bank account and if the interest you receive on it does not keep pace with inflation, the purchasing power of your saving declines.

Similarly, if you are a lender of money and inflation turns out to be higher than you anticipated when you lent, you would earn an interest rate on what you have lent that does not keep pace with inflation. Suppose you lent me $1000 for a year at 10 % interest but inflation turned out to be 20 % over the year. At the end of the year, I repay you $1000 plus 10 % of $1000 in interest, a total of $1100. However, because of the 20 % inflation, at the end of the year it now takes $1000 plus 20 % of $1000, which equals $1200, to buy what $1000 could have bought at the beginning of the year. The $1100 you receive from me at the end of the year has less purchasing power than the $1000 you lent me at the beginning of the year. You, the lender, have lost because of not correctly anticipating inflation and not charging a rate of interest high enough to compensate you for inflation decreasing the purchasing power of what you lent. As a borrower in this situation, I have gained because the purchasing power of what I repay you is less than the purchasing power of what I borrowed from you.

People holding currency lose as the purchasing power of their currency is eroded by inflation. If the inflation rate was 100 % a week, and you earned $40 each day but were paid at the end of the week, by the time you received your paycheck, the purchasing power of the $40 you earned the first day would be halved—for example, if a set of goods and services cost $40 at the beginning of the week, at the end it would cost $80 if the inflation rate for these was 100 % per week. It would be sensible for you to ask to be paid more often and for you to shop more frequently to quickly convert your money into commodities. This example suggests that as inflation intensifies, people would seek to engage in more frequent transactions to reduce their losses from inflation. The time and resources that have to be spent on these increased activities are called **shoe-leather costs**. Inflation increases the running around we do, so we can think of it as wearing down our shoe leather!

As inflation escalates, prices of supermarket items, catalog prices, restaurant menu prices, etc., have to be changed frequently. Rapid inflation also makes it difficult for those offering services of pay phones, parking meters and other coin-operated machines, since it is troublesome to frequently adjust these to accept new amounts of coins. Making these alterations uses up time and resources and is a rising cost as inflation ratchets up. The costs of inflation that result from prices having to be updated often are called **menu costs**.

These consequences of inflation become more pronounced as inflation intensifies. Also, as inflation quickens, those who have wealth can still afford to buy what they want. The poor, however, have little or no assets they can draw on to enable them to buy what they need. High inflation thrusts the poor into even greater want and despair. (It is always the poor who suffer the most when the economy worsens. This is why those who make policy should be ever cognizant that theirs is a sacred duty—failure to make good policies is often like a frightening crime, imposing severe suffering on people.)

EXERCISE 1

1. Suppose in Ruritania, our favorite country, inflation is as follows: 2000: 3 % ; 2001: 3.5 % ; 2002: 4.1 % ; 2003: 10 % ; 2004: 20 % ; 2005: 1250 % ; 2006: 4 % ; 2007: 3 % ; 2008: 1 % ; 2009: –1 % ; 2010: 0.5 %. Cite time periods in which each of the following occurred: i. Creeping inflation; ii. Galloping inflation; iii. Hyperinflation; iv. Disinflation; v. Deflation; vi. Reflation.

2. A lender will not be penalized by inflation if
   a. Inflation is unanticipated by the lender
   b. The lender correctly anticipates inflation and charges a nominal rate of interest that takes account of the anticipated inflation
   c. The lender suffers from money illusion
   d. Inflation is unanticipated by the borrower

3. Which one of the following statements is correct? Unanticipated inflation:
    a. Increases the real value of savings
    b. Increases the purchasing power of currency
    c. Benefits those receiving fixed incomes
    d. Penalizes those who have lent money

THE CAUSES OF INFLATION

From the AD-AS model, we know that any factor that increases AD or decreases AS can push up the price level. Among the factors that can increase AD are increases in consumer optimism, business optimism, government spending, exports, transfers, and the money supply, and decreases in tax rates that cause people to spend more. Among the factors that can decrease AS are increases in the price of a widely used input, deterioration of technology that increases inefficiencies in production, increases in taxes that increase unit costs of production, and increases in government regulations that increase unit costs of production.

An increase in the price level resulting from a rise in AD is called **demand-pull inflation**. An increase in the price level due to rising costs of production (which decrease AS) is called **cost-push inflation**.

Any of the factors just listed can cause inflation. For example, rising government spending can push up aggregate demand and the price level and cause inflation. However, we will now argue that if inflation is persistent and rapid,[52] the ultimate source of this is rapid increase in the money supply.

To see why this is so, recognize that if the price level is moving up rapidly, then the factor causing this must also be changing rapidly. But, considering the factors that increase AD or decrease AS, it is impossible to imagine consumer optimism,

---

[52] To get a sense of what persistent, rapid inflation is, note that inflation of a few percentage points a month would be extraordinarily high by US standards, where core CPI inflation over the last 10 years has averaged about 1.9 % **per year**.

business optimism, exports, transfers, tax rates, government regulations, or technology changing at continuous very high rates.

Increases in the price of inputs also cannot be the cause of continuous, high levels of inflation. It is impossible for the supply of, or demand for, a widely used input like labor or oil to change so much and continuously as to cause the price of the input to rise at continuous very high levels to cause sustained, rapid inflation.[53]

Also, government spending can only rise at the very high rates necessary to cause sustained high levels of inflation if the government is able to obtain the funds to finance its spending. The central bank is the only lender that can continually create money to lend to the government. Lenders other than the central bank have only limited amounts to lend. The central bank, however, can continually purchase bonds issued by the government and issue money to pay for these.

This issuing of money by the central bank in return for bonds increases the money supply (as we learned in Chapter 7). As the government continually borrows large sums from the central bank, the money supply increases sharply causing very high levels of inflation.[54]

Rapid increase in the money supply is the ultimate cause of persistent, rapid inflation. Any factor that increases AD or decreases AS can cause inflation, but persistent, high levels of inflation is caused by rapid increase in the money supply. To deal with such inflation, there is only one remedy—the growth of the money supply must be reduced.

---

[53] If the price of an input did rise perpetually and sharply it would be because some other factor is causing very high levels of inflation and so pushing up, at phenomenal rates, the price of the input (as well as the price of other goods and services). We will soon see that such a factor is rapid increase in the money supply.

[54] In some countries, unlike in the US, the central bank is under the control of the executive branch of the government—the President or the Prime Minister. The political leader can give orders to the central bank to lend to the government. The central bank prints money that it lends to the government. This situation is frequently referred to as the central bank "**printing money**" to finance government spending. In the US, however, the President cannot give orders to the Fed.

THE EQUATION OF EXCHANGE

The **equation of exchange** gives us further insights into the role of money in causing inflation.

Suppose in 2012 the total amount of purchases (or sales—purchases must equal sales because whatever is a purchase for a buyer is a sale for a seller) in an economy was $500 million, and the money stock was $100 million. Then on the average each dollar of the money stock was used 500/100 = 5 times in paying for the transactions during 2012.

As money moves from person to person when purchases and sales occur, the same currency note gets used many times in making payments. Let's say I pay you $15 for a good I purchase from you, and you then use this $15 to pay for your purchases from another person, who then uses them to pay another person. The same $15 are used 3 times in making these transactions, so on the average each dollar of these 15 is used 3 times in making payments. The average number of times each dollar of the money stock is used in paying for transactions is called the **velocity of circulation of money**, or just velocity of circulation or **velocity** for short.

If, in a given time period in an economy, Q is the total amount of goods and services bought or sold and P is the average price level, then the dollar value of transactions equals PQ. If M is the money stock, then the velocity of circulation, V, is PQ/M. Therefore, MV = PQ. In calculations of V, nominal GDP is generally used as an approximation for PQ, which means Q is approximated by real GDP. This happens because GDP figures are readily available in statistical sources.

MV = PQ, or MV = Nominal GDP, or MV = P times real GDP, is called the **equation of exchange**. This equation can be used to examine the role of money in causing inflation. By simple mathematical manipulation, the equation of exchange, MV = P times real GDP, can be re-expressed as:

Inflation rate = Growth rate of the money stock
                        + Growth rate of velocity
                        − Growth rate of real output.[55]

Real GDP is frequently referred to as real output. If n is the inflation rate and m, v and q are the growth rates of the money stock, of velocity and of real output respectively, $n = m + v - q$.

Table 1 gives numerical illustrations of the connection between the inflation rate, and the growth rates of the money stock, velocity and real output.

TABLE 1
$n = m + v - q$

n	m	v	q
6	7	2	3
140	90	48	−2
1000	802	195	−3

n = inflation rate; m, v and q are the growth rates of the money stock, of velocity and of real output respectively. The inflation rate is obtained by adding the growth rates of the money stock and velocity and subtracting the growth rate of real output.

The formula $n = m + v - q$ shows that an increasing money stock, increasing velocity and declining output each result in rising inflation. But it is impossible for output to decline at continuous, very high levels. After all, if a society's output

---

[55] Taking logarithms (to base e) of both sides of MV = PQ, we have: ln M + ln V = ln P + ln Q , so ln P = ln M + ln V − ln Q. Taking derivatives with respect to time, (1/P)dP/dt = (1/M)dM/dt + (1/V)dV/dt − (1/Q)dQ/dt. These terms are respectively, the inflation rate, the growth rate of the money stock, the growth rate of velocity and the growth rate of real GDP. So we have: **Inflation rate = Growth rate of the money stock + Growth rate of velocity − Growth rate of real output**.

declined by 100 %, the society would have no output at all—an impossibility. So very high and rising levels of inflation cannot be due to declining output. Of the two other possible causes of inflation, growth of the money stock and growth of velocity, it is rapid growth of the money stock that causes very rapid rates of inflation. In fact, as the money stock grows rapidly and speeds up inflation, this causes people to want to get rid of money swiftly by buying goods and services. If people held on to money as inflation occurs, they would lose purchasing power. So they quickly use their money to buy goods and services in order to avoid or reduce the loss of purchasing power. This is what increases velocity—which measures the average number of times each dollar of the money stock is used in making payments. So it is large increases in the money stock that is the ultimate cause of very high levels of inflation.

If you became a political leader and you were inclined to have your government borrow from the central bank to finance very large increases in spending, bear in mind that the central bank by issuing money this way increases the money stock. If these increases in the money stock occur in very large and rising amounts, this will cause high levels of inflation, even hyperinflation. If, after reading this book, you know this lesson alone you will be wiser than many political leaders the world has very painfully endured.

EXERCISE 2

1. A sharp rise in the price of oil can cause hyperinflation. True or false? Explain.

2. Which of the following, *ceteris paribus*, can increase inflation?
    i.   Rising consumer spending
    ii.   Falling velocity of circulation of money
    iii. Increased government regulations on business
    iv.   A declining money supply

UNEMPLOYMENT

For any country in which you are interested, if you check with the country's agency that is responsible for compiling employment statistics, you will be able to get the specific criteria that agency uses to determine who is counted as employed, unemployed, or not in the labor force. In the US, the unemployed are those 16 years and older who do not have jobs, are available for work and are seeking work, or are laid off from a job and expecting to be recalled to it. So a person without a job is only counted as unemployed if the person meets conditions like those just stated.

The employed are those who have jobs. The jobs do not have to be full time. In the US, if a person did any work at all for pay or profit during the survey reference week,[56] or worked at least fifteen hours for no pay in a family member's business, he/she would be counted as employed.

- The **labor force** consists of those who are employed, e, and those who are unemployed, u.

- The unemployment rate is [u/ (u + e)] X 100 %. The **civilian labor force** excludes those who work in the military.[57] The **civilian unemployment rate** is unemployed civilians as a percentage of the civilian labor force.

- If a person is not employed and also does not meet the conditions to be considered unemployed, that person is not a part of the labor force. **A person can be classified as employed, unemployed or not in the labor force.**

---

[56] The survey reference week is the week in each month when the survey to determine employment/unemployment is done by the US Bureau of the Census for the Bureau of Labor Statistics. This week typically includes the 12th of the month.

[57] Those in penal and mental institutions and in homes for the aged are also not counted as part of the civilian labor force.

Frictional Unemployment

No matter how well an economy is performing, there will always be some unemployment in it. There will be persons entering the labor force as they reach working age or as they graduate from college, persons leaving jobs to seek better ones, or relocating and having to find new jobs. These processes are not instantaneous. It takes time for people to be matched with jobs because of the "frictions" of real life such as people not having perfect information on where the jobs they want are available. Until these persons secure jobs, they will be counted as unemployed. This type of unemployment is called **frictional unemployment**.

Structural Unemployment

Structural unemployment occurs when there is a mismatch between the skills people have and the jobs that are available, and from institutional practices and social habits that cause unemployment.

Structural changes in an economy such as technological changes (e.g., automation) put some workers out of jobs by making their skills irrelevant for the available jobs. Or as demand for some products fades away while other products become the craze, some industries decline as others arise, leading to unemployment for some, and the availability of new jobs for which they don't have the skills. This is likely to entail far more prolonged unemployment than a case of frictional unemployment, as it is likely to take considerable time for people to acquire the new skills needed to fill vacant positions.

Institutional practices like minimum wage laws (that make it necessary for firms to pay wages above a certain level) could add to structural unemployment as they make firms unable to afford low-skilled workers—a category into which many teenagers fall. Social habits, such as unemployed persons delaying finding jobs because they are paid what they view as generous unemployment benefits, could also add to structural unemployment.

Seasonal Unemployment

This occurs in occupations that are seasonal. Farms produce crops during certain times of the year, ski-resorts might be operational only in winter, etc. Laborers in these occupations are likely to face **seasonal unemployment** in the out-of-season periods.

The Natural Rate of Unemployment

The percentage of unemployment due to frictional, structural and seasonal causes constitute the **natural rate of unemployment**.[58] The natural rate of unemployment for the US in 2009 was said to be around 5 %.[59] The US Congressional Budget Office estimated it to be about 5.2 % for each of 2009 to 2012.[60]

However, determining what is the natural rate of unemployment is not at all hard science, so no one can claim to know for sure what it is. It is worth noting that in the US for 2006 and 2007, unemployment averaged 4.6 % per month, substantially below the presumed natural rate of around 5 %, and these were times when the subprime/credit crunch crisis was intensifying, wreaking its havoc on the economy, leading to the start of a recession in the US in Dec. 2007. (As was explained in Chapter 3, in the US, the Business Cycle Dating Committee of the National Bureau of Economic Research determines the dates of the start and end of a recession. On Dec. 1, 2008, this committee announced that a recession had started in the US in Dec. 2007.)

When the unemployment rate in an economy is at the natural rate, the economy is said to be at **full employment**. So at full employment the unemployment rate would be greater than zero. The level of output of an economy when the economy

---

[58] There is some fuzziness in the discussion of these concepts. Some economists do not mention seasonal unemployment as a part of the natural rate of unemployment, and others include frictional unemployment as a part of structural unemployment, etc.

[59] Paul Krugman (Nobel Prize, Economics, 2008), for example, has said that the natural rate of unemployment "clearly means an unemployment rate near 5" percent. See Krugman, P. (2009, Jan. 6). Stimulus arithmetic (wonkish but important), *The New York Times*.

[60] Congressional Budget Office. (2011, Jan.). *The budget and economic outlook: Fiscal years 2011 to 2021*.

is at full employment is called **potential output** (or potential GDP)—the economy is achieving its potential in terms of output.

The level of the natural rate of unemployment varies over the course of time. Younger workers have higher rates of frictional unemployment, and it is believed that in the US since the 1970s the declining share of younger workers in the labor force has contributed a decrease of about 1 % in the natural rate of unemployment. The growth of temporary-help employment services and Internet job finding sites has made jobs searches more efficient and may have contributed to decreasing the natural rate of unemployment. Factors like these are believed to have caused a decrease in the natural rate of unemployment in the US from the levels of the 1970s.

Cyclical Unemployment

Cyclical unemployment is due to the fluctuations in economic activity associated with the economy's business cycle (the business cycle was discussed in Chapter 3). As an economy weakens, unemployment rises. As an economy moves through recession, unemployment continues to rise. Eventually, as the economy emerges from the recession and strengthens, unemployment falls.

Cyclical unemployment, unlike frictional, structural and seasonal unemployment, is not part of the natural rate of unemployment. Cyclical unemployment is caused by aggregate demand and/or aggregate supply[61] being less than enough to keep employment at the full employment level. When cyclical unemployment occurs, an economy's output is below potential.

---

[61] Some economists refer to cyclical unemployment as caused by only aggregate demand being less than enough to keep unemployment at the full employment level. However, as we saw in the AD-AS model, fluctuations in aggregate supply can also cause fluctuations in output and employment.

EXERCISE 3

1. Elvis has quit his job and is seeking a better job. His unemployment should be categorized as:
    a. Structural
    b. Cyclical
    c. Frictional
    d. Seasonal

2. The unemployment that results from the decreased demand for goods and services as a recession occurs is:
    a. Structural
    b. Cyclical
    c. Frictional
    d. Seasonal

3. Britney has lost her job in the textile industry due to cheaper textiles coming in from China. She is acquiring skills to get one of the jobs available at Apple. Her unemployment would be categorized as:
    a. Structural
    b. Cyclical
    c. Frictional
    d. Seasonal

4. When an economy is at its natural rate of unemployment,
    a. It has only frictional unemployment
    b. Its potential output exceeds its actual output
    c. It has only cyclical unemployment
    d. Its actual output equals its potential

5. When an economy is at full employment, its unemployment is said to be at the natural rate, and it has zero
    a. Frictional unemployment
    b. Structural unemployment
    c. Cyclical unemployment
    d. Seasonal unemployment

UNEMPLOYMENT AND GDP GROWTH

In a country like the US, the population and the labor force are growing over the course of time. As people reach the age when they are ready to be part of the labor force, if there are no jobs for them, they join the ranks of the unemployed, and the unemployment rate rises. For the unemployment rate to stay constant, the economy has to be growing to create jobs for the new people being added to the labor force.

This means there has to be real GDP growth, because this will typically be associated with more jobs becoming available as workers will be needed to produce the increased output of goods and services. So if the labor force is growing, a certain amount of real GDP growth is necessary to create jobs just to keep the unemployment rate constant. Suppose the unemployment rate is 9 %, and that as the labor force grows over a year, annual GDP growth of 2 % is needed just to create new jobs to keep unemployment constant. Then if GDP grows 2 % over the course of a year, the unemployment at the end of the year would still be 9 %.

No one knows for sure what level of GDP growth is necessary to keep the unemployment rate constant. Any attempt to figure out what it is depends on data for previous years. But as the economy evolves, any relationship based on past data may not capture what is relevant for the present and future.

Many factors influence this relationship. For example, if the economy is emerging from a recession but businesses are not sure of the strength of the recovery, they might meet increased demand for their goods and services by utilizing their existing workers more, rather than by hiring new workers. In this situation, real GDP growth could be rising, and high enough to cause unemployment to fall, and yet unemployment could continue to rise because of this reluctance of businesses to hire more people. Another factor that affects how many jobs GDP growth creates is productivity—the amount of output produced by a unit of input such as labor, machinery, etc. Increasing productivity enables the economy to produce more goods and services with less labor than it needed in the past. This causes GDP growth to contribute less to decreasing unemployment than would have occurred in an economy with lower productivity.

The relationship between the level of unemployment and GDP growth gets great attention when an economy has experienced a recession and unemployment is high. Then the news is full of policy makers, businesspersons and pundits speculating on what level of economic growth would push down the unemployment rate.

Okun's Law

Arthur Okun served in the 1960s on the Council of Economic Advisers (a group that advises the US President on economic matters). He specified a relationship between unemployment and output that has come to be known as **Okun's Law**. This "law", however, is more of a rough approximation. There are different versions of this "law", and the empirical relationship it indicates changes over the years as the economy evolves. As was explained earlier, many factors influence the change in unemployment that would be associated with a change in GDP growth. It was also noted that a certain amount of GDP growth is necessary just to keep the unemployment rate constant. If this amount of GDP growth is X % per year, then annual GDP growth above this X % level could bring down unemployment. No one knows exactly how much unemployment will fall for each percent of GDP growth above this level of growth of X %. Krugman, for example, suggests that in the US, 2 to 3 % in growth above this X % level would bring down unemployment by 1 %.[62] This statement of the empirical relationship between GDP growth and unemployment is a version of Okun's Law.

THE PHILLIPS CURVE

A.W. Phillips, an electrical engineer turned economist, published a paper in 1958 in which he showed for decades of data on the United Kingdom that there was an inverse relation between unemployment and a measure of inflation. The claim that there was this relation between unemployment and inflation came to be known as the **Phillips curve**. A Phillips curve would look like Figure 1.

---

[62] See Krugman, P. (2009, Jan. 6). Stimulus arithmetic (wonkish but important), *The New York Times*.

FIGURE 1

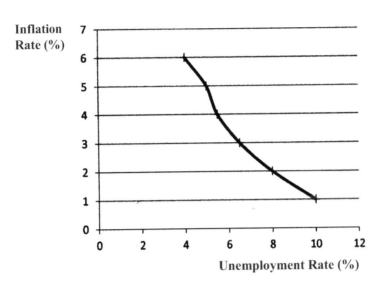

**The Phillips curve shows an inverse
relation between inflation and unemployment.
(Hypothetical data are displayed here.)**

From the AD-AS model, we know: AD→ => P↑, Y↑ and AD← => P↓, Y↓.
Recall that inflation is the percentage change in P, and rising/falling output can
mean decreasing/increasing unemployment. With changes in AD, it is possible for
rising inflation to be associated with decreasing unemployment, or for falling
inflation to be associated with rising unemployment. Inflation and unemployment
can have an inverse relation when changes in the price and output levels are due to
changes in AD.

However, as you can readily check using the AD-AS model, when changes in AS
are changing the price level, output and unemployment, then inflation and
unemployment can rise and fall together. We learned, for example, that if AS
decreases, the price level rises and output falls. This could mean that both inflation
and unemployment would rise. If AS is increasing, the price level falls and output
rises. This could result in both falling inflation and unemployment. The Phillips
curve relation depicted here does not hold when changes in AS are causing
changes in the price level, output and unemployment.

In the 1970s and 80s, there were several years when this simple Phillips curve relation did not hold for the US. Decreases in AS due to oil price increases in 1973–74 and 1978–80, and increases in AS due to oil price declines during 1982–86, were among the reasons for this. For much of the 1990s also, in the US unemployment declined substantially but inflation declined contrary to what the simple Phillips curve relation suggests. Chapter 11 presents a more sophisticated version of this relationship, the **expectations-augmented Phillips curve,** and also the **long-run Phillips curve**.

THE MISERY INDEX

Arthur Okun, mentioned above when Okun's Law was discussed, referred to the sum of the inflation and unemployment rates in the US as the <u>discomfort index</u>. In the 1976 US presidential contest, Jimmy Carter gave it a more vivid name, the **<u>misery index</u>**, in attacking President Ford's management of the economy. Ronald Reagan used the misery index to flay President Carter, and the index has continued to be used in presidential campaigns. Table 2 shows levels of the misery index for years in which US presidential elections occurred.

TABLE 2
The Misery Index

Presidential Candidate (*= incumbent, or from incumbent's political party)	Year	Inflation Rate (CPI, annual rate)	Unemployment Rate	**Misery Index**
Ford* defeated by Carter	1976	5.5	7.7	13.2
Carter* defeated by Reagan	1980	12.8	7.5	20.3
Reagan* reelected	1984	4.3	7.4	11.7
George H.W. Bush* succeeds Reagan	1988	4.2	5.4	9.6
Clinton defeats Bush*	1992	3.2	7.3	10.5
Clinton* reelected	1996	3.0	5.2	8.2
George W. Bush defeats Gore*	2000	3.4	3.9	7.3
George W. Bush* reelected	2004	3.2	5.5	8.7
Obama defeats McCain*	2008	3.7	6.5	10.2
Obama* defeats Romney	2012	2.2	7.9	10.1

Source: Bureau of Labor Statistics, US Department of Labor
Data are for October of each year, the month before the US Presidential election.

THE TAYLOR RULE

In Chapter 7, we said that central banks are deeply concerned with keeping inflation at acceptable levels and with fostering conditions for economic growth. They constantly monitor economic occurrences to advocate the right policies for meeting these objectives.

John Taylor[63] articulated a rule that central banks can follow to help them set their interest rate targets. For the Federal Reserve, the US central bank, the **Taylor rule** stipulates that:

$$i = 1.5\,n + 0.5\,y + 1$$

In this formula, i is the fed funds target rate, n is the inflation rate, and y is the output gap—the growth rate of real GDP minus a measure of the growth rate of potential output (the full employment level of GDP).

Of course, there are challenges with attempting to apply this rule. Some of these are: What measure of inflation should be used? Should the inflation rate be the current rate, the average rate over some past period, or an anticipated future rate?

Rules versus discretion

Advocates of a rule for guiding policy believe this safeguards policymakers from mistakes, as a rule is based on objective considerations and on what historical experience suggests is optimal. Those who are less enthused about rules have advocated **discretion**, the freedom to exercise judgment in response to circumstances. They have cautioned that what happened in the past is not necessarily a good guide to dealing with the present and the future, when there might be issues that did not exist in the past.

In particular, a central bank needs to have flexibility to take account of unforeseen circumstances and special events. For example, suppose inflation increased substantially but a central bank views this as due to a surge in energy prices that

---

[63] Taylor, J. (1993). Discretion versus policy rules in practice. In *Carnegie Rochester Conference on Public Policy* (pp. 195-214). Amsterdam: North-Holland.

was likely to last a few months then dissipate. If the Taylor rule suggested the bank's target rate should be increased sharply in response to this inflation surge, a central bank that had committed to this rule would be hard pressed to explain why it did not raise interest rates. Advocates of the rule have countered that the rule provides a sound underpinning for policy and is not meant to be followed mechanically, that it does not prevent a central bank from exercising discretion in special circumstances.

WHY THE FED SEEKING A ZERO INFLATION RATE CAN EXACERBATE UNEMPLOYMENT

Paul Volcker and Alan Greenspan, who have both been very famous Chairpersons of the Fed, often spoke of the desire to have a zero inflation rate in the US. To have a zero inflation rate, the price level has to be unchanged. Suppose the price level is P_1 (Figure 2) and the Fed wanted to keep it there to have a zero inflation rate. If a change occurred (e.g., a sharp rise in the price of oil) that decreased AS and increased the price level to P_2 (with output falling to Y_2 and unemployment rising), the Fed would have to decrease the money supply if it wanted to get the price level back to P_1 ($Ms\leftarrow => AD\leftarrow => P\downarrow, Y\downarrow$).

If this is done, so that the price level fell back to P_1, output would now be at the level Y_3, even lower than Y_2—the level of output immediately after the decrease in AS. Unemployment would now be even higher than immediately after the decrease in AS. The price paid for decreasing the money supply to get a zero inflation rate is higher unemployment.

Unemployment is far more painful to people than a little inflation. However, as the analysis we have just done shows, the Fed decreasing the money supply to keep the inflation rate at zero may remove the irritant of inflation but only at the cost of higher unemployment, and the population will face the question of whether this is a price worth paying for zero inflation. This is an interesting consideration with which to end this chapter.

FIGURE 2

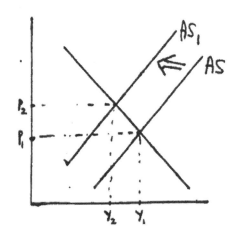 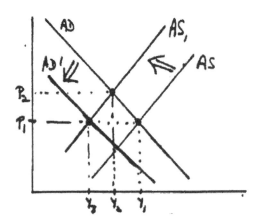

A decrease in AS causes P to
rise to P_2 and Y to fall to Y_2.

After AS decreases to AS_1, the
Fed decreases the money supply
to get the price level back to P_1,
so AD decreases to AD_1 and Y
falls further from Y_2 to Y_3,
increasing unemployment to more
than after the decrease in AS.

**How the Fed seeking a zero inflation
level can exacerbate unemployment**

EXERCISE 4

1. Use the following data to find: i. Velocity; ii. The growth rate of the money
   stock; iii. The number of employed; iv. The size of the labor force; v. The
   unemployment rate; vi. The misery index.

   > Money stock = $300 million
   > Nominal GDP = $3300 million
   > Inflation rate = 10 %
   > Growth rate of velocity = 5 %
   > Growth rate of real output = – 2 %

Part-time employed = 10 million
Full-time employed = 70 million
Unemployed = 20 million

2. Suppose annual GDP growth of 2.25 % is needed just to keep a country's unemployment rate constant, and every annual percent increase in growth above this 2.25 % level causes a fall in unemployment of 0.5 %. If unemployment is 10 % at the start of a year and growth over the year is 4.25 %, what will unemployment be at the end of the year? What happens to unemployment if growth over the year is –0.75 %?

3. What would be your response to the following statement? "Unemployment in our country is 7 %, our economy is expected to grow 3 % in the year ahead, and each percent of growth will bring down unemployment."

4. According to the Taylor rule, what should be the fed funds target rate if the inflation rate is 1.5 % and the output gap is –5 %?

ANSWERS

EXERCISE 1

1.   i.   Creeping inflation: 2000–2
       ii.   Galloping inflation: 2003–5
      iii.   Hyperinflation: 2005
       iv.   Disinflation: 2006–8
        v.   Deflation: 2009
       vi.   Reflation: 2010

2. b

3. d

EXERCISE 2

1. False. A rise in the price of oil causes a decrease in aggregate supply that increases the price level and causes inflation. However, hyperinflation is defined as inflation of over 1000 % per year. It is impossible for the price of oil to rise so rapidly to cause such a high level of inflation. Hyperinflation is caused by extremely high levels of growth of the money supply.

2. Inflation could be increased by i and by iii. From the formula $n = m + v - q$ we learned in this chapter, we know that declining V and declining M will bring down inflation, so ii and iv, *ceteris paribus*, cannot cause inflation to rise.

EXERCISE 3

1. c
2. b
3. a
4. d
5. c

EXERCISE 4

1. i.   Velocity = nominal GDP / money stock = 3300/300 = 11
    ii. Growth rate of the money stock = inflation rate minus growth rate of velocity plus growth rate of real output = 10 % – 5 % + –2 % = 3 %
    iii. Number of employed = part-time employed plus full-time employed = 10 million + 70 million = 80 million
    iv. Size of labor force = employed plus unemployed = 80 million plus 20 million = 100 million
    v.   Unemployment rate (%) = (unemployed/labor force) X 100 = (20/100) X 100 = 20 %
    vi. Misery index = inflation rate plus unemployment rate = 10 + 20 = 30

2. Growth over the year is 4.25 %, which is 2 % above the 2.25 % level needed to keep unemployment steady and would reduce unemployment by 2 times 0.5 % = 1 %. Unemployment at the end of the year would be 9 %.

    If growth over the year is –0.75 %, not only is the economy not getting the 2.25 % growth needed to keep unemployment steady, but it is also losing jobs from the decline in growth of 0.75 %. Growth over the year is 3 % (2.25 + 0.75) below the level needed to keep employment constant and, if a fall in growth of 1 % causes a 0.5 % decrease in unemployment, then unemployment would increase by 3 x 0.5 percent = 1.5 %. Unemployment at the end of the year would be 11.5 %.

3. If this country has a growing population and labor force, a certain amount of economic growth would be necessary just keep unemployment steady. Only growth above this amount would contribute to decreasing the unemployment rate, as was explained in this chapter. A part of the 3 % growth would be needed just to keep unemployment steady and only the economic growth above this part would contribute to decreasing unemployment. The claim in the statement that "each percent of growth will bring down unemployment" is therefore likely to be erroneous.

4. The Taylor rule specifies that the fed funds target rate should be 1.5 times the inflation rate plus 0.5 times the output gap plus 1 = 1.5 X 1.5 + 0.5 X (–5) + 1 = 0.75 %.

CHAPTER 9
THE BALANCE OF PAYMENTS ACCOUNTS

INTRODUCTION

A country's economic transactions with the rest of the world can have significant consequences. For example, we know from the AD-AS model that if foreigners buy more of our country's goods and services, this increases its exports and aggregate demand, pushing up its output and price levels. Every day the news is full of references to economic transactions between countries—trade deficits, exchange rates, etc. Unless we know what these are, we can feel that life is passing by without us understanding much of it.

To learn about how an economy is managed, or just to understand the economic links between countries, we must learn terms, concepts and causal connections relating to a country's transactions with the rest of the world. This chapter begins to provide this knowledge.

THE BALANCE OF PAYMENTS ACCOUNTS

A country's **balance of payments accounts** is a systematic record of the country's economic transactions with the rest of the world for a specific time period, e.g., a quarter or a year. For the US, this set of accounts is called the International Transactions Accounts (ITAs). As long as you learn the basic system for constructing the balance of payments accounts, you will be able to comprehend variations of it that you encounter. As was the case when we studied GDP accounting in an earlier chapter, the aim here is to enable you to understand important concepts and avoid the minutiae of accounting that are not essential for our purpose.

First, we will learn about the sections of the balance of payments accounts and what type of transactions is entered in each. Then we will see how double entry bookkeeping is used to record transactions.

The current account

The **current account** is one of the main sections in the balance of payments accounts. It is a record of transactions in merchandise (goods), services, income and some types of transfers[64]. In a country's current account, the money value of a transaction that causes the country to receive a payment, or to receive a transfer, is recorded with a positive sign. The money value of a transaction that causes the country to make a payment, or to give a transfer, is recorded with a negative sign.

A country's merchandise exports are the goods it sells to the rest of the world. These sales cause the receipt of payments by the country and are recorded with a positive sign in the country's current account. If the US sells $100 million of goods to Germany, this $100 million is recorded with a positive sign under merchandise exports in the US current account. Merchandise imports are goods bought from the rest of the world. These purchases cause payments to be made to the rest of the world and are recorded with a negative sign in the importing country's current account. If the US buys $1 billion of goods from Canada, this is recorded as minus $1 billion under merchandise imports in the US current account.

The value of merchandise exports minus the value of merchandise imports equals the **merchandise trade balance**.

Services exports are services sold to the rest of the world. Examples of services are travel, transportation, communication services and financial services. If a foreigner buys a ticket from an American airline, this is an American service bought by a foreigner, so it is an American service export. Service exports result in the receipt of payments by the exporting country and are recorded with a positive sign under services exports in that country's current account.

If an American visits London, UK, and pays for a British hotel, this is an American import of a British service of hotel accommodation. A country's services imports result in payments to foreigners and are recorded with a negative sign under services imports in the country's current account.

---

[64] The term "transfer" was first encountered in Chapter 2. Examples of transfers in the balance of payments accounts are given a few paragraphs later in this chapter.

The value of services exports minus the value of services imports equals the **services trade balance**.

The sum of the merchandise trade balance and the services trade balance is called the **goods and services balance**.

Income in the balance of payments accounts refers to payments such as the interest on bonds or other loans, dividends on stocks, income from the country's businesses operating abroad or from foreign businesses in the country, and compensation of employees who are working outside of their country. Income payments received by Americans from abroad are recorded with a positive sign in the income section in the US current account. Income payments made by Americans to foreigners are recorded with a negative sign. Summing these positive and negative amounts gives net income.

Transfers recorded in the current account cover goods, services and assets that go from residents of one country to those of another without anything of economic value being provided in return. If a person in the US sends a gift of food or money to his family abroad, this is a transfer. Government grants and pensions paid to those abroad are also examples of transfers that are included in this section of the current account. In these transfers, parties in one country are giving to those in another, but not getting any kind of payment in return. So you may see these transfers referred to as unilateral. This means "one-sided"—not involving both parties giving something to each other in an exchange.

A transfer received by a person in the US from someone abroad is recorded with positive sign under transfers in the US current account. Transfers made by someone in the US to anyone abroad are recorded with a negative sign. Summing these positive and negative amounts gives net transfers. Net transfers are also called net unilateral transfers.

The sum of the merchandise trade balance, the services trade balance, net income and net transfers is called the **current account balance**.

When any one of these balances is negative, there is said to be a **deficit**. For example, if the merchandise trade balance is negative, this is referred to as a merchandise trade deficit. If a balance is positive, it is called a **surplus**. For example, a positive current account balance is called a current account surplus.

The example below illustrates these data for the United States of America:

EXAMPLE
Current Account, United States, 2012

Current account	$ billions
Merchandise exports	1564.1
Merchandise imports	-2299.4
Merchandise trade balance	-735.3
Services exports	630.4
Services imports	-434.6
Services trade balance	195.8
Net income	198.6
Net transfers	-134.1
Current account balance	-475

Source: US Department of Commerce, Bureau of Economic Analysis, preliminary data

For the US in 2012, there was a merchandise trade deficit of $735.3 billion, a current account deficit of $475 billion, etc. The parts of the current account in surplus were services (the services trade balance was $195.8 billion) and net income (surplus of $198.6 billion).

The capital account
The **capital account** is a record of international transactions in items such as natural resources (land, mineral rights, forestry rights, fishing rights, etc.) and intangible assets (trademarks, copyrights, domain names, etc). These items are

<u>nonproduced, nonfinancial assets</u>—they are not items created in a production process and they are not financial.

Transfers such as debt forgiveness (when a country forgives the debt of another country) and migrant transfers (the value of the belongings, assets and liabilities immigrants/emigrants bring/take when they arrive in or depart from a country) are also among the items included in the capital account.

NOTE
You might come across balance of payments accounts that use an older format in which the capital account as we have just presented it does not exist. This older style does have a capital account but it is like what is described as the financial account, which we discuss next.

The International Monetary Fund has advocated the modern method for the presentation of balance of payments data outlined here, which has three main sections—the current account and the capital account as we have defined them, and the financial account as we describe it next.[65] The older style has two main sections in the balance of payments accounts—the current account and the capital account, which cover the transactions we have listed here for the current, capital and financial account.

The financial account
The **<u>financial account</u>** is a record of transactions with other countries in assets such as bonds, stocks, currency, loans, and the purchase or sale of businesses. The

---

[65] One reason for this new format with the current, capital and financial account sections in the balance of payments accounts is that some of the transactions now included in the capital account were previously in the current account. This new format lets the current account adhere more accurately to the definition of the subcomponents of goods and services balance, net income and net transfers as they have been mentioned in this chapter.

net amount of all these transactions is called the <u>financial account balance</u>.[66]

Any acquisition of US financial assets by foreigners is recorded with a positive sign in the US financial account. When we presented the current account, we noted that exports of goods and services have a positive sign in the current account. Similarly, foreigners acquiring US assets is like an "export" of assets and has a positive sign in the balance of payments accounts.

Any acquisition of foreign assets done by US residents is recorded as a negative in the US financial account. Just as imports of goods and services have a negative sign, as we learned when discussing the current account, US residents acquiring foreign assets is like an "import" of assets and has a negative sign.

A reduction in our assets held by foreigners is also recorded as a negative in our financial account. A reduction in foreign assets we hold is recorded as a positive in our financial account. These principles should become clearer to you when you study the following sub-section of this chapter on how double entry bookkeeping is used in the balance of payments accounts.

Double entry bookkeeping

Double entry bookkeeping is used in recording the balance of payments accounts. This means every transaction that occurs between countries has two entries associated with it, one a credit (recorded with a plus sign) and the other a debit (recorded with a minus sign). If US residents buy $1 million of cars from Japan, the value of cars bought is recorded as an import of $1 million (as minus $1 million under merchandise imports in the US current account). But the US residents have to pay for the cars. The payment of $1 million that they must make for the cars, if is it made in US dollars, increases foreign holdings of US assets (dollars in this case) and is recorded as a positive in the US financial account. If, instead of being made in dollars, the payment is made in yen the US residents

---

[66] Central banks frequently engage in financial account transactions such as the buying or selling of foreign currency to influence exchange rates. (We learn more about this when we discuss exchange rates in the next chapter.) These transactions are called <u>official reserve transactions</u>.

owned, this decreases US holdings of foreign assets and is recorded as a positive in the US financial account. The payment is like an "export" of assets.

Suppose China buys $10 million of wheat from the US. This is recorded as plus $10 million in US merchandise exports. Then the payment China makes is recorded as a minus $10 million entry in the US financial account. If China pays in US dollars, foreign holdings of US assets decrease, which is recorded as a negative entry in the US financial account. If China pays in some currency other than the US dollar, US holdings of foreign assets increase, which is recorded with a negative entry in the US financial account. However the payment is made, it leads to a negative entry in the US financial account. It is like an "import" of assets and is recorded with a negative sign.

For some transactions, these two entries will be in the same section of the account. If China buys $1 billion in bonds from the US, the purchase of the bonds is a plus $1 billion in the financial account of the US balance of payments (like an "export" of assets) and the payment of $1 billion for the bonds is a minus $1 billion in the financial account (it's like an "import" of assets). So in this case both entries in this double entry system are in the same account.

Let's say a British resident bought stocks in an American company and paid for the stocks in pounds. This increases foreign holdings of US stocks and is recorded as a positive in the US financial account. However, the British resident paying for these stocks increases US holdings of pounds (or any other foreign currency in which the British resident pays), which is recorded as a negative in the US financial account. (If she pays with dollars, this decreases foreign holdings of dollars, which is also recorded as a negative in the US financial account.) So here we have another example of both entries associated with a transaction going into the financial account.

If the US gives a gift of $1 million of wheat to Bangladesh, $1 million is put as a negative entry under transfers in the current account, and $1 million is recorded as a positive entry under merchandise exports in the US current account. In this case the double entry is made by treating the wheat given to Bangladesh as if it were a merchandise export (the entry under exports), but Bangladesh didn't have to pay for it (the entry under transfers).

If an American tourist in London spends $300 on British hotel accommodation, this is recorded as minus $300 under services imports in the US current account. The fact that foreign holdings of our currency have increased by $300 is recorded as plus $300 in the US financial account.

These are just a few examples to make you more familiar with the system of double entry bookkeeping used in balance of payments accounting. You don't have to worry about all the technicalities of doing this as our purpose here is to get an overall understanding of what the various components of the balance of payments contain and mean. If you ever have to work at putting together these accounts, you will get extensive guidelines from your employers on the relevant rules.

Because every transaction has two entries associated with it in the balance of payments accounts, with one of the entries positive and the other negative, if all these entries are recorded correctly, the balance of payments must sum to zero. Consequently, **the current account balance plus the capital account balance plus the financial account balance must equal zero.** Because recording the balance of payments is a complex process involving so many transactions, there are always errors and omissions. **If the three balances in the accounts do not sum to zero, it is because of these errors and omissions (frequently referred to as a "statistical discrepancy").**

Excluding the statistical discrepancy, the current account plus the capital account balances will be of equal magnitude but opposite sign to the financial account balance.

A SUMMARY OF THE RELATIONS AMONG
THE COMPONENTS OF THE BALANCE OF PAYMENTS ACCOUNTS

Merchandise exports minus merchandise imports
= Merchandise trade balance

Services exports minus services imports
= Services trade balance

Merchandise trade balance plus services trade balance
= Goods and services balance

Merchandise trade balance plus services trade balance plus net income plus net transfers = Current account balance

Goods and services balance plus net income plus net transfers
= Current account balance

Current account balance plus capital account balance plus financial account balance = 0 (ignoring errors and omissions)

Total of the current account plus the capital account balances is equal in magnitude but opposite in sign to the financial account balance (ignoring errors and omissions)

For any of the accounts in the balance of payments, a positive account balance is called a **surplus**. A negative account balance is called a **deficit**. For example, if a country has a financial account surplus, this simply means that in the country's balance of payments accounts the financial account balance is positive. Frequently, you may hear people referring to "balance of payments deficits" or "surpluses." What they mean is the balance on one of the main categories of the accounts, and you would have to delve further into what they are saying to find out which balance they have in mind.

Usually the generic term **trade deficit/surplus** is used to refer to a deficit/surplus in merchandise trade, or in goods and services or in the current account. The context usually makes clear precisely which one of these deficits/surpluses in being referred to.

EXERCISE

Each of the exercises below lists data from balance of payments accounts. Find the missing values (for the items in bold) and answer the questions that follow.

1.   Country A, 2012

	$ Millions
Merchandise exports	500
Merchandise imports	−200
Merchandise trade balance	
Services exports	80
Services imports	−80
Services trade balance	
Net income	−1
Net transfers	−9
Current account balance	
Capital account balance	0
Financial account balance	

What is the amount of merchandise imports made by country A in 2012? In 2012, did country A have: a. a merchandise trade deficit; b. a services trade surplus; c. a current account surplus?

2.   Country B, 2012

	$ Millions
Merchandise exports	400
Merchandise imports	
Merchandise trade balance	−100
Services exports	
Services imports	−60
Services trade balance	20
Net income	0
Net transfers	
Current account balance	
Capital account balance	0
Financial account balance	100

What is the amount of services imports for country B in 2012? Did country B have a current account deficit in 2012?

3. Looking at Country X's balance of payments accounts for 2009, in which the new standards advocated by the IMF for presenting data had not yet been adopted, I see loans listed in a section titled the "Capital Account". In balance of payments accounts that follow the new standards, what would be the title of the section in which loans are listed?

FUNDING A CURRENT ACCOUNT DEFICIT

If I am a US resident and I want to import goods from China, I arrange to pay my dollars for the goods. When these dollars are received by the Chinese exporter, they are typically changed into the local currency (yuan) and end up in the central bank of China.[67] China now owns these dollars and can do what it wants with them. The US runs huge current account deficits with China ($333 billion in 2012), so China ends up with large amounts of US dollars.

This process, in which China willingly accepts dollars for the products the US buys from it, is referred to as China "financing" the US current account deficits. The word "financing" as used here does not mean the same as when it is used in everyday conversation. If I said I was financing your studies, this means I am giving you loans or gifts for you to be able to fund your studies. "Financing" as used here, however, does not at all mean that China is actually lending the US funds to enable the US to import products from China. In the example in the previous paragraph, the import began with me wanting the products and getting my dollars to the Chinese exporter. China did not lend me anything. The only sense in which China is "financing" this transaction is that China is willing to take the dollars. Regrettably, people often think the term "financing" means China is actually lending the US to fund the imports the US makes from China. This is a misconception in which the term financing is confused with the way it is used in everyday conversation.

---

[67] Because of Chinese government restrictions on the use of the yuan outside of China, one would typically not be able to convert dollars into yuan to send to the Chinese exporter and would have to pay in dollars.

To have a sensible perspective, it is also useful to keep in mind that China is not doing the US a favor by accepting dollars for its products. Think of what would happen to China if the US did not want to buy its products. Chinese enterprises would lose their markets and have to lay off large numbers of workers, and economic growth in China would be diminished.

From the dollars it receives from the US, China has traditionally invested large amounts in buying US Treasuries, which the US government issues to fund the US budget deficits. So the US government has been borrowing from China to fund its expenditures. One can say that China is financing the US budget deficit, with financing here closer to its meaning in everyday speech. However, as we have noted, we cannot say that China is financing the US current account deficit, if we are using the term "financing" in the sense of its everyday meaning. Moreover, China has not been buying US Treasuries as an act of kindness to the US. China needs safe investments in which it can put its current account surpluses. US Treasuries have so far provided that safety.

IS A TRADE DEFICIT BAD? IS A SURPLUS GOOD?

The aim here is to point out some key considerations, not to go into an exhaustive discussion of all the relevant issues.

When a country has a persistent trade deficit, it is habitually selling less to the rest of the world than it is buying from the world. Some media pundits portray this as a negative signal about the country's economy—that its goods and services are not very desirable. The truth is far more complex. To better assess the significance of a country's trade deficit, one has to know the context in which it occurs. Consider the following situations—a country is running large trade deficits because:

1. It is importing large amounts of machinery and inputs to improve its productive capability.

2. Its consumers buy a lot from abroad because imports are cheap.

In 1, the trade deficit seems to be for a worthy purpose: improving the country's productive capability. Assuming its economic plans are well formulated and efficiently executed, this country could later have a much more vibrant economy as a result of the machinery and inputs obtained from abroad.

In 2, the country's consumers benefit from getting goods and services more cheaply from abroad. But the country's industries that have to compete with these cheaper imports have most likely had to lay off workers. Some businesses may even have moved from this country to enhance their profits by using cheaper foreign labor and resources. A lot of the imports of this country are probably being made by firms that once operated in the country but that are now located abroad. Two key elements are evident in this situation:

- The country's consumers benefit from the lower costs they incur due to the availability of the cheaper imports.

- Jobs will have been lost in this country as a result of the competition from the cheaper imports and from businesses moving abroad to utilize cheaper foreign inputs. Some jobs might be created in this country from the importation and distributions networks for the goods and services coming from abroad. But these jobs created are typically far fewer than the jobs lost due to cheaper production available abroad.

Jobs losses cause severe pain to those who become unemployed, especially when alternative employment is hard to find. But it has been a trend of the world economy that businesses move to where they can substantially lower their cost of production. The same businesses that have shifted production from the US to China will shift to Vietnam, Mexico, Brazil, etc. as they can increase profitability by doing so.

US trade deficits

It is important to understand some distinguishing characteristics of US trade deficits. To see the first of these, let us contrast an economically less developed country running a trade deficit with the US running one.

Most international trade is invoiced (priced and has to be paid for) in US dollars. When economically less developed countries have to pay for imports, their own currencies are typically not accepted by exporters. They usually have to pay in US dollars and other foreign currencies. If one of these countries is running a deficit on its current account, it is paying more to other countries than those countries are paying to it. It will have to get dollars or other foreign currency to pay for the amount of the deficit. It can get this from foreign currency it has or from borrowing. If it runs growing current account deficits, it will have to get increasing amounts of foreign currency to pay for these and the question will arise as to whether these current account deficits are sustainable, i.e., can it find the foreign currency necessary for continuing to fund these deficits?

In the case of the US, however, since the currency used in the US is dollars created by the US central bank, the US doesn't face this problem of having to find foreign currency to pay for its imports. Countries around the world readily accept US dollars. The US can run persistently large current account deficits and not face the difficulty of paying for them that was just described for less developed countries.

Also, by running large trade deficits the US boosts demand for the goods and services of other countries. If the US were to cut back on its imports, other countries would suffer a fall in demand for their products, lowered incomes and higher unemployment. By running large trade deficits, the US confers a benefit on the rest of the world of boosting economic growth abroad. Regrettably, media pundits often seem not to be cognizant of this benefit to the rest of world of the US running trade deficits.

Do a country's huge trade surpluses imply that its economy is performing very well overall?

Looking at a country's huge trade surpluses and concluding that its economy must be a stellar performer is like looking at a student who is outstandingly good in one subject and concluding that he must be doing very well overall. A telling cautionary note about this is provided by Japan. In the 1970s and 80s, as the US ran growing current account deficits, Japan ran huge surpluses with the US and with the rest of the world. The news media regularly quoted pundits who believed that Japan was going to become the dominant economic power in the world and who cited its huge current account surpluses as a sign of its economic dominance.

By 1990, the Japanese economy fell into a crisis from which, more than two decades later, it has not yet emerged. Japan still runs large current account surpluses with the US ($94 billion out of a total US current account deficit of $475 billion, in 2012), but nowadays there is no claim in the news media that this is a sign of Japan's economic superiority relative to the US—Japan's prolonged economic crisis has ended such talk.

China's current account surpluses with the US have rocketed up from $73 billion in 1999 to $333 billion in 2012, and economic growth in China has been very high by historical standards. This has captured the popular imagination, and China has taken the place of Japan in a well-touted view that China will become the dominant economy in the world. As was the case with Japan, it would be wise to take a comprehensive look at China's economy and not allow some of its successes to lead to rash conclusions about China's prospects.

China's large trade surpluses are associated with a grim situation of relatively inadequate consumption in China. Consumption as a percentage of GDP is about 34 % in China, but about 60 % in countries like Brazil and India, indicative of the relatively low consumption in China.[68] Because of very meager provision of government unemployment insurance, old-age and retirement pensions, healthcare, education and housing, Chinese have to save to meet these needs. This severely restricts what they can spend on consumption, and deprives them of necessities that could make their life more comfortable. If their consumption levels were higher, some of what is exported would have been used in China, reducing China's exports surplus. This is widely recognized as a challenging "imbalance" in China's economy and the government of China has repeatedly stated the importance of correcting it.

So, to properly assess the significance of trade deficits and surpluses, we have to examine the wider economic context. This is a suitable thought with which to end this chapter.

---

[68] World Bank. (2011). World Development Indicators Online (WDI) database.

ANSWERS

All the units are in $ millions.

1.   Merchandise trade balance = 500 – 200 = 300

Services trade balance = 80 – 80 = 0

Current account balance = merchandise trade balance + services trade balance + net income + net transfers = 300 + 0 + –1 + –9 = 290

Financial account balance = minus (current account balance + capital account balance) = – (290 + 0) = –290

Amount of merchandise imports made by country A = 200. Country A had: a. Not a merchandise trade deficit, but a merchandise trade surplus (300); b. Not a services trade surplus, but a zero services trade balance; c. A current account surplus (290).

2.   400 minus amount of merchandise imports = –100.
Therefore, amount of merchandise imports = 500.
Entry for merchandise imports must be –500.

Services exports minus 60 = 20. Therefore, services exports = 80. Entry for services exports must be 80.

Net transfers = Current account balance minus merchandise trade balance minus services trade balance minus net income. But current account balance = minus financial account balance (because the capital account balance is zero) = –100. Therefore, net transfers = –100 – (–100) – 20 – 0 = –20.

The current account balance, as we just noted, = minus the financial account balance (because the capital account balance is zero) = –100.

The amount of services imports made by country B = 60. Country B had a current account deficit of 100.

3. According to the new standards, loans would be listed in the financial account. This account would contain much of what is in the capital account in Country X's 2009 balance of payments accounts.

CHAPTER 10
EXCHANGE RATES

If you are in the US and you make a purchase from the United Kingdom (UK), you are likely to have to convert your dollars into pounds sterling, the currency of the UK, to pay the seller. If you pay in dollars, the seller is likely to convert the dollars into pounds for use in the UK. Transactions between countries in goods, services and assets give rise to the need to convert funds into different currencies.

An <u>exchange rate</u> is the amount of one currency that must be paid for another. It is the price of a currency. If the US $ per British pound rate is 2, this means 2 dollars must be paid for a pound, or 1/2 pound must be paid for a dollar. If the yen per US $ rate is 125, this means 125 yen (the Japanese currency) must be paid for a dollar, or 1/125 dollar must be paid for a yen.

Transactions in the foreign exchange market total trillions per day when expressed in US dollars, about four trillion US in 2010. The London foreign exchange market is the largest in the world, with currency trades equal to about 1.48 trillion US dollars per day, according to the *Triennial Central Bank Survey*.[69] The New York market is next in size with about 0.7 trillion dollars in daily trades.

Flexible; Fixed

There are two main kinds of exchange rates—**<u>flexible exchange rates</u>** and **<u>fixed exchange rates</u>**.

Flexible rates are also called <u>floating rates</u>. When the exchange rate of one currency for another is determined mainly by the market forces of demand and supply, the exchange rate is said to be flexible. In a flexible exchange rate system, every time there is a change in the demand for, or supply of, a currency, the amount of another currency that must be paid for that currency changes. The US

---

[69] Bank for International Settlements. (2010, Dec.). *Triennial Central Bank Survey—Report on global foreign exchange market activity in 2010*. Because this is a triennial survey, the most recent one available is from 2010.

dollar and the yen are traded for each other in a flexible exchange rate system. Throughout the business day, the amount of yen that must be paid for a dollar, or the amount of a dollar that must be paid for a yen, changes as demand and supply for these currencies change. Currencies like the US dollar, the Canadian dollar, the yen, and the British pound are among many traded for each other in flexible exchange rate systems.

Fixed rates, however, as the word "fixed" suggests, are set at specific levels by governmental authorities and legal purchases and sales of these must occur at the fixed levels. We will soon discuss how a fixed exchange rate system works.

Depreciation; Appreciation; Devaluation; Revaluation

If A and B are two currencies and the amount of A that must be paid for a unit of B is increasing (which implies that the amount of B to be paid for a unit of A is decreasing), A is said to be **depreciating** relative to B, and B is said to be **appreciating** relative to A. If the yen per $ rate moves from 100 to 102, more yen have to be paid for a dollar, so this is **depreciation** of the yen relative to the dollar. This also implies that less of a dollar now has to be paid for the yen, which is **appreciation** of the dollar relative to the yen.

When referring to fixed exchange rates, the terms **devaluation** and **revaluation** are frequently used, instead of depreciation and appreciation, to refer to changes in the levels at which governmental authorities set these rates. If, for example, a country's fixed exchange rate is 3 pesos per US $ and this is then changed to 4 pesos per US $, this is devaluation of the peso—now more of it has to be paid to get a US dollar.

HOW A FIXED EXCHANGE RATE SYSTEM WORKS

There are various kinds of fixed exchange rate systems. However, in the typical one, a country's central bank sets the exchange rate of its currency against another country's currency, allowing it to move only within a narrow range. The central bank then <u>intervenes</u>, buying or selling currency as is necessary to maintain the rate. **Intervention** is the purchase or sale of currencies by a central bank in an attempt to influence the level of exchange rates.

Let's say Country X's fixed exchange rate is set at between 3.9 and 4.1 pesos for the dollar. X's central bank will let the peso move between 3.9 and 4.1 pesos for the dollar. If demand for pesos became strong enough that the peso threatened to move to less than 3.9 pesos for the dollar, X's central bank would intervene to buy dollars and offer pesos for them thus increasing the availability of pesos and weakening the peso. This would keep the peso at more than 3.9 pesos per dollar and within the band of 3.9 to 4.1 pesos per $.

If people wanted to get out of pesos and into dollars causing the peso to move in the direction of more than 4.1 pesos per $, X's central bank would intervene to buy pesos offering dollars in return. This would strengthen the peso and keep the peso per $ rate in the accepted range of 3.9 to 4.1 pesos per $.

The central bank of a country with a fixed exchange rate must be ready to engage in intervention—buying or selling currency as is necessary to keep the exchange rate within the fixed range. To be able to intervene, the central bank must have **official reserves**, foreign currency that it can use to facilitate its intervention. In the example just cited, if X's central bank had to prevent the peso from weakening to more than 4.1 pesos per $, it must have dollars to offer for pesos it buys up to strengthen the peso. If it ran out of reserves for doing this, it would have to allow the peso to go weaker than 4.1 pesos per $ by either one of two courses of action:

- It could devalue the peso by setting a new range for the fixed rate of the peso in which more pesos have to be paid for a dollar, e.g., a fixed rate range such as 4.4 to 4.7, or whatever level it would then be able to hold the peso per $ rate at.

- Or it could abandon the fixed exchange rate and let the peso float against the dollar. If it abandoned the fixed exchange rate, it would free itself of the burden of having to intervene to keep the rate within a certain range.

FACTORS THAT CHANGE THE PRICE OF A CURRENCY IN A FLEXIBLE EXCHANGE RATE SYSTEM

In a flexible exchange rate system, currency exchange rates are determined mainly[70] by the interaction of demand and supply of people and businesses who want to buy or sell the currency. Any factor that changes demand for and/or supply of a currency will alter the amount of foreign currency that has to be paid for it. For example, a factor that increases demand for a currency increases the price of the currency—the amount of foreign currency that has to be paid for it. This causes the currency to appreciate.

Now we will look at some specific factors that affect **daily movements** in flexible exchange rates. **As we consider each factor, keep in mind that it is viewed as occurring *ceteris paribus*. This way, for pedagogical purposes, we are able to hold other factors constant and single out the effect each factor has.** What if in real life you see a particular factor occurring but an exchange rate moves differently from what the discussion below suggests should happen? What this means is that there are other factors at work more than offsetting the impact of the factor you are looking at.

Interest rates

Financial investors seeking the highest interest rates across the globe are very active in short term speculative activity in foreign exchange markets. If a country's central bank is expected to push up the interest rates it controls, this increases the expected earnings from short-term interest bearing assets, making them more attractive to currency speculators. As speculators from around the globe seek to buy these assets, they have to acquire the country's currency to make their purchases. This boosts demand for the country's currency, increasing the amount of foreign currency that has to be paid for a unit of it. The currency appreciates.

---

[70] Central banks sometimes intervene to buy or sell currencies to influence flexible exchange rates. For example, if a government believes that speculators in the currency market have driven a flexible exchange rate currency away from levels that the government feels is appropriate, the government may have its central bank intervene by buying the currency (if the government wants to strengthen the currency) or selling it (if the government wants to weaken the currency).

The reverse happens if a country's central bank is expected to lower rates, or not to raise rates as early and/or by as much as had been expected. If these interest rates are declining in a country, or are perceived as likely to be lower than previously anticipated, this makes acquiring the country's short term interest earning assets seem less attractive to financial investors. This, *ceteris paribus*, decreases demand for the currency causing it to depreciate. So a looser monetary policy that lowers interest rates in a country causes, *ceteris paribus*, depreciation of its currency. For example, on Feb. 10, 2010, the pound (the British currency) weakened against the euro after UK data showed inflation to be tamer than expected and the Bank of England (the UK Central Bank) indicated it would have a looser monetary policy that would keep interest rates lower than had previously been expected by the foreign exchange markets.

Economic growth

News that economic growth is higher than expected that boosts confidence in a country increases demand for the country's assets. This raises demand for the country's currency for use in buying those assets. The currency appreciates. Similarly, better than expected news on consumer confidence, retail sales, manufacturing strength, the strength of the services sector, employment, etc. that increases optimism about a country's growth prospects will, *ceteris paribus*, cause its currency to appreciate.

News that a country's economic growth is less than expected that diminishes confidence in the country's economy decreases demand for the country's currency. The currency depreciates. For example, on Feb. 12, 2010, the euro fell to a nine-month low against the dollar on news that GDP growth in the euro area was weaker than expected.

Worse than expected news on consumer confidence, retail sales, manufacturing strength, the strength of the services sector, employment, etc. that increases pessimism about a country's growth prospects will, *ceteris paribus*, cause its currency to depreciate.

Talking-up, talking-down

Governments sometimes attempt to influence exchange rates through statements made by officials. US officials who want to see the dollar appreciate on foreign exchange markets may, for example, speak of their intent to see the dollar stronger, hoping their remarks would impart strength to the dollar by increasing demand for it. This is called **"talking-up"** the dollar. **"Talking-down"** a currency refers to statements aimed at causing it to depreciate.

Safe-haven

The greater the expectation that an economy will have economic and political stability, the stronger will be the desire of financial investors to hold assets in that economy. This factor causes the currency to appreciate. If instability develops within a country, *ceteris paribus*, this leads to loss of confidence in the country's currency, which depreciates. On Feb. 12, 2010, the Argentine peso fell to an eight-year low against the US dollar as turmoil over economic policy caused investors to want to get out of pesos and into US dollars. This investor demand for dollars is an example of **safe-haven demand**—anytime a currency is bought to get out of one that is from a country experiencing turmoil, the currency that is bought is a "safe-haven". The US dollar, the Swiss franc and the yen are frequently safe-havens when other countries experience turmoil.

Risk-on, risk-off

If investors become more willing to take on risk, they move out of safe-haven assets such as the US dollar and into riskier assets like stocks. Let's say investors have been fearful about the US economic future and then a piece of economic data comes out that boosts optimism about the US economy. The increased optimism about the US economy by itself would cause the dollar to appreciate, as we discussed a few paragraphs earlier. But if this rise in optimism causes investors to become willing to take on more risk, and to move out of their safe-haven holdings of dollars and into riskier assets such as stocks, then the positive economic news could cause dollar depreciation as stock prices rise. The term **risk-on trade** refers to investors moving out of a safe-haven asset such as the US dollar and into riskier assets such as stocks. A **risk-off trade** occurs when investors get out of riskier assets such as stocks and move into safe-haven assets such as the dollar.

Commodity currencies

A **commodity currency** is the currency of a country that is highly dependent on the export of raw materials. The Australian dollar and the Canadian dollar are examples of commodity currencies as Australia and Canada are very important commodity exporters.

When investors become more optimistic about world economic growth, they expect this growth to boost demand for commodities, so commodity currencies strengthen. Commodity currencies weaken if investors become more pessimistic about world economic growth.

Exchange rate models

In economics, there are several models[71] of what determines the levels of exchange rates. In these models, a few economic variables (e.g., output, money supply and interest rates) are cited as the factors determining exchange rate levels. It should not surprise you that these models often do not do well in explaining exchange rate levels. At any point in time, a variety of factors, including non-economic factors such as fears/optimism over a country's future, affect exchange rate levels. Any attempt to specify just a very few economic factors as affecting exchange rates leaves out a lot of other relevant factors. To the extent that these omitted factors are exerting influence on exchange rate movements, the models that omit them will not do well in explaining those movements.

For example, if there is a political crisis in a country, this is likely to cause depreciation of its currency if it has a flexible exchange rate system, or to cause pressure for devaluation if it has a fixed exchange rate. A model that focuses on a few economic factors that affect exchange rates will not take account of a non-economic factor like this.

When models of exchange rates have been tested, they have generally not held for data different from that for which they were originally found to hold. This should not be surprising given the variety of factors that affect exchange rates—factors that are relevant at one point in time may be supplanted by other factors at another time period. Some of these factors may even be non-economic and not measurable. This is why you may encounter the expression **"exchange rate models do not fit out of sample."** This simply means these models typically do not work well to

---

[71] Chapter 1 discussed what a model is.

explain exchange rate movements when tested on data different from that for which the models were originally developed.

EXERCISE 1

1. If the $ per euro rate moves from 1.25 to 1.2, which currency is appreciating? How much of a euro must be paid for a dollar when the $ per euro rate is 1.2?

2. Which of the following are likely to cause the dollar to depreciate relative to the yen? View each of these as occurring *ceteris paribus*.
   i.   The Fed is buying yen
   ii. The expectation develops that the Bank of Japan (the central bank of Japan) will raise interest rates
   iii. A new report shows US output to be growing more rapidly than had previously been expected
   iv. The US money supply is being sharply increased

3. In iii in the previous question, it is stated that "A new report shows US output to be growing more rapidly than had previously been expected." Suppose that when this news comes out, investors become more willing to take on risk. Could the US dollar depreciate in this situation?

4. As the world was engulfed in an economic crisis in the fall of 2008, the US dollar strengthened against the euro and other currencies, even though the US was in very serious economic trouble, with widespread fears that it was headed for another Great Depression. Why do you think the dollar strengthened?

5. If investors become more willing to take risks, what is likely to happen to the US dollar and the Australian dollar?

6. On May 22, 2012, financial markets were rocked by fears that a Greek exit from the Eurozone would cause a world financial panic. In Japan, the Bank of Japan announced it was keeping monetary policy unchanged, contrary to the

expectations of investors, who had been expected further monetary easing from the Bank of Japan. What do you think happened to the:

    i. US dollar relative to the euro

    ii. Australian dollar relative to the US dollar

    iii. Yen relative to the US dollar

WHY A COUNTRY CHOOSES A FIXED/FLEXIBLE EXCHANGE RATE SYSTEM

Fixed rate system

Let's say Country X's currency is the peso. If a resident of X borrowed $1000 from a US bank, and the peso per $ rate were 4, the resident would owe 4000 pesos. If the exchange rate were flexible, and the peso per $ rate went to 6 a month later, the resident would owe 6000 pesos. A fluctuating exchange rate causes the risk that the resident would face increased domestic currency cost of repaying the loan. If X's exchange rate were fixed, this risk would not exist for transactions in the currency against which X's currency was fixed. One benefit of a fixed exchange rate is that it removes **exchange-rate risk**—the risk that a fluctuating exchange rate would raise the cost of an economic transaction.[72]

With a fixed peso per dollar exchange rate, residents of X would also not have to worry that fluctuations in the peso per $ rate would cause changes in import and export prices in terms of peso. If an item cost a $1 in the US, with the peso per $

---

[72] As was explained earlier in this chapter, fixed exchange rates are often not set at an exact level such as 4 pesos for the dollar. They are usually set within a narrow range, such as 3.8 to 4.2 pesos per dollar. So the movement of the fixed rate currency within this range will still pose a little of the types of risk we discuss here. (For example, suppose the fixed rate can move between 3.8 and 4.2 pesos per $1. If you borrow $1,000 when the fixed rate is 3.9 pesos, you have borrowed 3,900 pesos. If when you have to repay, this rate has moved to 4.1 pesos for the dollar, you will owe 4,100 pesos.) But these risks are likely to be far less with this type of fixed exchange rate than with a flexible exchange rate because with a flexible system the movement in exchange rates are typically far bigger than in the fixed system.

rate at 4, the item costs 4 pesos to residents of X (ignoring transport costs, etc.). If residents of X sold a good for 4 pesos to someone in the US, they know they would get $1. If the exchange rate fluctuated, however, a good that cost $1 in the US would cost varying amounts in pesos depending on the exchange rate. Also, residents of X would not be sure of what they would get in dollars for their exports. An export that has a price of 4 pesos sells for $1 with the exchange rate at 4 pesos for a dollar, but with the exchange rate at 8 pesos for the dollar it sells for only 50 US cents. This uncertainty about the price of imports in terms of X's currency, or about what X could get in terms of US dollars for its exports, is called **trade-price uncertainty.** A fixed exchange rate removes trade-price uncertainty for trade with the country against which X's currency is fixed.

Let's say that X imports a variety of goods from the US, and that the US prices of these have very low inflation, so that the US prices of these imports increase only very slowly over time. Then, with the peso fixed against the dollar, these imports would barely go up in price in terms of peso.

If, however, X had a flexible exchange rate, even though the prices of the imports were almost constant in terms of US dollars, they could fluctuate wildly depending on how the flexible exchange rate changed. If an import cost $1, it would cost 4 pesos if the exchange rate were 4 pesos for the dollar. But a month later, if the exchange rate were 8 pesos for the dollar, the item that still cost US $1 would cost 8 pesos.

By choosing a fixed exchange rate relative to the US dollar, X is able to keep the prices of its imports at the inflation rate they have in the US. If there were little or no inflation in the US, the prices of these imports would have little or no inflation. X, by choosing a fixed exchange rate relative to the dollar, is said to <u>anchor</u> the price inflation of these imports to that of the US. When this purpose of keeping inflation low is served by a fixed exchange rate, the fixed exchange rate is said to be an **inflation anchor**.

Eliminating exchange-rate risk and trade-price uncertainty, and using the exchange rate as an inflation anchor, are key reasons why a country chooses a fixed exchange rate.

Flexible rate system

A flexible exchange rate provides a country with a "self-correcting" mechanism to facilitate economic adjustment. If Country Y is running a trade deficit that causes increased demand for foreign currencies (as Y's residents buy more from abroad than foreigners are buying from Y), this, *ceteris paribus*, will cause Y's currency to depreciate. The higher demand for foreign currencies strengthens the foreign currencies relative to Y's currency, so Y's currency depreciates. This depreciation, however, makes Y's goods and services cheaper to foreigners. So it sets in train a mechanism that could increase foreign demand for Y's products and help to reduce the trade deficit. This is an example of the "self-correcting" aspect of a flexible exchange rate. Having the benefit of this self-correcting mechanism is a key reason for a country to choose a flexible exchange rate system.

Another reason for having a flexible exchange rate system is that managing a fixed exchange rate can be quite burdensome. When a country has a fixed exchange rate, it has to be able to intervene to maintain this rate. As was explained earlier in this chapter, a country has to have foreign currency reserves to facilitate this intervention. Any sign that reserves are not enough to keep the exchange rate at its fixed levels could cause speculators[73] to bet that the fixed exchange rate would not hold. The bets of the speculators would make it more difficult to maintain the fixed rate or even hasten its demise. Factors like political uncertainty and rumors that the fixed rate may be unsustainable will cause people to want to get out of the currency that is fixed and acquire foreign currency. These make the task of maintaining the fixed rate onerous. Having a flexible exchange rate removes these burdens.

---

[73] Speculators are likely to borrow the local currency and sell it for foreign currency. This would further weaken the local currency making it increasingly difficult for the country to maintain the fixed rate. (Borrowing an asset and selling it in the hope of buying it back later when its price has decreased and then repaying what was borrowed is called "shorting" the asset or "going short.") When the currency devalues, the speculators are able to repurchase it at a much cheaper rate than at which they borrowed it. They then repay what they borrowed and gain a substantial profit.

INTERVENTION AND STERILIZED INTERVENTION

Earlier in this chapter, we discussed the role of intervention in maintaining a fixed exchange rate system. Central banks also intervene in flexible exchange rate systems to influence the level of exchange rates. The Fed in the US did this often in the 1980s to decrease the price of the dollar on foreign exchange markets.[74] The US government was influenced by the belief that dollar depreciation would make US products cheaper to foreigners (since they would have to pay less foreign currencies for these) and would make foreign products more expensive to Americans (by causing Americans to have to pay more dollars for them). The US felt this would increase its exports, decrease its imports and lead to a reduction in the huge trade deficits the US ran with Japan and Germany.

Coordinated intervention, also called **concerted intervention**, occurs when several countries coordinate their intervention to influence exchange rate levels. For example, in March 2011, the G-7 countries (US, Canada, France, Germany, Italy, Japan and the UK) intervened to weaken the yen. It was believed that weakening the yen would help economic recovery in Japan. It would increase demand for Japanese exports by making them cheaper to foreigners. Japan needed this help as it had just suffered a horrendous earthquake and tsunami that had actually caused the yen to strengthen. The yen had strengthened because, after the disasters occurred, Japanese brought home assets they had been holding abroad. They converted these into yen to meet expenses they had to incur in Japan as a result of the catastrophes. For example, Japanese insurance companies had to bring in assets from abroad and convert them to yen in order to pay claims for damage due to the natural disasters. As the Japanese converted their foreign-held assets into yen, this increased demand for yen, causing the yen to appreciate.

---

[74] In the US, the US Treasury Department decides what is to be done about the value of the dollar on foreign exchange markets. The US Treasury then instructs the Fed on what intervention the Fed must make.

Sterilized intervention

If the Bank of Japan (BOJ), Japan's central bank, wanted to depreciate the yen relative to the dollar, it could sell yen, buying dollars in exchange. This would decrease the price of the yen and increase the price of the dollar, causing depreciation of the yen relative to the dollar.

Intervention, however, could change the money supply. If the BOJ is selling yen, this increases the amount of yen outside of the BOJ. If the yen the BOJ sold stayed in Japan, the Japanese money supply increases. If the BOJ sold foreign currencies and took yen in return for those foreign currencies, the amount of yen outside of the BOJ decreases. This could decrease the Japanese money supply if the yen taken in by the BOJ came from within the Japanese banking system.

If the BOJ has to intervene to affect the value of the yen on foreign exchange markets but it does not want to affect the Japanese money supply, it can engage in **sterilized intervention**. Sterilized intervention is intervention combined with an OMO (Open Market Operation, discussed in Chapter 7) to offset the impact of the intervention on the money supply.

Suppose the BOJ intervenes to sell yen (buy foreign currencies, paying for these with yen), and this increases the Japanese money supply. If the BOJ at the same time sells bonds in an appropriately sized OMO, it could decrease the Japanese money supply enough so that the combined effect of the intervention and the OMO leaves the money supply unchanged. This is an example of sterilized intervention.

Now suppose the BOJ intervenes buying yen in exchange for other currencies (to appreciate the yen) and this decreases the Japanese money supply. To sterilize this intervention, the BOJ must at the same time engage in an OMO to buy bonds to increase the Japanese money supply. To fully sterilize the intervention, the OMO must be of sufficient size so that the combined effect of the intervention and the OMO leaves the Japanese money supply unchanged.

EXERCISE 2

1. If the US Treasury wanted the Fed to intervene to depreciate the dollar but the Fed was bent on fighting inflation in the US, might the Fed be reluctant to carry out this intervention?

2. If the Bank of Japan was purchasing euros by offering yen for them, what must it do to sterilize this intervention?

3. Suppose the US wanted the yen to appreciate relative to the dollar but the Japanese Prime Minister wanted the money supply in Japan to be increased to stimulate output in Japan. Is there a conflict between these objectives?

REAL EXCHANGE RATES

To be clear about what is a real exchange rate, we must first grasp what is meant by **real**.

Real

To get an understanding of what the term "real" means, let us consider some examples of nominal and real variables. We have encountered nominal and real GDP. Nominal GDP is the value in terms of money of final goods and services produced in a given time period. As we learned earlier in this book, it can be found by taking all the final goods and services produced, multiplying each by its price and finding the total money value. Real GDP, however, is found by taking the relevant goods and services and multiplying each by a base period price. With the goods and services measured in terms of the prices of this base period, inflation is controlled for. So a change in real GDP can only occur if the volume of goods and services produced has changed. Any occurrence that changes only the prices of goods and services will change nominal GDP but not real GDP.

We have also encountered the nominal and real interest rate. The nominal interest rate is just the actual price you pay for borrowing money. If you borrow $1000 at

5 % per annum, the nominal interest rate is five percent. If the expected inflation over the year is 2 %, then the real interest rate is 5 minus 2 percent.

These examples illustrate that a nominal variable is a price or is measured in a currency amount that has been unadjusted for inflation. A real variable, however, is measured in terms of a price or currency value that has been adjusted for inflation (e.g., the real interest rate is the price of borrowing money after an adjustment for inflation has been made, and real GDP is the currency value of output after an adjustment for inflation has been made by holding prices constant). A real variable is also one whose measure does not involve a price or currency value (e.g., unemployment—which is measured as a percent of the labor force).

Nominal exchange rates
In the media, you will often see exchange rate quotations, e.g., 98.2 yen per US dollar. These quotations show the rates at which currencies are being traded for each other. They are called **nominal exchange rates**. Let's say you are looking at the Mexican peso. You might see a quote like 12.8 pesos per dollar. This is the nominal exchange rate of the peso for the dollar.

Real exchange rates
There is another kind of exchange rate that is important in economic analysis. It is called the **real exchange rate**. While nominal exchange rates are always in the news, real exchange rates are not. The real exchange rate is something that economic analysts calculate.

Let's say you wanted to find the real exchange rate of the Mexican peso in terms of the US dollar. To get this real exchange rate, you would take the nominal peso per dollar exchange rate, multiply it by the US price level, and then divide it by the Mexican price level. Let's say:

E = Nominal peso per $ exchange rate
P* = US price level
P = Mexican price level

Then the real exchange rate of the peso in terms of the dollar is:

EP*/P   (the product of E and P* divided by P)

A question you may have is: What do we mean by "US price level" or "Mexican price level", represented by P* and P in the formula for the real exchange rate? When economists are calculating a real exchange rate, they determine what measures they will use for the price levels needed to do their calculation. Earlier in this book, you were introduced to measures of the price level like the CPI and the PPI. Analysts also use other kinds of price levels, e.g., the price level of goods and services a country exports. Because our purpose here is to get an understanding of what is meant by the real exchange rate, and not to get into the intricacies of its calculation, we do not have to worry about issues such as what price levels are used in the calculation of the real exchange rate.

(Some analysts define the real exchange rate as the inverse of what we have here. They put E as the $ per peso rate, P as the Mexican price level, and P as the US price level. We will use the formula we have stated because it facilitates a better focus on how real exchange rate changes affect the non-US country—Mexico, in these examples—which is often a significant issue in international economics.)*

Look at what our real exchange rate formula for the peso does. It takes the US price level, which is a measure of US prices in dollars, and it multiplies it by the peso per $ exchange rate. What this does is to convert the US price level into Mexican pesos. So EP* is the US price level expressed in pesos.

P represents the Mexican price level. So when we take EP* and divide it by P, we are measuring the US price level expressed in peso relative to the Mexican price level.

What happens if this ratio is increasing? It means EP* is increasing relative to P, that is, US goods and services expressed in terms of pesos are becoming relatively more expensive compared to Mexican goods and services, so Mexican goods and services are becoming cheaper relative to US goods and services. **When this happens, the peso is said to be having real depreciation relative to the dollar.** This means Mexico's goods and services are becoming **more competitive** in terms of price compared to US goods and services, and this can cause US buyers to want more of the Mexican goods and services.

If the ratio of EP* to P is falling, P is increasing relative to EP*. Mexican goods and services are becoming more expensive relative to US goods and services. **When this happens, the peso is said to be having real appreciation relative to the US dollar.** This tells us that Mexico's goods and services are becoming less **competitive** in terms of price compared to US goods and services, and this can cause US buyers to want less of the Mexican goods and services.

Here are key points about what a movement in E alone means and what a movement in EP*/P means:

If the nominal peso per dollar exchange rate (E) is **increasing**, this means the Mexican peso is depreciating—

- The Mexican **CURRENCY** is becoming **cheaper** in terms of dollars.

But if the real peso per dollar exchange rate (EP*/P) is **increasing**, this is a real depreciation of the peso relative to the dollar—

- Mexico's **GOODS AND SERVICES** are becoming **cheaper** relative to those from the US, so Mexico is becoming **more competitive** relative to the US.

If the nominal peso per dollar exchange rate (E) is **decreasing**, this means the Mexican peso is appreciating—

- The Mexican **CURRENCY** is becoming **more expensive** in terms of dollars.

But if the real peso per dollar exchange rate (EP*/P) is **decreasing**, this is a real appreciation of the peso relative to the dollar—

- Mexico's **GOODS AND SERVICES** are becoming **more expensive** relative to those from the US, so Mexico is becoming **less competitive** relative to the US.

EXERCISE 3

1. In the following statement, make the correct choice from the options in parentheses: If I go to a bank to exchange pesos for dollars and a bank employee tells me that the exchange rate is 10 pesos per dollar, this rate is a **(nominal exchange rate, real exchange rate)**. If the rate last week was 9 pesos for the dollar, this means the peso is **(appreciating, depreciating).** After leaving the bank, I see my crazy economics professor, and he tells me that the real peso per dollar exchange rate shows peso appreciation. This means Mexican goods and services are becoming **(less, more)** competitive.

2. Look at the real exchange rate data below on Country X. Is the real exchange rate of Country X appreciating or depreciating? Is Country X becoming less or more competitive?

Year	Real Ex. Rate
2008	101
2009	104
2010	109
2011	110

3. What happens to the peso real exchange rate relative to the dollar as we have defined it, and to Mexican competitiveness, if each of the following is occurring **alone**:
   a. The nominal peso per $ exchange rate shows the peso is appreciating
   b. The US price level is falling
   c. The Mexican price level is rising

4. What is the difference between a nominal exchange rate change and a real exchange rate change?

5. Can the nominal yen per $ exchange rate show the yen to be appreciating but the real yen per $ exchange rate show the yen to be depreciating?

6. In the news media, there have been many discussions in recent years of the US government's desire to get the Chinese government to appreciate the Chinese

currency (yuan). The media discussions focus on the nominal exchange rate. Which one of the following best reflects what the US wants?

    a. A nominal yuan appreciation
    b. A real yuan appreciation
    c. The prices of Chinese exports to the US to fall
    d. The prices of US exports to China to rise

PURCHASING POWER PARITY (PPP) THEORY

Purchasing power parity (PPP) theory is a theory of exchange rate determination which states that the exchange rate between two currencies should be the ratio of the domestic to the foreign costs of the same basket of goods. (Here we will frequently use goods as a short hand for goods and services.) For example, if the identical basket of goods costs 400 pesos in Mexico but $100 in the US then the exchange rate of the peso to the dollar should be 4 for 1. According to PPP theory, when the exchange rate is at this level, equal to the ratio of the prices of the two baskets of goods, it is said to be at **equilibrium**.

The notion that at any point in time a good would have the same price no matter where it is sold is called the **law of one price**. The law of one price gives rise to PPP. If the law of one price held and a good costs $1 in the US and 2 pesos in Mexico, the peso per dollar exchange rate has to be 2, so that the good costs the same no matter where it is sold: $1 (= 2 pesos) in the US, or 2 pesos (= $1) in Mexico.

The law of one price and PPP theory assume perfect arbitrage. **Arbitrage** is trading to make profit when one can buy an item in one market and sell it for a higher price in another market. Arbitrage, ignoring transport and transaction costs, ensures the equalization of the price of the same basket of goods across countries. If the same pen sells for a dollar in the US but sells for 2 pesos in Mexico, and the peso per dollar exchange rate is 4, then we can buy a pen in Mexico for 2 pesos, equal to 50 US cents, and sell it in the US for a dollar, equal to 4 pesos.

Arbitrageurs, those who seek to profit from price differences like this, will change dollars into pesos, buy pens in Mexico and sell them in the US. The increased demand for pesos to use to buy pens from Mexico will strengthen the peso relative to the dollar. The increased demand for the pen in Mexico will push up the price of the pen there. The increased availability of pens in the US due to pens being brought in from Mexico will push down the price of the pen in the US. This process only stops when the peso per dollar exchange rate is equal to the peso price of a pen in Mexico divided by the US dollar price of the pen in the US, so that the pen costs the same no matter where it is sold.

The limitations of PPP theory

PPP theory assumes that people have perfect information available to them to facilitate arbitrage. Also, viewing arbitrage as a means of ensuring PPP ignores non-traded goods and services (that cannot be traded or are not traded over long distances, e.g. cleaning services, fast food, etc.), since it is impossible or difficult to buy them in one market and sell them in another to take advantage of a price differential. Further, PPP theory ignores international differences in tastes and buying habits. For example, if product X is loved in one country and its use is critical in the culture of that country, but X is not at all liked in another country, the much greater demand for X in the first country relative to the second country is likely to cause it to have a higher price in the first country. The law of one price, which as explained earlier underpins PPP theory, will not hold for product X.

As discussed earlier in this chapter, there are many factors that cause exchange rates between currencies to fluctuate. News of political instability in a country could cause its exchange rate to depreciate sharply. Or if investors become enthused about shifting funds into a country to earn the higher interest rates available there, a country's currency could appreciate. As we saw when we discussed factors that can cause a flexible exchange rate to change, daily news and expectations can cause sharp fluctuations in exchange rates. Events like these that alter exchange rates have nothing to do with just the relative price of baskets of goods between countries, which is the sole determinant of exchange rates in PPP theory.

PPP is said to hold in the "long run", which is a rather vague term in this context that implies there will be a tendency for exchange rates to move toward PPP levels over the course of time. Given the variety of factors that affect exchange rates, do not be surprised that for long periods of time actual exchange rates differ from what analysts feel should be the PPP levels.

USES OF PPP THEORY

PPP theory is one of the methods economists use to determine if a currency is **<u>overvalued</u>**, **<u>undervalued</u>**, or at an appropriate level relative to another currency. Other methods can be used to make these determinations. Some analysts make these assessments using complex models involving a variety of factors that influence exchange rates. See, for example, the discussion of exchange rate models earlier in this chapter.

<u>**Overvaluation**</u> means a currency is more expensive than it should be. If analysts believe the Swiss franc per US dollar rate should be 1.4 but the actual market exchange rate of the Swiss franc to the dollar is 1, then these analysts would say that the Swiss franc is overvalued. You pay less of it to get foreign currency—you would pay only 1 Swiss franc to get a US dollar when you should be paying 1.4. Another way of thinking about overvaluation is that foreign currency buys less of the overvalued currency than it should—a US dollar buys 1 Swiss franc instead of buying 1.4 Swiss francs.

<u>**Undervaluation**</u> means a currency is cheaper than it should be. If the market exchange rate of the Swiss franc is 1.2 Swiss francs per US dollar, but analysts believe the rate should be 0.9, these analysts would view the Swiss franc as undervalued. You pay 1.2 Swiss francs for a US dollar when you should only be paying 0.9 of a Swiss franc. A US dollar buys you 1.2 Swiss francs when it should only get you 0.9 of a Swiss franc.

The concept of **equilibrium** was mentioned at the start of our discussion of PPP theory. Equilibrium to a PPP theorist means the exchange rate between two currencies corresponds to the level PPP suggests. Suppose the same basket of goods costs $100 US in the United States but 600 yuan in China, and a PPP theorist feels this basket accurately reflects purchasing power. Then a yuan per dollar rate of 6 would be considered an equilibrium rate by this theorist. If the actual exchange rate in the foreign exchange markets is more than 6 yuan per dollar, this theorist would consider the yuan to be undervalued. If it less than 6, this theorist would view it as overvalued.

EXERCISE 4

1. The identical basket of goods costs $100 in the US but 400 pesos in Mexico, and the exchange rate of the peso to the dollar is 4 for 1 (a lucky coincidence!). Then the price of this basket of goods changes so that it costs $110 in the US and 550 pesos in Mexico. If these were PPP levels, what should be the new exchange rate between the peso and the dollar, according to PPP theory?

2. According to PPP theory, if a basket of goods costs $1000 in NY and 1250 euros in Paris, this means the euro per dollar rate should be 1.25. True or false? Explain.

3. Suppose a very reputable economist writes an article in the *Wall Street Journal* suggesting that the PPP level of the yen per $ rate is 100, when the yen per $ rate is 80. Can you conclude from this that the yen is overvalued relative to the dollar (and the dollar undervalued relative to the yen)?

The Big Mac index

The *Economist* magazine collects data on the price of the McDonald's Big Mac hamburger[75] and uses this data to make PPP calculations. If PPP held for the Big Mac, its price when converted into US dollars should be about the same around the world. Converting the price of this burger into US dollars using market exchange rates provides a very rough approximation of the extent to which the market exchange rate has a country's currency overvalued (too expensive) or undervalued (too cheap).

---

[75] It has done this since 1986. Big Macs are not sold in India, so the *Economist* uses the price of a Maharaja Mac, which is made with chicken instead of beef.

Table 1 shows data from the *Economist* for the Big Mac Index in early 2012. To calculate the PPP Swiss franc per US dollar exchange rate based on this Big Mac index, we take the Swiss franc price of the Big Mac and divide by the US price of the Big Mac: 6.5 / 4.2 = 1.55. So PPP theory suggests, using this very simple measure comparing Big Mac prices, that the Swiss franc per US dollar rate should be 1.55.

However, as the third column of the table shows, the market exchange rate of the Swiss franc to the dollar at the time these data were collected was 0.96, not the 1.55 suggested by PPP theory. A US dollar could only buy 0.96 of a Swiss franc when PPP theory suggested it should be able to buy 1.55 Swiss francs. So in reality the Swiss franc was more expensive than PPP suggested it should be—it was overvalued.

TABLE 1
Big Mac Prices and Currency Exchange Rates

Country	Big Mac price in local currency	Market exchange rate of country's currency per US $	Big Mac price in US $	Currency over/ under valuation
US	4.20 dollars	--	4.20	--
Switzerland	6.50 Swiss francs	0.96	6.81	Overvalued
Brazil	10.25 reals	1.81	5.68	Overvalued
Japan	320 yen	76.9	4.16	Undervalued
China	15.4 yuan	6.32	2.44	Undervalued
South Africa	19.95 rand	8.13	2.45	Undervalued
India	84 rupees	51.9	1.62	Undervalued

Source: *The Economist*, Jan. 12, 2012

If PPP held, a US dollar would be able to buy the same amount of Big Mac everywhere, so in each country the Big Mac would cost the equivalent of US $4.20, the same as in the US. If the price of a country's Big Mac when converted into US dollars is greater than $4.20, this means each unit of the country's currency is equal to more in US dollars than it would be if PPP held. So the country's currency is overvalued. If the price of the local Big Mac when converted into US dollars is less than $4.20, this means each unit of the country's currency is equal to less in US dollars than it would be if PPP held. So the country's currency is undervalued. According to the *Economist* data cited here, Switzerland and Brazil had overvalued currencies, and Japan, China, South Africa and India had undervalued currencies.

EXERCISE 5

1. If PPP held for the Big Mac in Table 1, what would be the US dollar price of the Big Mac in each country?

2. If the US dollar price of the Big Mac in a country is more than the price of the Big Mac in the US, does this tell you that the country's currency is overvalued?

3. From the data in Table 1, what should be the PPP yuan per US dollar and the PPP rupee per dollar exchange rates?

GDP IN TERMS OF PPP EXCHANGE RATES

Suppose the real GDP of a country in its own currency is 20,000 pesos. If the peso per US dollar market exchange rate is 4 for 1, the country's real GDP is $5,000 when converted into US dollars.

But let's say what sells for 2 pesos in that country would actually sell for $1 in the US. Then the PPP exchange rate is 2 pesos per dollar, and expressed in terms of PPP of the dollar, the real GDP of the country would be 10,000 dollars, which is much more (double) than the GDP found using the regular exchange rate.

In many of the poorer countries of the world, labor is very cheap. Labor is a very important input in the creation of goods and services. For goods and services that are created locally, their production costs are much less than would be the case for the same goods and services produced in the US. What sells for the local currency equivalent of a US dollar at the market exchange rate would cost a lot more in the

US. For example, a meal in India that costs 10 rupees, equivalent to 20 US cents (when the rupee per $ market exchange rate is 50 rupees for a dollar), would probably cost 8 dollars in the US. For a taxi ride that costs 25 rupees in India, a similar ride in New York would probably cost 20 dollars.

So if we want to compare the GDP of countries and we use market exchange rates, we can end up undervaluing the GDP of countries where production costs are much lower. GDP calculated using PPP exchange rates seeks to overcome this problem.

If the peso per dollar rate moves to 5, the GDP of the country in the earlier example when expressed in US dollars would now be $4,000 (20,000 pesos/5 pesos per dollar). If, however, 2 pesos worth of goods and services in that country can still be bought for a dollar, then the GDP of the country in terms of the PPP of the dollar would still be 10,000 dollars. As we learned earlier in this chapter, market exchange rates are affected by a variety of factors—news, political developments, etc. These rates can sometimes be quite volatile. When GDP is calculated using market exchange rates, it could fluctuate a lot just because of exchange rate gyrations. Finding GDP in terms of PPP exchange rates avoids this problem. If we want to compare the sizes of various countries' economies, using GDP at PPP exchange rates is likely to give us a better comparison than using GDP at market exchange rates.

Of course, it is very difficult to compute PPP exchange rates. One cannot just compare prices of one or a few goods and services between two countries to get the PPP exchange rate of their currencies. What should be in the basket of goods and services that is compared across these countries? How does one take account of goods and services in a country that do not exist in the other country? These are some of the very difficult questions that have to be struggled with when attempting to calculate GDP in terms of PPP exchange rates.

The International Comparison Program (ICP) has to grapple with these issues as it produces GDP data in terms of PPP for about 180 countries. The ICP was started in 1968 by the United Nations Statistical Division (UNSD) and the International Comparisons Unit of the University of Pennsylvania. In 1993, the World Bank became the international coordinator of the program to provide it with more effective management.

ANSWERS

EXERCISE 1

1. The dollar is appreciating. 1.2 dollars for one euro means 1 dollar for 1/1.2 euro = 0.83 euro.

2. i, ii and iv

3. There would be two factors at work here. First, if the news of US output growing more rapidly than expected increases optimism about the US economy, this, *ceteris paribus*, causes the US dollar to appreciate. Second, if the news makes investors more willing to take on risk, they are likely to move out of the safe haven of the dollar and buy investments such as stocks, which, *ceteris paribus*, depreciates the dollar. So if this second factor is strong enough relative to the first, the dollar depreciates after this news.

4. Even though the US was in a severe economic crisis, the US government has a solid history of making the payments due on its bonds. US government bonds were a safe asset to buy when there was turmoil around the world, causing increased demand for dollars for purchasing these bonds, so the dollar appreciated relative to currencies such as the euro.

5. A risk-on trade causes investors to move out of safe-haven US dollars, so the US dollar would weaken. A risk-on trade also means investors are more optimistic about the prospects for world economic growth and would be expecting stronger demand for commodities, so the currency of a commodity exporting country like Australia would strengthen.

6.
   i. The US dollar is a safe-haven currency and strengthened relative to the euro as investors wanted to get out of euros and into dollars.
   ii. The Australian dollar weakened relative to the US dollar as investors became more pessimistic about world economic growth and decreased their holdings of commodity currencies like the Australian dollar.

iii. With the tighter than expected monetary policy in Japan, the yen strengthened relative to the dollar.

EXERCISE 2

1. Yes, the Fed might be reluctant because intervention to depreciate the dollar would mean making more dollars available, which would increase the US money supply if those dollars went into the US banking system. The Fed wanting to fight inflation necessitates decreasing the US money supply.

2. If the Bank of Japan is purchasing euros and selling yen, to sterilize this intervention it must engage in an OMO to take in yen, i.e., sell bonds.

3. Yes, there could be a conflict because increasing the money supply in Japan, *ceteris paribus*, will depreciate the yen relative to the dollar.

EXERCISE 3

1. nominal exchange rate; depreciating; less

2. depreciating; more competitive

3.
   a. In the formula for the real exchange rate, the nominal exchange rate E alone is changing. It decreases, so EP* falls. With P unchanged, the real exchange rate EP*/P decreases. This is peso appreciation and Mexican goods and services become less competitive.

   b. If the US price level is falling, but E and P are unchanged, EP*/P decreases. The peso appreciates in real terms and Mexican goods and services become less competitive.

   c. With the Mexican price level rising, EP*/P falls. This means peso appreciation in real terms and a decline in Mexican competitiveness.

4. A nominal exchange rate change is a change of E alone (referring to the formula EP*/P). A real exchange rate change occurs when EP*/P as a whole is changing in value. To see whether a real exchange rate is changing, you have to look at not just E but also P* and P.

5. Yes. The real yen per $ exchange rate depends on the nominal rate, the US price level, and the Japanese price level. So even though the nominal rate (E in our formula) is falling (the yen is appreciating), P could be falling by enough relative to P* to cause EP*/P to increase, i.e., the yen depreciates in real terms even as it is appreciating in nominal terms.

6. b.   What the US administration actually wants is for the **real** yuan per $ exchange rate to show yuan appreciation, making Chinese goods and services more expensive and therefore less competitive relative to US goods and services. The US government hopes this would lead to a reduction in US purchases of Chinese products and more purchases of US products by China, reducing the huge US trade deficit.

EXERCISE 4

1. The peso per dollar rate would be 5 pesos per dollar (550 pesos/110 dollars).

2. True, if we assume that it is the "long run" so that all adjustments (e.g., arbitrage) have occurred to ensure that PPP holds. With PPP holding, the exchange rate would be 1250 euros / $1000 = 1.25 euros per dollar.

3. If you accept this analyst's view, then the yen should be at 100 yen per dollar. But it is actually at 80 yen per dollar. So you pay less yen to get a dollar than should be required. So the yen is overvalued, if you determine overvaluation based on this PPP level.

EXERCISE 5

1. The price in US dollars for the Big Mac would have to be the same in each country, so it would be $4.20.

2. Yes, if we assume comparing Big Mac prices is an appropriate way of assessing PPP and we are assessing overvaluation in terms of PPP.

3. The PPP yuan per dollar exchange rate is the yuan price of the Big Mac in China divided by the price of the Big Mac in the US = 15.4 / 4.2 = 3.67. The PPP rupee per dollar exchange rate is the rupee price of the Big Mac in India divided by the price of the Big Mac in the US = 84 / 4.2 = 20.

CHAPTER 11
VERSIONS OF THE AD-AS MODEL

INTRODUCTION

So far we have used a version of the AD-AS model in which the AD curve is negatively sloped and the AS curve is positively sloped. In this version, which we will call the **general AD-AS model** from now on, a change in AD or AS changes both the price level, P, and the output level, Y. It is applicable to situations in which changes in both P and Y are relevant concerns.

We must learn versions of the AD-AS model applicable to other situations such as when change in one of P or Y is not a concern. By learning these versions we enhance our capacity to use the AD-AS model to understand the world.

THE KEYNESIAN VERSION

We will now study a version of the AD-AS model called the **Keynesian version** because it embodies views associated with John Maynard Keynes, who studied situations of high unemployment such as existed during the Great Depression in the 1930s. Keynes expressed the views on which this model is based in his book *The General Theory of Employment, Interest and Money,* first published in 1936 and usually referred to for short as *The General Theory.*

In this version of the AD-AS model, wages and prices are taken to be constant. This is because in the situations to which this model applies unemployment is high enough to enable businesses to get all the labor they want at the existing wage— high unemployment makes it impossible for workers to bargain for higher wages. At the same time, workers, like any of us, resist cuts in their wages. Wages can therefore be viewed as constant. Wages are a very important cost of production. With these production costs constant, the theoretical abstraction can be made[76] that

---

[76] In Chapter 1 we discussed the role of abstraction in theory formulation.

whatever amount of output is produced can be offered for sale at the same price. In this case, the AS curve is horizontal and wages and prices are constant.[77] Because there is high unemployment, output is below potential.

Figure 1 shows a diagram representing this model[78] and lists the characteristics of the situation to which the model applies.

FIGURE 1
THE KEYNESIAN VERSION OF THE AD-AS MODEL

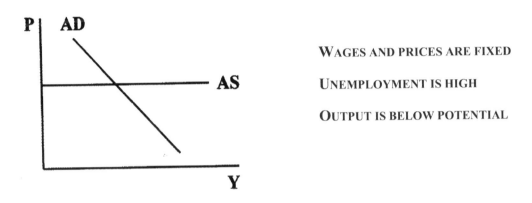

WAGES AND PRICES ARE FIXED

UNEMPLOYMENT IS HIGH

OUTPUT IS BELOW POTENTIAL

Another reason wages and prices could be constant is that they are established by contracts. Frequently, workers have contracts with employers stipulating their wages, and businesses have contracts with customers stipulating their prices. These contracts generally cannot be legally changed, or are costly and disruptive to change, in a short period of time. For a short time period, wages and prices would be constant. Consequently, this Keynesian model, which holds wages and prices to be constant, is frequently referred to as a short-run model.

---

[77] Note that Keynes did not hold that wages and prices are always constant. However, if wage and price changes are not a serious concern, and if we want to focus exclusively on how changes in AD affect output and employment, wage and price changes can be ignored.

[78] Each of the versions of the AD-AS is often referred to as a model. In Chapter 1, we noted that "model" has the same meaning as "theory".

This model draws attention to the role of aggregate demand in changing output and employment. If the government engages in expansionary fiscal policies, this increases aggregate demand and increases output and employment (Figure 2).

FIGURE 2

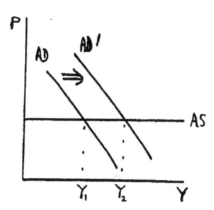

**Policies that increase AD boost
output and employment.**

This result is similar to what we learned in the general AD-AS model in Chapters 2 and 3 except that now the price level remains constant because the AS curve is horizontal.[79] The Keynesian version of the AD-AS model focuses attention on the role government can play in using fiscal and monetary policy to increase aggregate demand and so increase output and employment. **Keynesians** feel government should attempt to manipulate aggregate demand to change output and employment. Policies to manipulate aggregate demand are called **activist policies**. Keynesians believe in activist policies.

When the price level is not a serious concern, the Keynesian model can be used for analysis and policy prescription. During the Great Depression, output and

---

[79] Of course, if output and employment continued to increase workers would be able to agitate for higher wages and the AS curve would no longer be horizontal. For such higher levels of output and employment, the general AD-AS model, or one of those to be learned later in this chapter, would be applicable.

employment had fallen sharply. The price level had also fallen sharply. The concern then was with increasing output and employment; increases in the price level were not a worry. The Keynesian model was quite relevant for analyzing that situation. It made clear immediately that increasing AD would increase output and employment. (Of course, decreasing AD would decrease output and employment.)

We can use this Keynesian model for theoretical analysis when we want to ignore price changes, even if such changes are occurring in the real world. We may want to ignore these changes because our purpose is to focus on what happens to output or some other economic variable without having to clutter our analysis with worry over what is happening to the price level. It would be a great mistake, however, to use this version of the AD-AS model for analyzing a situation in which inflation is a serious concern.

In APPENDIX, Part III *at the end of this book*, **there is a discussion of an algebraic version of the Keynesian model.** It:

- Shows how a model based on Keynesian notions can be constructed to do actual calculations to determine output and other variables.

- Gives you some insight into how this is done without spending time on details you will probably never need—as it is unlikely that the typical reader of this book will have to do these calculations in the course of his/her career.

- Introduces you to terms like the Keynesian multiplier, the marginal propensity to consume, the marginal propensity to save and the paradox of thrift.

THE CLASSICAL VERSION

Some economists before Keynes, called **classical economists**, held that wages and prices were **perfectly flexible**, meaning that they change very rapidly, and this causes the economy to always be at full employment. This view is the basis of what came to be known as the **classical model**. According to the classical model, any attempt to raise the level of output increases the demand for labor and pushes up wages and so immediately discourages increased employment. As a result, output remains at the original level. Any tendency to decrease output decreases the demand for labor, makes workers willing to take lower wages to get or keep jobs and so encourages increased employment. This keeps output at the original level. These wage level adjustments occur instantaneously.[80]

Any tendency for employment to fall below or rise above the full employment level immediately sets in motion the adjustment processes just described. Employment remains at the full employment level, and the unemployment rate remains at the natural rate. If unemployment is always at the natural rate, the economy does not depart from its full employment level of output (potential output). Because output is always at potential, the AS curve is represented by a vertical line at the potential output level.

Figure 3 shows a diagram representing this model and lists characteristics of the situations to which it applies. The diagram makes obvious that changes in AD do not at all change output in this classical version. Whether the AD curve shifts up or down, output remains at Y*. There is no reason for government to engage in fiscal or monetary policy to affect output and employment because any such change has no effect on these variables. This classical version suggests that the economy left to itself will be at full employment. It does not need government interference to get to full employment.

This model is frequently called a model of the <u>long run</u>. The term "long run" used in this context should not be viewed in terms of calendar time but as the time when output is at potential. This model is appropriate if we are dealing with a situation in

---

[80] The classical economists recognized that in reality these wage adjustments might take a little time. The point is, however, they occurred quickly enough so that for theoretical purposes we could view them as happening instantaneously. Also, the price of output depends on the cost of producing it. Wages are a most important cost of production. With these perfectly flexible, prices would also be perfectly flexible. So in the classical model, wages and prices are perfectly flexible.

which the economy is at full employment and it is reasonable to think that prices and wages change very rapidly.[81]

FIGURE 3
THE CLASSICAL VERSION OF THE AD-AS MODEL

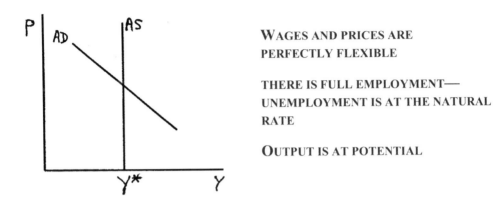

WAGES AND PRICES ARE PERFECTLY FLEXIBLE

THERE IS FULL EMPLOYMENT—UNEMPLOYMENT IS AT THE NATURAL RATE

OUTPUT IS AT POTENTIAL

The classical dichotomy

In the classical model, changes in the money supply do not affect output, employment or any other real variables.[82] In terms of Figure 3, changes in the money supply would shift AD but leave the economy's output and employment at the full employment level. Because real variables are not affected by the money supply in the economy, we can study how they are determined without a consideration of nominal variables like the money supply. We can then analyze nominal variables like the money supply to determine what the price level would be. That real and nominal variables can be analyzed separately, is called the **classical dichotomy**. That changes in the money supply have no effect on real variables is called **money neutrality**.

---

[81] The classical model is generally referred to in textbooks as we have just described it. However, people differ in what they mean by the term "classical economists." According to Keynes, Karl Marx invented the term to refer to Ricardo, James Mill and their predecessors. Keynes, however, used the term to also include followers of Ricardo such as Marshall, Edgeworth and Pigou.

[82] In Chapter 10, we discussed what are real and nominal variables.

The Keynesian model versus the classical model

As we have noted, the classical economists believed the perfect flexibility of wages and prices keeps output at the full employment level. The classical economists also believed **supply creates its own demand**. By this they meant that the value of output produced and supplied equals what is earned by those producing the output. These earnings will be spent on the goods and services produced. The amount people spend (the quantity of aggregate demand) will equal the amount supplied (the quantity of aggregate supply) and will be determined by the amount supplied. This means supply creates its own demand.

If \$1 billion worth of output is produced, people in the economy earn \$1 billion from the production and sale of this output. They will spend \$1 billion—the amount of demand will be \$1 billion. If the amount supplied is \$2 billion, the amount of demand will be \$2 billion. The amount of aggregate supply determines the amount of aggregate demand. This is what the classical economists meant by the view that supply creates its own demand—a notion called **Say's Law**, after Jean-Baptiste Say (1767-1832), the economist who is credited as its originator.

Even if people do not spend all they earn but save some of it, Say's Law still holds, according to the classical economists. They believed what is saved will be borrowed by businesses for investment (in equipment, machinery, factories, etc.). Savers earn the interest that businesses pay for borrowing these savings. It is the interest rate that provides the incentive for saving. If there is any tendency for businesses to want to invest less, which will make them want to borrow less, this causes savers to take a lower interest to get their funds loaned out (rather than not have their funds loaned out and earn no interest). The lower interest rate creates less of an incentive for people to save, so what is not saved anymore will now be spent by people. The decreased investment by businesses is offset by the increased spending by people. In this situation, the total quantity of aggregate demand remains unchanged and equal to the quantity of aggregate supply—as Say's Law suggests.

According to the classical economists, the perfect flexibility of wages and prices ensured that the level of output produced was equal to potential, and Say's Law ensured that the quantity of output demanded equaled the quantity of output supplied. The economy would always be at equilibrium in a situation of full employment.

In reality, however, when the Great Depression occurred and there was a prolonged period of rising unemployment and decreasing output, it became clear that the classical model was not a good approximation of the way the macro-economy worked. As Keynes noted in *The General Theory*[83], classical economists were:

> apparently unmoved by the lack of correspondence
> between the results of their theory and the facts
> of observation;—a discrepancy which [ordinary
> people have] not failed to observe....

> It may well be that the classical theory
> represents the way in which we should like our
> economy to behave. But to assume that it
> actually does so is to assume our difficulties
> away. (pp. 33-34)

He noted in Chapter 1 of *The General Theory* that the characteristics of the classical theory "happen not to be those of the economic society in which we actually live, with the result that its teaching is misleading and disastrous if we attempt to apply it to the facts of experience." (p.3)

Keynes believed that if businesses became very pessimistic about the future this causes a sharp fall in their investment and in aggregate demand. This decreases the quantity of aggregate demand to much less than potential output and drives up unemployment, unlike what the classical economists believed.

Keynes also believed that as unemployment increased wages would not fall[84] as the classical economists held. Falling wages would therefore not exist to encourage

---

[83] Keynes, J.M. (1936). *The general theory of employment, interest and money.* (1974 ed.). London: Macmillan.

[84] Earlier in this chapter we discussed the Keynesian view on why wages would be rigid.

employment of more labor and help the economy move back to full employment as the classical economists envisaged. The economy, according to Keynes, could be stuck for long periods of time at high unemployment. Government action would be necessary to stimulate increases in aggregate demand to increase output and employment. These views are in sharp contrast to those of the classical economists that the economy would be at full employment and that no government intervention was necessary to ensure this.

A VERSION OF THE AD-AS MODEL WITH
ADJUSTMENT TO THE LONG-RUN EQUILIBRIUM

This is a generic version that depicts how the economy moves to full employment. In this version, it is held that if actual output is less than potential output, wages fall.[85] If actual output is greater than potential output, wages rise.[86] This wage adjustment mechanism is called the economy's <u>self-correcting mechanism</u>.

This version has the usual negatively sloped AD curve but has two AS curves—the upward sloping one we have been using since we introduced the AD-AS model in this book and a vertical one, like the one in the classical model, called the <u>long-run AS curve (LRAS)</u>. The upward sloping AS curve in this model is called the <u>short-run AS curve (SRAS)</u>. Do not let this terminology cause you to confuse it with the AS curve of the Keynesian model (because the Keynesian model, as we noted earlier, is called a short-run model).

Consider the situation depicted in Figure 4. Here actual output, corresponding to the point where the AD curve and the SRAS intersect, is y, and potential output is

---

[85] Unemployment above the natural rate makes workers willing to take lower wages in order to get jobs.

[86] Workers on the job will have to work overtime at higher wage rates. Or those who might otherwise have left their jobs to seek other employment might be induced to stay if their demand for higher pay is met. Factors like these cause wages to rise when output is above potential and unemployment is below the natural rate.

Y*, where the long-run AS is located. Because y is less than potential output, unemployment is above the natural rate and wages will be falling—workers will be willing to take lower wages in order to get employed. Falling wages cause the SRAS to shift to the right—just as we have learned in this book since we first discussed what shifts the AS curve.

As long as y < Y*, if the economy is left to itself, this SRAS curve will shift to the right until it intersects AD on the LRAS line at Y*. At that point, y = Y*, unemployment is at the natural rate, and wages cease falling. According to this model of adjustment to the long run, when output is below potential, wages fall. This increases SRAS, enabling the economy to reach full employment, when unemployment is at the natural rate.

FIGURE 4
AN ILLUSTRATION OF THE AD-AS MODEL
WITH ADJUSTMENT TO THE LONG-RUN EQUILIBRIUM
STARTING WITH UNEMPLOYMENT ABOVE THE NATURAL RATE

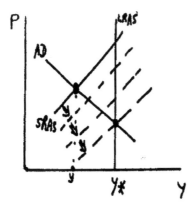

With y < Y*, wages fall, causing the SRAS to shift to the right until SRAS and AD intersect on the vertical AS—full employment is reached.

Figure 5 depicts a situation in which actual output (y_1) is above potential output (Y*). Unemployment is below the natural rate, so wages will be rising. As wages increase, the SRAS shifts to the left until potential output is reached (point A in the figure) and unemployment is back at the natural rate.

FIGURE 5
AN ILLUSTRATION OF THE AD-AS MODEL
WITH ADJUSTMENT TO THE LONG-RUN EQUILIBRIUM
STARTING WITH UNEMPLOYMENT BELOW THE NATURAL RATE

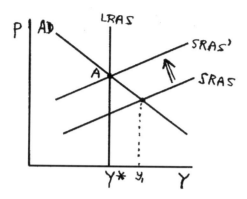

NAIRU

The natural rate of unemployment is also called the **nonaccelerating inflation rate of unemployment (NAIRU)**. As we have seen in this model, if unemployment goes below the natural rate, workers seek and get higher wages. This decreases short-run AS and brings unemployment back to the natural rate level. As this occurs, inflation rises, and the price level in the end is higher than it was initially. Once unemployment reaches the natural rate, there is no impetus for workers to increase their wage demands, and therefore for inflation to accelerate. So the natural rate of unemployment is the rate of unemployment at which inflation is not accelerating (or decelerating)—the nonaccelerating inflation rate of unemployment, NAIRU.

THE EXPECTATIONS-AUGMENTED PHILLIPS CURVE

In Chapter 8, we discussed the Phillips curve—the inverse relation between inflation and unemployment. According to the simple Phillips curve relation depicted there, lower/higher unemployment would be associated with higher/lower inflation. In this simple relation, **the level of inflation depends on the level of unemployment** and is inversely related to it.

We described there one set of circumstances under which this inverse relation would not hold. From the general AD-AS model, we know that if changes in aggregate supply occur, inflation and unemployment could move in the same direction. For example, a decrease in aggregate supply could mean higher prices (more inflation) and lower output (higher unemployment). So inflation and unemployment could be positively related.

Now consider another scenario. Suppose workers begin to **expect** a higher level of inflation. For example, they become convinced that government policies will cause prices to shoot up faster than they had originally thought. Then they will seek higher wages to compensate them for the higher prices they expect to pay for goods and services, and this leads to a higher level of inflation. So no matter what is the existing level of unemployment, if inflation expectations rise, this causes actual inflation to go up.

Inflation depends not just on the level of unemployment but on expectations of inflation. Economists Milton Friedman (Nobel Prize, Economics, 1976) and Edmund Phelps (Nobel Prize, Economics, 2006) independently proposed this notion, which is referred to as the **<u>expectations-augmented Phillips curve</u>**.[87]

THE LONG-RUN PHILLIPS CURVE

From the AD-AS model with adjustment to the long run that we have just learned, we see that in the long run unemployment would be at the natural rate. For example, any attempt to decrease unemployment below that natural rate would simply lead to higher wages that decrease short-run aggregate supply and bring the economy to a new equilibrium but at a higher price level.

---

[87] Friedman, M. (1968). The Role of Monetary Policy. *American Economic Review*, 58 (1), 1-17; Phelps, E. S. (1968). Money-Wage Dynamics and Labor-Market Equilibrium. *Journal of Political Economy*, 76 (4), 678-711.

To the extent this model holds, in the long run, no matter what the level of inflation is, unemployment will be at the natural rate. Just as the long-run aggregate supply curve is vertical, so the **long-run Phillips curve** is vertical. That the long-run Phillips curve is vertical at the natural rate of unemployment is referred to as the **natural rate hypothesis,** or the **Phelps-Friedman hypothesis,** as it was proposed by Edmund Phelps and Milton Friedman.

WHAT LIES AHEAD

In Chapter 12, we discuss other schools of thought in economics to understand why they differ in their views of the economy and in their policy prescriptions. We will extensively use the AD-AS model with adjustment to the long run introduced in this chapter to highlight key features in these schools of thought.

If you would like an algebraic treatment of the Keynesian model presented in this chapter, you can read the **END OF BOOK APPENDIX, Part III.** It provides essential notions and avoids details for which you are likely to have no practical use.

EXERCISE

1. Suppose workers begin to **expect** a higher level of inflation and take this into account as they bargain over wage contracts. Using the general AD-AS model, explain what will happen to AS. Is it likely that both inflation and unemployment will rise?

Use the AD-AS model with adjustment to the long run to answer 2 to 4:

2. Suppose the economy is at full employment but the government believes the price level is too high, so it drastically reduces AD, and then leaves the self-correcting mechanism to bring the economy back to full employment. Explain how the adjustment back to full employment occurs. (This method of drastically reducing AD to fight inflation is called the **cold-turkey approach**. In contrast,

the method of gradually reducing AD to reduce inflation is called the **gradualist approach**. A government pursuing a gradualist approach might be seen as hesitant and fearful of the adverse consequences of reducing AD. Its policy to fight inflation could therefore suffer from lack of credibility, causing inflationary expectations to continue to rise because people don't really believe the government will persist in the fight against inflation.)

3. Draw a diagram to represent an economy in which there is considerable unemployment with actual output below potential. Show how the adjustment to full employment will occur if this economy is left to itself. Could there be prolonged periods of unemployment above the natural rate if the economy is left to itself to reach full employment?

4. Suppose there is an influx of skilled immigrants into an economy that was suffering from a shortage of skilled labor. What happens to potential output? Does the LRAS shift to the right? If the economy was at full employment before the influx of labor, explain how it reaches a new equilibrium at full employment after the influx of skilled immigrants. (Assume AD does not change.)

5. What relationship does the long-run AS curve depict? What relationship does the long-run Phillips curve depict?

ANSWERS

1. Workers will seek higher wages to compensate them for the higher prices they expect to pay for goods and services. The short-run aggregate supply curve will shift to the left. Using the general AD-AS model diagram, we can depict this situation as in the figure below. It shows a lower level of output and a higher price level resulting (as AS shifts to the left to AS"). In this scenario, inflation could rise at the same time as unemployment increases.

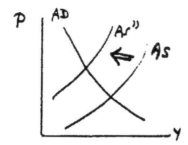

2. The figure below depicts the situation in which the economy is initially at G and then the government drastically reduces AD to AD', bringing the economy to H. At H, output is less than potential and unemployment is above the natural rate, so wages fall, causing SRAS to shift to the right to SRAS' until output reaches potential at I. The price level is now lower than initially at point G.

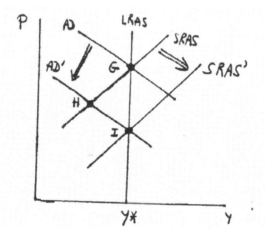

3. The diagram will be like Figure 4 in this chapter, which is reproduced on the next page for convenient reference. If the economy is left to itself, according to the AD-AS model with adjustment to the long run, wages will fall, causing the SRAS to shift to the right until potential output is reached. There could be prolonged periods of unemployment if the self-correcting mechanism works slowly to bring the economy to potential output.

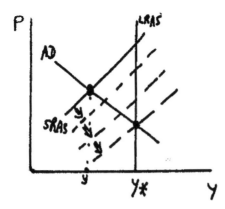

With y < Y*, wages fall,
causing the SRAS to shift
to the right until SRAS and
AD intersect on the vertical
AS—full employment is
reached.

4. With more skilled labor now in the economy, potential output increases, so
LRAS shifts to the right to LRAS'. Suppose the economy was initially at R (in
the figure below). After LRAS shifts to LRAS', at R output will be below
potential and unemployment will be higher than the natural rate, so wages will
fall, and SRAS will shift to the right until a new equilibrium is reached at S.

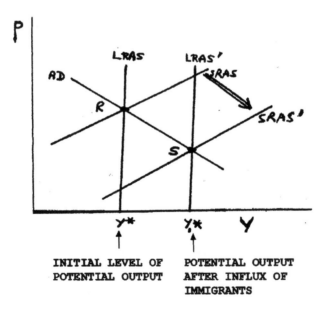

(You were told to assume AD does not change. However, if you want to think
of what happens to AD, consider the following: The demand for goods and

services from the skilled immigrants is likely to increase AD. If it does, the AD curve shifts up, and intersects the LRAS' curve at a point higher than S. SRAS will shift to the right, as described earlier in this answer, and, in the new equilibrium, SRAS' will intersect the new AD curve where the new AD curve intersects LRAS'. So if AD increases, the new equilibrium level of output will still be Y_1^*, but the new equilibrium price level will be higher than at S, corresponding to the point where the new AD curve intersects LRAS'.)

5. The long-run AS curve shows a relationship between the price level and output, with output at potential for all price levels. The long-run Phillips curve shows a relationship between the inflation rate and the unemployment rate, with unemployment at the natural rate for all inflation rates.

We have learned that the various schools of thought [in economics] all have important elements of truth in them. But none of them is by itself a sufficient explanation of what goes on in the economy.

—Michael Boskin, Chairperson of the US President's Council of Economic Advisors, 1989-1993

Fortunately, I was encouraged to join the debate team in my junior year of high school and participated actively in speech competitions around the state. Learning debate was an important early impact on my ways of thinking. You are taught that there are always at least two sides to public policy questions, and you have to learn a good argument for both sides as well as knowing how to critique both sides.

—Elinor Ostrom, Nobel Prize, Economics, 2009

CHAPTER 12
SCHOOLS OF THOUGHT IN ECONOMICS

INTRODUCTION

In this chapter we discuss five schools of thought—**monetarism, new classical macroeconomics**, **new Keynesianism**, **real business cycle theory** and **supply-side economics**—on how the macroeconomy works and on policies suitable for obtaining full employment and potential output. We will frequently refer to the AD-AS model. This extends the discussion started in the previous chapter in which we looked at the Keynesian and classical models.

MONETARISM

Monetarists hold that of the factors that cause changes in aggregate demand, change in the money supply is the main one. Because of the emphasis they put on the role of money in the economy, it is not surprising they are called monetarists and that their view on the role of money is called **monetarism**.

Monetarists believe in the **quantity theory of money**. Recall (from Chapter 8) the equation of exchange, $MV = PQ$, where M = money supply, V = velocity, P = price level, and Q = real GDP (so PQ = nominal GDP). To move from this equation to their quantity theory of money, monetarists hold that V is predictable. Changes in M therefore have predictable effects on PQ (nominal GDP). To understand what happens to nominal GDP, monetarists focus on determining what happens to M and V because any percentage change in MV must lead to an equal percentage change in PQ.

Of all the factors we learned in Chapter 2 that can affect AD, M is the one that enters directly into the equation of exchange and the quantity theory. The others can affect nominal GDP only indirectly through any effects they have on M and/or V. This is why monetarists hold changes in the money supply are the main cause of changes in AD.

Like the classical economists, monetarists believe that the economy is inherently stable and has a tendency to move toward full employment because the self-correcting mechanism (explained in Chapter 11) works effectively.

They also believe that attempts by governments to use monetary and fiscal policy to affect output and employment generally destabilize the economy. Monetarists feel this is so because of lags in the recognition, formulation, implementation and effects of policy. It takes time, referred to as a **recognition lag**, before a government recognizes a problem in the economy. It takes time to formulate a policy to deal with the problem—a **formulation lag**. It takes time to get the policy implemented—an **implementation lag**. While economic theory informs us about the possible effects of policies, no one has knowledge of exactly when these effects will occur or what will be their precise magnitude over the course of time—an **effects lag**.

Consequently, a government policy implemented now may become effective when it is no longer needed because the problem it seeks to address is long past. The government is like a doctor checking you, learning you had a fever three months ago but prescribing aspirin for it now! According to the monetarists, the government is guilty of severe malpractice in managing the economy.

Because of their confidence in the effectiveness of the economy's self-correcting mechanism and because of the lags just described, monetarists feel that government's attempt to manipulate aggregate demand to change output and employment destabilizes the economy. They do not believe in activist policies.[88]

Monetarists believe the government should not manipulate fiscal policies in an attempt to change output and employment. Instead, a suitable set of stable fiscal policies should be decided on and pursued by government.

---

[88] Recall from Chapter 11 that policies to manipulate aggregate demand are called activist policies.

Monetarists also do not believe government should keep altering money supply growth to adjust aggregate demand, output and employment. They feel government attempts at this manipulation of the money supply destabilize the economy because of the lags we have described. Monetarists advocate a constant growth rate of the money supply. They feel the central bank should set money supply growth at a level consistent with the money needed by a growing economy and should avoid contracting or expanding the money supply to manipulate AD. This view of the monetarists is called the rule or the **constant growth rate of the money supply rule.**

Some of the prominent names that have been associated with advocacy of monetarism are: Milton Friedman (Nobel Prize, 1976), Karl Brunner, Phillip Cagan, David Laidler, Thomas Mayer, Allan Meltzer, Michael Parkin, Anna Schwartz and Alan Walters.

Monetarists versus Keynesians
Monetarists differ sharply from Keynesians. Keynesians believe the economy's self-correcting mechanism is not effective because of the rigidity of wages and prices. They advocate activist government policies—the manipulation of both fiscal and monetary policy to change output and employment. Suppose the economy was experiencing high unemployment, as represented in Figure 1 with output at Y_1 and unemployment above the natural rate. The Keynesians would argue that the economy could remain at output level Y_1 for a long time unless government acted to increase AD and bring the economy to full employment—by increasing AD to AD', for example.

The monetarists would claim that what is necessary is a constant growth rate of the money supply and a stable set of fiscal policies. If the governing authorities have such policies in place and output is still below potential, then the economy's self-correcting mechanism will work to bring output to potential. (Recall from Chapter 11, if the self-correcting mechanism works, when output is below potential wages would fall increasing SRAS until Y^* is reached, as is shown here in Figure 2.)

FIGURE 1

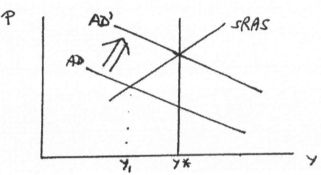

IF OUTPUT IS BELOW POTENTIAL, THE KEYNESIANS
WOULD ADVOCATE EXPANSIONARY POLICIES TO
INCREASE AD AND ENABLE THE ECONOMY TO REACH
POTENTIAL OUTPUT AND FULL EMPLOYMENT.

FIGURE 2

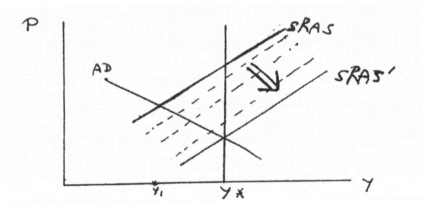

IF OUTPUT IS BELOW POTENTIAL, THE MONETARISTS
WOULD ADVOCATE A CONSTANT GROWTH RATE OF THE
MONEY SUPPLY, A STABLE SET OF FISCAL POLICIES
AND LETTING THE ECONOMY'S SELF-CORRECTING
MECHANISM WORK TO BRING THE ECONOMY TO FULL
EMPLOYMENT AND POTENTIAL OUTPUT.

NEW CLASSICAL MACROECONOMICS

As the term "new classical" suggests, new classical macroeconomists have views based on notions of the classical economists that wages and prices adjust rapidly and the economy is typically at full employment. They hold that people form their view of the future based on **rational expectations**. People having rational expectations means they take account of all available information in forming their view of what is likely to exist in the future. Also, they do not make systematic errors in predicting the future. It is not that they never make errors in their predictions. But if they do make errors, knowledge of the errors they made is used to correct their assessment of what is likely to be in the future.

To see the effects of economic policy when people have rational expectations, consider the following. Suppose the government increases aggregate demand, from AD to AD' in Figure 3. If people have rational expectations, and if this government action is anticipated (known in advance), workers will know the increase in AD will increase the price level and raise their cost of living and they will immediately demand higher wages. Firms will know they will get higher prices for their output and will pay the higher wages.

FIGURE 3

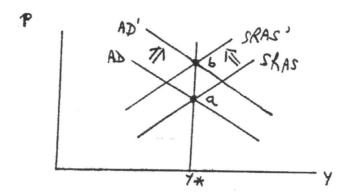

ACCORDING TO THE NEW CLASSICAL MACRO-
ECONOMISTS, AN ANTICIPATED INCREASE
IN AD DOES NOT INCREASE OUTPUT OR EMPLOYMENT.
THE ECONOMY MOVES INSTANTANEOUSLY FROM a to b.

According to the new classical economists, if people have rational expectations, the increase in AD immediately causes wages to increase and SRAS to decrease rapidly from SRAS to SRAS'. The economy moves quickly from the equilibrium labeled *a* to the one labeled *b* in Figure 3. For theoretical purposes, the economy is viewed as moving instantaneously from *a* to *b* by the new classical macroeconomists if the increase in AD is anticipated. By similar analysis, if a decrease in AD is anticipated, it causes the economy to move to a new equilibrium instantaneously—from *c* to *d* in Figure 4.

FIGURE 4

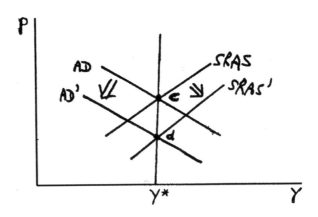

ACCORDING TO THE NEW CLASSICAL MACRO-
ECONOMISTS, AN ANTICIPATED DECREASE IN AD
DOES NOT DECREASE OUTPUT OR EMPLOYMENT.
THE ECONOMY MOVES INSTANTANEOUSLY FROM c to d.

Suppose now the increase in AD is unanticipated—the government implements a policy change without people being aware of it. AD increases from AD to AD' (Figure 5), and the economy moves from *f* to *g*. According to the new classical macroeconomists, because the increase in AD is unanticipated, it takes time, but a relatively short period of time, for workers and firms to learn of the policy change. The economy remains at *g* while people learn of what has occurred. As workers become aware of what has happened, they demand higher wages to help them cope with the higher cost of living due to the higher price level. Firms raise prices as they learn of what has happened and to cope with the higher wage demands, so each level of output is now offered for a higher price. SRAS decreases to SRAS' and the economy moves to *h*.

FIGURE 5

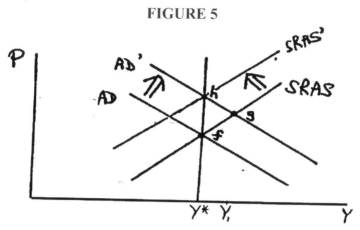

ACCORDING TO THE NEW CLASSICAL MACRO-
ECONOMISTS, AN UNANTICIPATED INCREASE
IN AD CAUSES OUTPUT TO RISE ABOVE
POTENTIAL TEMPORARILY.

According to the new classical macroeconomists, an unanticipated policy change causes a change in the level of output and employment for a brief period of time. In the case of the unanticipated increase in AD we just examined, output rises above potential to Y_1, and then falls back to Y*. Unemployment falls below the natural rate before increasing back again to the natural rate when output returns to Y*. By similar analysis, you can show that an unanticipated decrease in AD will cause output to temporarily fall below potential before rising back to potential level.

The Lucas supply curve
The <u>**Lucas supply curve**</u>[89] is a short-run aggregate supply curve that looks like the SRAS curve in Figure 5, but the explanation for its shifts is done in terms of the actual price level, P, and P^c, the price level expected by firms and laborers. The

---

[89] This curve was given this name because it is based on ideas developed by Robert Lucas. See Lucas, R. E., Jr. (1973). Some international evidence on output-inflation tradeoffs. *American Economic Review*, *63*(3), 326-334.

Lucas supply curve offers a deeper explanation of why an unanticipated change in policy can cause output and employment to move, for a short period of time, from the full employment level.

If AD increases and the price level P rises, and firms don't know this is a rise in the general price level but think that they are getting better prices for their products, they would be willing to produce more. For them the price level P is higher than the price level P^e they would expect to receive in these circumstances. If workers think that their wages are higher than they would expect, they would be willing to supply more labor. Firms wanting to produce more and workers willing to supply more labor makes possible a higher level of output. There is a movement along the SRAS curve such as from *f* to *g* in Figure 5.

This misperception of the price and wage levels by firms and workers occurs because employers and workers are more familiar with their particular firms and industries than with the whole economy. So as suppliers of products and of labor, they might misinterpret "general price movements for relative price changes" (Lucas, 1973, p. 333). They think they are getting better prices and wages when, in fact, prices and wages are up throughout the economy.

As workers realize that prices in general have gone up so that their cost of living is higher, offsetting any gains they thought they had from their increased nominal wages, they will want higher wages. As firms recognize that the price increase was not only for the products they sold but economy wide so that they don't have a price advantage, and with their workers wanting more wages, the firms would want a higher price level for any level of output they are offering for sale. The SRAS shifts to the left, as it does in Figure 5 to SRAS'. As P minus P^e goes to zero, the economy reaches a point like *h* in Figure 5, with output back to where it was before the gap between P and P^e started.

The policy ineffectiveness proposition
According to the new classical macroeconomists, government policies to manipulate aggregate demand just result in changes in the price level. If the policies are anticipated, output and employment very quickly get back to the long-run level, as we have explained. If the policies are unanticipated, output and employment may, only for a short period of time, differ from the long-run level. So

policy is ineffective in causing any enduring change in output and employment. This is referred to as the **policy ineffectiveness proposition**.

The Lucas critique

If Policy A caused certain outcomes when it was first introduced, you cannot hold that it will cause the same outcomes when used again. People's expectations of how that policy will work are likely to have been affected by their knowledge of how it worked the first time. These expectations will affect outcomes, just as we have seen in examples of the new classical model we have discussed so far.

In traditional macroeconomic forecasting, however, empirical relationships observed in the past between macroeconomic variables are used to make future projections as if those relationships would hold in the future. The **Lucas critique**[90] is that incorrect forecasts are likely to result from this. A relationship between macroeconomic variables that held in the past occurred when people had specific expectations. As people's expectations change, it is unlikely that the relationship would repeat itself. As a result of the Lucas critique, it has become more common for macroeconomic forecasters to take account of changes in expectations.

The nature of expectations

There is dispute, of course, over whether people have rational expectations. Also, because of the widespread use of contracts establishing wages and prices, wages and prices may not adjust as rapidly as the new classical macroeconomists suggest.

However, the question of how people form their expectations is a very important one to which there is no easy answer. Theorists who make specific assumptions about expectations formation help to give us scenarios of how the economy would perform if in fact those specific assumptions held. While the world may not behave exactly as these theorists suggest, these theories do deepen our understanding of the role of expectations and of what will happen under various scenarios.

---

[90] Lucas, R. E., Jr. (1976). Econometric policy evaluation: A critique. In *Carnegie Rochester Conference on Public Policy* (pp. 19-46). Amsterdam: North-Holland.

Among prominent contributors to the development of new classical macro-economics are Robert Lucas (Nobel Prize, 1995—mentioned in Chapter 1 and cited in this section), Robert Barro, Thomas Sargent (Nobel Prize, 2011), and Neil Wallace.

NEW KEYNESIANISM

In Chapter 11, we mentioned why Keynes felt wages and prices could be viewed as constant. The new Keynesians are Keynesians who seek more sophisticated explanations than those given by J.M. Keynes and his early followers for the **stickiness** (the constancy or slow adjustment over time) of wages and prices. They examine, in greater depth than Keynes and his early followers did, the behavior of firms and workers that could cause stickiness.

One of the new Keynesian explanations for the stickiness of prices is that **menu costs** (first mentioned in Chapter 8) inhibit firms from changing prices. When a firm adjusts its prices, it may have to print new catalogs, change billing systems, inform and reassure customers, change its advertisements, and so on. All of these are costly activities that may cause the firm to be hesitant to change prices.

New Keynesians also argue that wages may not be cut when unemployment is rising. Lowering wages could **decrease** a firm's profits by encouraging its workers to shirk or by reducing the capacity of workers to acquire the basic necessities of life, diminishing their ability to work energetically and productively. In fact, new Keynesians argue, firms may even pay wages above the market rate to encourage workers to be more efficient. Wages above the market rate paid by firms to maintain or increase efficiency are called **efficiency wages**.

The new Keynesians point out another reason why wages may change slowly—wages are frequently set in long-term labor contracts. These contracts are generally long-term because wage negotiations cost firms and workers money and time, and are often associated with the threat of a strike and tension at the work place. The stressful and time-consuming nature of such negotiations make normal people want to have them infrequently. This is achieved by making long-term contracts that do not have to be renegotiated until after a few years.

Even when there are no written contracts between workers and firms, there may be **implicit contracts**—verbal understandings between workers and firms on the wages and terms of employment. These understandings foster trust and a better work atmosphere. Making these implicit contracts can entail dialogue, negotiations, tension and frustration. It is inconvenient for workers and managers to be constantly changing them. This reluctance to change implicit contracts frequently also accounts for the stickiness of wages.

A key difference between the Keynesians and the new Keynesians is that the latter engage in extensive research to find what in worker and firm behavior can account for the stickiness of prices.

Like the new classical macroeconomists, new Keynesians focus on how the behavior of workers and firms affect macroeconomic policy. So in both of these schools of thought, they focus on the micro-foundations (the behavior of workers and firms) of macroeconomic behavior, but these two schools differ in their view of how these micro units behave. The rapid adjustment of prices and wages that occurs in the new classical macroeconomists' view of the world does not occur in the new Keynesian view. So the new Keynesians feel, just like the Keynesians, that government policy can be effective in changing output and employment.

New Keynesian theory sprouted in the 1970s. Among those who have contributed to its development are: George Akerlof (Nobel Prize, 2001), Olivier Blanchard, Stanley Fischer, Nobuhiro Kiyotaki, Gregory Mankiw, Edmund Phelps (Nobel Prize, 2006), David Romer, Joseph Stiglitz (Nobel Prize, 2001), John Taylor, Michael Woodford and Janet Yellen.

REAL BUSINESS CYCLE THEORY

To get an understanding of what is real business cycle (RBC) theory, we must remind ourselves of what the terms "business cycle" and "real" mean.

Business cycle

As was explained in Chapter 3, "business cycle" refers to the fluctuations in economic activity an economy experiences. Sometimes economic activity is declining, and this decline might be severe enough to become a recession. At other times economic activity is increasing, as when the economy is recovering from a recession, or experiencing substantial economic growth. In RBC theory, which we will learn shortly, the term "business cycle" is not at all meant to imply that there is any specific pattern to these fluctuations in economic activity. It just means that over the course of time the total output of an economy, and associated variables such as employment, fluctuate.

Real

As was explained in Chapter 10, a nominal variable is a price or is measured in a currency amount that has been unadjusted for inflation. A real variable, however, is one whose measure does not involve a price or currency value (e.g., unemployment—which is measured as a percent of the labor force), or is measured in terms of a price or currency value that has been adjusted for inflation (e.g., the real interest rate is the price of borrowing money after an adjustment for inflation has been made, and real GDP is the currency value of output after an adjustment for inflation has been made by holding prices constant).

Nominal shocks versus real shocks

In the AD-AS model, if the AS curve is vertical and AD alone changes, this causes the economy's price level to change but the output level remains the same, as at Y^* in Figure 6. The price level is a nominal variable, so this change in P alone is a nominal change. If AS changes, however, the price level, P, changes, but so does output, Y. Y here is a real variable, so the change in AS causes a real change (Figure 7).

FIGURE 6

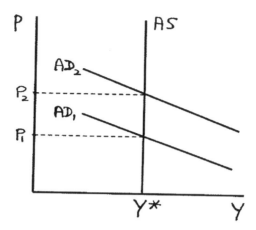

WITH THE AS CURVE VERTICAL, A CHANGE IN
AD (e.g., AN INCREASE IN AD FROM AD_1 TO AD_2)
CAUSES ONLY THE PRICE LEVEL TO CHANGE
(FROM P_1 TO P_2), WHILE OUTPUT REMAINS AT
Y*. THE CHANGE IN P IS A NOMINAL CHANGE.

FIGURE 7

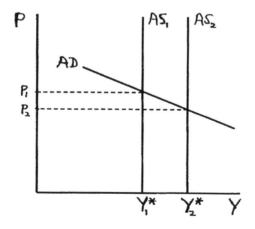

A CHANGE IN AS (FROM AS_1 TO AS_2) CAUSES
BOTH P AND Y TO CHANGE (FROM P_1 TO P_2;
FROM Y_1^* TO Y_2^*). THE CHANGE IN Y IS A
REAL CHANGE.

When the AS curve is vertical, a change in AD alone causes a change only in P, which is a nominal change, so some refer to a change in AD in these circumstances as a **nominal shock**. A change in AS, however, causes the real variable Y to change. A change in AS is a **real shock**. A nominal shock to the economy causes a change in only nominal variables (such as the prices of goods and services). A real shock causes a change in real variables (such as output and employment).

RBC theorists

Real business cycle theorists are so called because they focus on how real shocks cause fluctuations in output and employment and determine the economy's business cycle.

They hold that wages and prices are perfectly flexible, so the AS curve is vertical. They believe that people have rational expectations, and they are often described as a subset of the new classical macroeconomists (discussed in a section above). Perhaps the most famous of the real business cycle theorists are Finn Kydland and Edward Prescott, who both received the Nobel Prize in Economics in 2004. Robert King and Charles Plosser are among those who have made important contributions.

In RBC theory, because wages and prices are perfectly flexible and the AS curve is vertical, changes in AD alone cannot change the level of output of an economy. It is changes in AS that cause changes in output and employment. Factors that cause AS to shift are responsible for the business cycle. Examples of factors that shift AS are:

- Technology that changes productivity—the amount of output that can be obtained with a unit of input
- Resource availability (e.g., changes in the supply of a widely used input such as oil)
- Government regulations
- Climate conditions (droughts, floods, etc.)

RBC theorists have focused heavily on how technology changes produce real shocks by changing productivity and causing the AS curve to shift. They believe these supply shocks are typically random and cannot be predicted. Policy makers' attempts to forecast GDP and develop policies to try to reach targets for economic growth are therefore likely to be futile.

As an illustration of how RBC theorists view the world, consider the following. The price of oil shoots up causing a decrease in AS—a leftward shift of the AS curve. The resulting decrease in business activity causes businesses to borrow less from banks. This reduction in bank lending decreases the money supply (as we learned earlier in this book when we discussed how the behavior of banks, the public and the Central Bank affect the money supply). The chain of causation in this example starts from a real shock causing AS to decrease. This then causes a decrease in business activity that leads to a reduction in the money supply. This is in contrast to Keynesians and monetarists who believe the money supply affects AD, which then leads to changes in output and employment.

Also, because RBC theorists view the AS curve as vertical, if the government sees output and employment falling and engages in activist policies that increase AD, the increase in AD will have no effect on output and employment. This is quite different from the Keynesian and monetarist views of the world in which government policy, through its effect on AD, is seen as a major cause of changes in output and employment in the economy.

RBC theorists hold that government policy can only affect output and employment if it affects AS. In analyzing a change in government purchases, RBC theorists try to determine how these purchases might affect AS. For example, if the government spending increases demand for goods and services and leads to a rise in wages that motivates workers to work more hours, this increased amount of labor can shift the AS curve. Through this increase in AS, the government purchases can affect output and employment. Keynesians and monetarists, however, focus on how changes in government purchases affect AD, not AS.

RBC theorists also have a unique view of unemployment. Let's say a supply shock occurs (such as the price of oil shooting up) that makes it prohibitively expensive to operate some plant and equipment and this decreases productivity. With less being produced per hour, firms will offer lower wages. RBC theorists claim that anyone willing to work for these lower wages would have a job, so any unemployment would be voluntary—people simply choosing not to work at the available wage level. Not surprisingly, this RBC view of unemployment as being voluntary does not sit well with those who believe that unemployment has to be combated by government policy.

SUPPLY-SIDE ECONOMICS

Supply-side economics focuses on factors that shift the economy's short and long-run AS curves. As we know from the AD-AS model, increasing aggregate supply increases output and employment in an economy. Economists who emphasize policies for increasing aggregate supply are called supply-side economists. They have argued for tax cuts and the removal of burdensome government regulations as mechanisms for increasing aggregate supply, while advocating a disciplined monetary policy to keep inflation under control.

An early example of the contrast between supply-side policy proposals and those based on manipulating aggregate demand occurred in the 1970s. The Ford administration in the United States was insisting a tax increase was necessary to fight inflation as it would decrease aggregate demand. However, Robert Mundell (Nobel Prize, 1999), considered the guru of supply-side economists, advocated a tax cut and a tight monetary policy.[91] He argued the tax cut would increase aggregate supply, output, employment and income. The increase in income would get the US government more revenues from taxes and so reduce the government budget deficit, and the tight monetary policy would curb inflation.[92]

---

[91] Mundell, R. A. (1999). *Nobel Lecture—A reconsideration of the twentieth century*. Retrieved from http://robertmundell.net/nobel-prize/

[92] The Ford administration did not adopt the policies Mundell recommended. Supply-side economics became very prominent during the Reagan administration in the US when tax cuts were enacted with the aim of stimulating aggregate supply. As you can readily check on the Internet, there has been great controversy over whether or not these policies had their intended effects.

Government regulations

Opressive government regulations reduce aggregate supply by raising the costs of doing business. Government regulations are essential to the maintenance of law and order, to ensure the safety and fair treatment of workers, to limit the harm human activity does to the environment, etc. However, if these regulations become excessive so that businesses spend an inordinate amount of time and resources to meet them, this raises the costs of doing business to an extent that exceeds the benefits to society of the regulations.

The news media often discuss inefficiencies in economies around the world. In Greece, for example, it is estimated that about 7 % of GDP is spent on government bureaucracy, about double the average for the European Union.[93] The numerous regulations that have to be met, the variety of government offices from which permissions have to be sought even for simple business activities, and the enormous amount of time and other resources it takes to set up a business are a huge deterrent to business investment. Meanwhile, the Greek economy is mired in substandard performance.

Cutting back on oppressive regulations reduces business costs and increases aggregate supply. Everyone who is concerned about society becoming more efficient should thoughtfully consider what reduction in excessive regulations could be beneficial, lowering the costs of doing business and so increasing aggregate supply. In this sense, we should all be supply-side economists.

Much of the focus on supply-side economics, however, has been on controversies over tax policies. To follow the arguments, it is necessary to define a few concepts.

---

[93] Papastolou, A. (2012, Dec. 3). Greek red-tape costs 14 billion euros. *GreekReporter.com.* Retrieved from http://greece.greekreporter.com/2012/12/03/greek-red-tape-costs-14-billion-euros/

Marginal tax rates; Average tax rates

The marginal tax rate is the percent of tax that has to be paid on the last dollar of income. Let's say you have to pay taxes at the following rates:

20 % on taxable income less than or equal to $30,000
35 % on taxable income above $30,000

If you earned $30,000 or less, your marginal tax rate would be 20 %; if you earned above $30,000 your marginal tax rate would be 35 %.

The average tax rate is the total tax paid divided by taxable income. If you earned $40,000, your taxes would be 20 % of $30,000 plus 35 % of $10,000 = $9,500, and your average tax rate would be $9,500/$40,000 = 23.75 %

A tax bracket is a range of income and the tax rate that applies to it. In the example above there are two tax brackets: Income of $0 up to and including $30,000 which is taxed at 20 %, and income above $30,000 which is taxed at 35 %. It is usual to refer to tax brackets in terms of the tax rate for the bracket, so the two brackets just mentioned would be the 20 % and 35 % brackets.

Marginal tax rates and aggregate supply

Supply-side economists emphasize that marginal tax rates, not average rates, are what affects decisions on whether to work, save or invest more. Suppose your taxable income is $80,000 and the marginal tax rate for taxable income above $80,000 is 75 %. Let's say you got the opportunity to do an extra job over the course of a year and to earn annual taxable income of $40,000 for it. If you took this job, you would now have to pay 75 % of your additional income in taxes. Over a year, you would only be able to add $10,000 after taxes to the income you currently get. You would probably decide that it is not worth it to work more. So the high marginal tax rate could cause less of your labor to be available to the economy than if you faced lower tax rates. If this type of behavior occurs on a significant scale, aggregate supply for the economy is diminished, as less labor will be available compared to if the tax rates were lower. As we know from the AD-AS model, this causes lower output and a higher price level in the economy.

Higher marginal tax rates are likely to cause people to decline overtime work, move to locations where taxes are lower, or retire early. By reducing the gains to be had, high marginal tax rates discourage business investment and entrepreneurial activity. This diminishes not just business demand for goods and services but also the development of the economy's productive capabilities and its aggregate supply. High tax rates increase attempts at tax avoidance through, for example, increasing the incentive to hide income and to take tax deductions.

The higher the tax rate, the lower the cost to the business of expenditures it can deduct. If the tax rate is 55 %, and a business can take a tax deduction for an item costing $100, the business, in effect, only incurs a $45 cost ($100 minus the 55 % deduction) for that item. If the tax rate were 70 %, the business would only be incurring a cost of $30 for the $100 tax-deductible item. High tax rates encourage spending on deductible expenses like fancy offices, expensive travel, business entertainment, conferences at resorts, etc. These expenditures and the activities associated with them may have nothing to do with enhancing productivity and detract from the efficient use of resources. The inefficient use of resources decreases aggregate supply.

Government revenue and the tax rate
Suppose all income was taxed at a rate of zero percent. Then government revenue from taxation would be zero. If all income was taxed at a rate of 100 %, government tax revenue would also be zero. People would not work if a 100 % of what they earned had to be paid in taxes, so the tax base (the pool of income available to be taxed) would be zero and the government would get no tax revenue. Figure 8 shows how a government's tax revenue is related to the tax rate. The tax rate on the horizontal axis means all income is taxed at that rate. (In real life, of course, not all income is taxed at the same rate. For example, the first $30,000 of a person's income might be taxed at 15 %, the next $40,000 might be taxed at 20 %, etc.)

This figure is called the **Laffer curve**, after Arthur Laffer, the supply-side economist who popularized it. The point A corresponds to the maximum revenue R_m the government can obtain from taxation and to a tax rate of X %. If the tax rate is increased above X %, government revenue falls below the maximum level R_m, and goes to zero as the tax rate rises to 100 %. The Laffer curve depicts two key lessons:

FIGURE 8

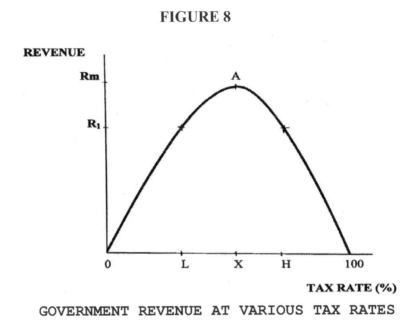

GOVERNMENT REVENUE AT VARIOUS TAX RATES

- If an economy has a tax rate above X %, the government can increase its revenue by decreasing the tax rate to X %. A higher tax rate will only mean higher revenue for the government if the tax rate is less than X %.

- Any level of government revenue less than R_m can be obtained by either of two tax rates. For example, the level of revenue R_1, can be obtained from the lower tax rate L or the higher rate H. To get a certain level of revenue, a government should consider not burdening the economy with a higher tax rate if a lower tax rate can give that same level of revenue.

Real economies are very complex and systems of taxation are not at all as simple as depicted in the Laffer curve, in which a single rate applies to all income. In reality, no one knows what is the shape of this Laffer curve for an economy. No one knows for sure what is the tax rate above which tax revenue declines.

Nevertheless, the awareness of the negative effects of high tax rates should cause policymakers to carefully consider the likely consequences for the economy of tax hikes, and especially what will be done with the additional revenue the government expects from the tax hikes. If this additional revenue will be spent to increase the productive capabilities of the economy, then this might create positive effects for the economy that outweigh any negative effects of the tax hikes. (Of course, it is possible that a government might plan a tax hike in the hope of getting additional revenue but end up with less revenue. This could happen if the tax hike causes tax evasion and other behaviors that lead to a reduced tax base. In terms of the Laffer curve, this would be like the tax hike taking the tax rate to above X %.)

Assessing the effects of tax rate changes

One of the great challenges in the real world is assessing the consequences of tax changes.[94] Let's say a tax cut occurs and the economy strengthens sharply. Suppose, at the same time as the tax cuts, the central bank is lowering interest rates, and there is new political leadership perceived as more competent than the previous one. Then it would be difficult to determine how much of the economy's success is due to the tax cuts. Could the economic boom have been mainly the result of the lower interest rates and/or the increase in business and consumer confidence due to the better political leadership?

Don't be surprised if, in a situation like this, controversy ensues over what were the effects of the tax cut. Research from those who favored the tax cut might show that it was a major cause of the boom. Research from those skeptical about the tax cut might show that it did not have much effect, or that it even harmed the economy. With many variables in an economy changing at the same time, researchers often find justification for the causal links their ideological views incline them to look for.

---

[94] Robert Lucas, mentioned earlier in this chapter for his contributions to the development of new classical macroeconomics, has argued that supply-side tax cuts can have very strong positive effects on an economy. He noted that this was a change from the belief in higher tax rates that he held earlier in his career. See: Lucas, R. E., Jr. (1990). Supply-side economics: An analytical review. *Oxford Economic Papers*, *42*(2), 293-316.

CONCLUSION

Each of the schools of thought focuses on a particular way of looking at the economy. When using a school of thought in our analyses, we have to keep in mind the assumptions underlying it. For example, let's say we want to analyze a real world situation using a model in which there is rapid adjustment to long-run equilibrium (e.g., a new classical model). We have to consider if there is rapid adjustment in the situation we are looking at. If there isn't, we have to ponder how actual behavior will diverge from what the model predicts.

The real world is likely to differ from any theoretical model. So we must be sensitive to what makes a particular theoretical perspective more/less relevant for analyzing a real world situation. With this awareness, we will be able to use each school of thought, not as a blind adherent, but perceptively.

EXERCISE

1. What are the differences/similarities between monetarists and new classical economists on the short-run and long-run effects of monetary policy?

2. What do you think of using a macroeconomic model based on empirical relationships between variables that were observed in the past?

3. A nominal variable is the
    a. Level of employment in an economy
    b. Goods and services consumed
    c. Economy's output measured in the price of a base year
    d. Price level

4. A real variable is
    a. The inflation rate
    b. The price level
    c. The money wages a person earns
    d. The interest rate adjusted for inflation

5. In RBC theory, which one of the following is correct?
   a. A real shock causes only a change in the price level
   b. Business cycles have regular patterns to them
   c. The fluctuations in output and employment do not follow any set pattern
   d. A nominal shock can cause a change in the economy's output

6. All of the following are held by RBC theory except:
   a. Wages are flexible
   b. All unemployment is voluntary
   c. Prices are fixed
   d. Monetary policy can change only the price level

7. How do supply-side economists differ from Keynesians in their assessment of government tax policy?

8. If a government lowers (raises) tax rates and there is an increase (decrease) in revenue the government collects, does this prove the Laffer curve effect occurred?

9. The use of activist fiscal and monetary policies is likely to be supported by which of the following?
   a. Supply-side economists
   b. RBC theorists
   c. Keynesians
   d. Monetarists
   e. New classical economists
   f. New Keynesians

ANSWERS

1.

	Monetarists	New classical macroeconomists
Short run	There are strong effects on output and the price level in the short run. The quantity theory of money states MV = PQ. Monetarists assume V is stable, so changes in M cause changes in P and Q.	If unanticipated, monetary policy causes output to change from the long-run level. But firms and workers relatively quickly adjust their expectations, and the economy soon reverts back to the long-run—full employment with only the price level changed. (If policy is anticipated, there is no short-run effect. The economy remains at the long-run, with just the price level instantaneously changed—see explanation of long-run effects in the next row of this table.)
Long run	Q is fixed at potential output, the full employment level of the economy, so M affects only P.	If the economy is at the long run and unanticipated policy occurs, it quickly reverts back to the long run, as explained in the row above. If monetary policy is anticipated, the economy immediately adjusts to a new price level at the full employment level of the economy. So with anticipated policy, the economy is always at the long-run level of output. The effect is the same as in the monetarist model in the long run: changes in M affect only P.

2. As the Lucas critique reminds us, models of the macroeconomy in which the causal links between variables are based on past empirical relationships are likely to be inappropriate for predicting what will happen in the future. Those past relationships held when people had specific expectations. Since people are

likely to have different expectations in the future, the empirical relationships observed in the past would be inappropriate for making predictions of the future.

3. d

4. d

5. c

6. c

7. Supply-side economists focus on the impact of tax policy on aggregate supply. Lower (higher) taxes could increase (decrease) aggregate supply and employment and lower (increase) the price level. Keynesians emphasize how tax policy affects aggregate demand, with lower (higher) taxes likely to increase (decrease) aggregate demand and therefore output, employment and the price level.

8. You would have to check what else was happening in the economy at the time of the lower (higher) taxes. For example, suppose economic growth picked up as new foreign markets were found for the economy's goods and services. Higher economic growth increases income, which could mean higher government tax collection. But if this higher economic growth was independent of tax cuts, then it would mean that the higher revenue collected by the government was not caused by the lower tax rates. Similarly, if the government raised taxes and this was followed by a decrease in government revenue collection, you would have to check whether any factor(s), other than the higher tax rates, caused the decrease in government revenue collection.

9. c, f

CHAPTER 13
GOVERNMENT SPENDING, BUDGET DEFICITS
AND GOVERNMENT DEBT

This chapter provides concepts essential for thoughtfully answering questions like: How much government borrowing is "too much"? Should a government always balance its budget—spend no more than the revenue it collects? Does government spending cause a reduction in investment by the private sector? These questions are at the heart of some of the most popular debates of our time. In the United States, Europe, and around the world they are a constant challenge to policy makers.

Among the concepts discussed are: primary deficit, structural and cyclical deficits, automatic stabilizers, crowding out, Ricardian equivalence, rolling over debt and monetizing debt.

GOVERNMENT SPENDING, REVENUE AND BUDGET DEFICITS

Government spending consists mainly of 3 categories:

1. Government spending on: the services of government employees, supplies for government offices, materials for highways and other infrastructure,[95] military equipment, etc.
2. Transfer payments—payments for which no services are given in exchange, like old age pensions, unemployment insurance, and welfare payments (financial assistance given to those in poverty).
3. Interest payments—the interest the government pays on its debt minus the interest it receives from loans it has made, e.g., student loans.

---

[95] **Infrastructure** is the physical and technical structures that facilitate living in a society—roads and highways, bridges, sewers, and water, electricity and telecommunications systems….

Government revenue is obtained from various taxes, such as personal income taxes, taxes paid by corporations, sales taxes, and contributions workers make to social insurance programs like Social Security in the US.

Deficit spending and debt

As we learned in Chapter 3, a government runs a budget deficit when its expenditures exceed its revenue. If expenditures exceed revenue, and the government does not have funds from previous budget surpluses to finance its expenditures, it has to borrow. When a government runs a budget deficit and borrows to fund its spending, this is called **deficit spending**. When a government engages in deficit spending, it borrows by issuing government bills, notes and bonds.[96] The issuing of these as a means of borrowing was described in Chapter 6.

A government's **debt** is its accumulated budget deficits minus its budget surpluses. In the US and many other countries, escalating budget deficits, and the resultant sharp increases in government borrowing and debt, have led to widespread concern with reducing budget deficits by curbing government expenditures and/or raising tax rates to increase revenue.

Primary deficit

If spending on categories 1 and 2 of the three kinds of government spending listed earlier exceed a government's revenues, the government runs a **primary deficit**. When a government runs a primary deficit, its revenues are not enough to fund its expenses for goods, services and transfer payments.

Suppose a government wants to default on its debt because it feels it cannot afford to meet the interest and/or principal payments, or as a tactic to get its creditors to make concessions and reduce the payments the government has to make. If the government is running a primary deficit, and it defaults and gets cut off from sources of borrowing, it will be unable to meet its daily expenses for goods,

---

[96] Accounting details that do not affect understanding of the key ideas presented here are omitted. They would encumber the presentation without adding insight. If you need all the minutiae on a country's deficits and debt, you can go to relevant sources, such as the Congressional Budget Office and the Office of Management and Budget, for information on the US deficit and debt.

services and transfer payments. This means that while the government would not have to make the payments due on its debt, it may create a lot of discontent in its country by being unable to fund daily operations of the government and the essential services the population needs. This consideration should be kept in mind whenever there is talk that a heavily indebted country should just default rather than strain excessively to make payments on its debt.

STRUCTURAL AND CYCLICAL BUDGET DEFICITS

For a given set of government spending and tax policies (fiscal policies), the budget deficit that would exist if the economy were at the full employment level of output and income is called the **structural deficit**.

The actual budget deficit consists of two parts: the structural deficit, which was just defined, and the **cyclical deficit**. The cyclical deficit is the part of the total budget deficit that depends on where the economy is in the business cycle. When an economy is booming, incomes rise and so do the taxes collected on those incomes. This increase in tax revenues decreases a cyclical budget deficit. With a given set of fiscal policies, the structural deficit is unchanged, so the cyclical deficit coming down due to the booming economy, brings down the overall budget deficit. Government payments for unemployment and welfare benefits are also likely to fall as an economy booms, and this too helps to reduce the cyclical deficit.

If the economy moves into recession, declining incomes decrease tax revenues, and government payments for unemployment and welfare benefits are likely to rise. This increases a cyclical budget deficit, and increases the overall budget deficit.

With the same set of fiscal policies, a government's budget deficit decreases/ increases if the economy is booming/contracting. It is the upturns/downturns in the economy that cause the cyclical deficit to decrease/increase, causing the actual budget deficit to decrease/increase.

Because a government's total budget deficit equals the structural deficit and the cyclical deficit, we cannot just look at the size of a government's budget deficit and reach a conclusion about how loose/tight are fiscal policies. The deficit might be large simply because the economy is weak and there is a higher cyclical budget deficit, due to decreased incomes leading to lower tax receipts and increased payments for government unemployment and welfare benefits.

To make an assessment about the looseness/tightness of fiscal policy, we have to look at the size of the structural deficit because this deficit is measured with the economy at full employment. It changes only if the government's spending and/or tax policies change.[97] Because the structural budget deficit is the deficit that would exist at full employment, it is sometimes referred to as the **full employment budget deficit.** The total budget deficit minus the cyclical budget deficit gives the structural budget deficit, so the structural deficit is also referred to as the **cyclically-adjusted budget deficit**.

As was explained in Chapter 8, there is no way of knowing precisely what is the level of output, income and employment that corresponds to full employment. So estimating what tax revenues and government expenditures would be if the economy were at full employment depends on the assumptions used in making this estimate. Consequently, the structural budget deficit is not something that is empirically observable. Analysts may differ on its level depending on the assumptions they make about what is the level of full employment output and income, and how much government spending and revenue will change if the economy were to move to full employment.

Automatic stabilizers
An **automatic stabilizer** is a policy or program that boosts aggregate demand when the economy is weakening and restrains aggregate demand when the economy is strengthening. For example, unemployment and welfare benefits paid by a government increase in a recession and fall when the economy is booming.

---

[97] It can also change if the economy's full employment level of output/income/ employment changes. As explained in Chapter 8, in the discussion of the natural rate of unemployment, what is full employment depends on factors such as frictional and structural unemployment. In the short run, however, full employment is considered fixed.

They boost aggregate demand as a recession occurs and restrain aggregate demand as the economy booms. They are automatic stabilizers.

In a country in which the percent of income that has to be paid in taxes increases with income, income tax is an automatic stabilizer. As a recession occurs, incomes fall and a smaller portion of income has to be paid in taxes. This reduction in tax payments mitigates the fall in aggregate demand. As the economy booms, the higher percent of income that has to be paid in taxes restrains aggregate demand.

Automatic stabilizers constitute **countercyclical** fiscal policy—spending and tax policies that help to counter the business cycle, dampening its effect on the economy.

Their effect on the cyclical deficit is to cause it to rise as the economy contracts and fall as the economy strengthens. For example, as the economy contracts, the government has to pay out more in unemployment and welfare benefits, and receives less taxes, causing a rise in the cyclical deficit.

EXERCISE 1

1. When a government borrows to spend more than it gets in revenue, it is
   a. Engaging in deficit spending
   b. Running a primary deficit
   c. Running a structural budget deficit
   d. Ensuring that the cyclically-adjusted budget deficit is zero

2. The cyclical budget deficit is
   a. Always larger than the structural budget deficit
   b. The part of the budget deficit that is due to the fluctuations in the business cycle
   c. Always smaller than the structural budget deficit
   d. Enlarged as the economy booms

3. If a government is running a primary surplus, this makes it easier to default on its debt than if it is running a primary deficit. True or false? Explain.

4. An automatic stabilizer
    a. Increases aggregate demand as the economy strengthens
    b. Causes the cyclical deficit to fall as the economy contracts
    c. Boosts aggregate demand as the economy weakens, and it is pro-cyclical fiscal policy that exacerbates fluctuation in a business cycle
    d. Is countercyclical fiscal policy and, as the economy strengthens, it restrains aggregate demand and causes the cyclical deficit to fall

SHOULD A GOVERNMENT HAVE A BALANCED BUDGET?

Governments tend to think short term, typically in terms of what is necessary to win the next election, and this often impels them to spend to satisfy supporters and win votes rather than to do what is in the best long term interest of a country. A government driven by this impulse will be motivated to spend and would have difficulty avoiding escalating budget deficits and debt. It is often argued that the only way to impose budgetary discipline on governments is to make it a legal requirement for them to have a **balanced budget,** which means government spending must equal revenue. However, having a balanced budget is full of challenges.

The taxes a government collects typically depend on the level of income in the economy. When an economy weakens, output and income decline, and the government gets less tax revenue. So the government would have to cut spending to keep the budget balanced. As we learned from the AD-AS model, reducing government spending will decrease output, employment and income, worsening the economic weakness.

If an economy is booming, government tax revenue increases as people and corporations have more income to be taxed. To keep its budget balanced, a government would have to increase spending or reduce taxes to offset the increased tax revenue. This would further increase aggregate demand, intensifying the economic boom. If the economic boom is pushing inflation too high, the increased government spending or tax cuts would push up the price level even more, exacerbating the inflation problem.

Pro-cyclical

In the discussion of automatic stabilizers, it was mentioned that these stabilizers constitute countercyclical fiscal policy. However, the requirement of having a balanced overall budget—that is, both the cyclical and structural deficits must be zero—makes fiscal policy pro-cyclical. In a recession, the government has to cut spending and/or raise taxes, worsening the recession. In a boom, the government has to increase spending or cut taxes, intensifying the boom.

Creating uncertainty

To keep its budget balanced, a government would have to engage in frequent changes of fiscal policy, cutting spending and/or raising taxes as the economy weakens and increasing spending and/or cutting taxes as the economy strengthens. These frequent changes in policy create instability—for example, businesses would be uncertain about the level of taxes they may have to pay and this uncertainty could cause them to be reluctant to expand their operations. The prospect of higher taxes as the economy weakens would discourage business investment.

Gimmicks

A government can also resort to gimmicks to meet its balanced budget requirement. Shifting payments from one fiscal year to another, changing the date by which taxes have to be paid, or selling assets to boost revenue are among maneuvers that can be used to balance a budget without really engaging in the **fiscal discipline** which the balanced budget requirement is intended to enforce. (Government spending and tax policy is called fiscal policy, so the term fiscal discipline refers to a government managing its finances well.)

Emergencies that require an unbalanced budget

If a nation faces a war, this would necessitate a sharp rise in spending to fund the war. A balanced budget requirement would hinder the government's ability to spend enough for such a cause. If the US had to have a balanced budget during World War II, this would have made it impossible for the country to fight tyranny.

A catastrophe such as a devastating earthquake is another example of an emergency that would be best dealt with by a government that is not restrained by a balanced budget.

Making exceptions

Of course, a law that a government budget be balanced can overcome some of the problems cited here by allowing the budget to be unbalanced in times of recession, war, catastrophes, etc.

Balancing only the structural deficit

Earlier in this chapter, we discussed what the structural budget deficit is. If a government has to balance just the structural budget deficit, it has to have a set of fiscal policies that would ensure a zero budget deficit if the economy were at full employment. The cyclical budget deficit would expand when the economy weakens and contract as the economy strengthens. The government would not have to take action to keep the cyclical deficit at zero. This would eliminate:

- The problem of fiscal policy being pro-cyclical, described under the heading **Pro-cyclical** on the previous page.

- The uncertainties resulting from frequent changes in fiscal policy required to balance the overall budget, described under the heading **Creating uncertainty** on the previous page.

But having to ensure the structural deficit is zero might necessitate a set of fiscal policies that could limit a government's flexibility to be able to spend enough to jump start an economy that is in severe recession and in times of war, catastrophe, etc.

Also, as was noted when we discussed structural deficits earlier in this chapter, determining the size of the structural deficit involves making a lot of assumptions about what is the full employment level of output and income, what tax revenues and government expenditures would be if the economy were at full employment, etc. There is no way of making these estimates precisely and opinions can vary a lot on what they should be.

THE IMPACT OF FISCAL POLICY

Crowding out

If government, businesses and individuals all need to borrow funds, they will compete with each other to get these funds. If there is a limited amount of funds, increased borrowing by a government leaves less funds available for businesses and individuals. Not only would less funds be available for the private sector to borrow, but the government demand for funds would push up the price (the interest rate) at which these funds are lent. Lenders seeing a great demand for the funds they have to lend will ask for a higher interest rate. In this situation, government borrowing to fund its expenditures makes it more expensive for the private sector to borrow to make investments, leading to less investment by the private sector. So increased government spending causes decreased investment. The possibility that government spending funded by borrowing could cause decreased investment is referred to as **crowding out**—the increased government borrowing crowds out business investment.

When crowding out is unlikely

Of course, if there is an enormous amount of funds available, then a government's borrowing will not prevent the private sector from borrowing as much as it wants and will have no significant effect on the interest rate at which the private sector can get loans. Crowding out is unlikely to occur in this scenario. Over the last few decades, the US government has engaged in massive borrowing to fund its spending. Huge amounts of funds available from countries like China and Japan has made this possible without any significant crowding out occurring.

Increasing business optimism and expansion

It is also possible that government spending could boost confidence in an economy's prospects, increasing business optimism. The government spending could create jobs and increase demand for goods and services, making possible a better business climate. For any given level of interest rate, businesses would be willing to invest more because of their greater optimism about the economy. So even if there is some crowding out due to government borrowing pushing up the interest rate at which funds could be borrowed, this crowding out could be more than offset by the boost in business optimism caused by the government spending. As economies around the world fell into deep recession in recent years, government spending packages, called **stimulus packages**, were devised to help revive the economies. These will succeed more to the extent that they boost business confidence.

There are often infrastructure projects that are too large for the private sector to take on, but which can boost a country's economy and the profitability and business expansion of the private sector. For example, let's say there are no good transportation links such as highways between where goods are produced and where they have to be marketed. If a government builds these links, this encourages business activity producing goods and transporting them to the areas where they can be marketed. A variety of businesses could then develop along the transportation routes (gas stations, restaurants, rest stops, motels…) and in the areas where the increased production and marketing occur (accommodations for workers, entertainment facilities…). The government, through appropriate infrastructure projects, can boost private sector expansion.

Ricardian Equivalence

The notion that consumers determine their spending based not just on their current income but also on the average stream of income they expect in the years ahead is called the **permanent income hypothesis**.[98] If people behave like this, and their disposable income increases now but is expected to go down in the future by an equivalent amount, it is likely that they will not change their consumption. The extra disposable income they get now will be saved to be spent in the future when disposable income decreases.

If people behaved as the permanent income hypothesis suggests and the government enacted a tax cut but maintained its level of spending by borrowing,

---

[98] Milton Friedman proposed this hypothesis. See Friedman, M. (1957). *A Theory of the Consumption Function*. New Jersey: Princeton University Press. A similar view of consumption called the life-cycle theory was developed by Franco Modigliani, Albert Ando and Richard Brumberg. See Modigliani, F. & Ando, A. (1963, March). The 'life-cycle' hypothesis of saving: aggregate implications and tests. *American Economic Review*, 53, 55-84. See Modigliani, F. & Brumberg, R. (1954). Utility analysis and the consumption function: An interpretation of cross-section data. In K. Kurihara (Ed.), *Post-Keynesian Economics* (pp. 383-436). New Brunswick, New Jersey: Rutgers University Press.

people will save the extra income they get from the tax cut. They will do so because they know that in the future the government will raise their taxes to repay what it borrowed. The tax cut does not change the level of permanent income and leaves consumption unchanged. Financing government spending by incurring debt now is equivalent to financing it by taxes that have to be raised later to repay the government debt.

This is called **Ricardian equivalence**, and is also referred to as the Ricardian equivalence hypothesis, proposition, theorem, theory, etc. This theoretical possibility was first considered by British political economist David Ricardo (1772-1823), who was one of the great classical economists, and this is why it has been named after him. It should be noted that Ricardo did not believe this theoretical possibility was likely to hold in the real world—so he did not believe in what came to be called Ricardian equivalence! He felt it would not hold because people were unlikely to think of tax obligations they might have in the distant future.[99]

Why Ricardian equivalence is not likely to hold

If the government enacted a tax cut so that we all now have more disposable income, how many of us would save that extra income because we anticipated we would have to pay higher taxes in the future? We may just not be farsighted and rational enough to take account of taxes that may be imposed on us in the future. Also, if the next generation will have to pay the taxes, we might not even care—it will be their problem, not ours. To the extent that the average person does not save to pay higher taxes that may be imposed in the future, Ricardian equivalence will not hold—when the government cuts taxes, it could lead to higher spending by consumers and so increase aggregate demand, output and employment.

Another reason Ricardian equivalence would not hold is that many people are not able to base their consumption on permanent income. If you estimate your consumption based on your permanent income should be $100,000 per year, but you are in the early stages of your career now and only earning $40,000, you may not have sources willing to lend you $60,000 to get your consumption up to the

---

[99] McCulloch, J. R. (Ed.) (1888). T*he Works of David Ricardo. With a Notice of the Life and Writings of the Author*. London: John Murray. p. 539.

$100,000 level. This inability to borrow leaves you with a **liquidity constraint**: your lack of funds constrains you to consuming at less than the level your permanent income would allow. Your income is not enough to give you the life-style you desire, so when you get extra income from a tax cut, you are likely to spend it, not save it as Ricardian equivalence suggests.

EXERCISE 2

1. If a government always balanced its budget, during a recession it would
   a. Decrease both its spending and taxes
   b. Increase both spending and taxes
   c. Keep spending and taxes unchanged
   d. Reduce spending and/or raise taxes

2. If Ricardian equivalence held and a government enacted a $50 billion tax cut but maintained its level of spending by borrowing $50 billion to finance the tax cut, what effect would the tax cut have on the economy's output and price levels and on private saving?

   Suppose data shows private saving did not increase even as a government cut taxes and borrowed to keep up its spending. Does this data support the Ricardian equivalence theory?

3. Ricardian equivalence is not likely to hold if people
   a. Face no liquidity constraints
   b. Determine their current spending by taking into account the future tax obligations they and their descendants are likely to face
   c. Do not worry about what tax obligations they may face in the future as a result of current government policy
   d. Consume based on their permanent income

THE PUBLIC DEBT

The government debt is the total accumulation of government budget deficits minus surpluses. As we have noted, when a government engages in deficit spending, it funds the spending by issuing bills, notes and bonds. Its total debt is the amount of these securities in existence.[100]

In the US, workers and their employers are required to pay Social Security and Medicare contributions to the federal government from which workers can be paid pensions and health benefits when they retire or if they become disabled. The funds in these government-run insurance programs are invested in US government securities.

If we subtract from the total US government debt the amount held by government entities (called **intragovernmental holdings**) such as the Social Security and Medicare funds, we are left with the **public debt**—the government debt held by individuals, commercial banks, insurance companies, state and local governments, the Federal Reserve, mutual funds, private pension funds, and foreigners. At the end of calendar year 2012, the debt of the US was about $16.43 trillion. Of this, $4.85 trillion was intragovernmental holdings. So the public debt was $(16.43 minus 4.85) trillion = $11.58 trillion.[101] Of this, about $5.31 trillion was held by foreigners.[102]

Historically, the US budget deficit and debt have climbed during wars and recessions and decreased after these events. These peaked in World War II, but in

---

[100] Keep in mind what was stated in an earlier footnote in this chapter. Accounting details that do not affect understanding of the key ideas presented here are omitted. They would encumber the presentation without adding insight. If you need all the minutiae, you can go to sources such as the Congressional Budget Office and the Office of Management and Budget for information on the US deficit and debt.

[101] Data from treasurydirect.gov.

[102] Data from Treasury Bulletin, Dec. 2012. The latest estimate available there was for June 2012

recent years have gone to levels last seen in the aftermath of World War II as the financial crisis and recession that started in 2007 decreased government revenues and forced increased government spending. These high levels of deficit and debt have sparked concern that the interest payment on the debt could eventually become so high and use up so much of government revenue that too little would be left for necessary government programs. There is also the fear that if the debt continues to escalate, lenders might become worried about the government's capacity to repay and be reluctant to make funds available to the government.

US GOVERNMENT ANNUAL PUBLIC DEBT (UPPER LINE) AND BUDGET DEFICIT (LOWER LINE) AS PERCENT OF GDP

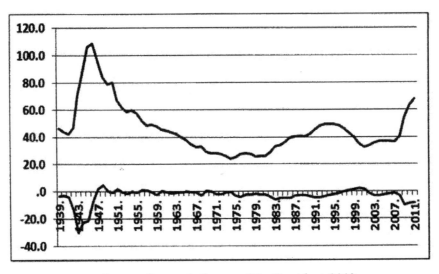

Source: *Economic Report of the President, 2012*

Note: The years shown in this chart are fiscal years. In the US, the fiscal year begins on October 1 and ends on September 30 of the following year. A fiscal year is called by the calendar year in which it ends, so the 2012 fiscal year ended on September 30, 2012. Before fiscal year 1977, the US government fiscal year started on July 1 and ended on June 30 of the following year.

THE BURDEN OF THE PUBLIC DEBT

Interest payment

One way to think of interest on the public debt is as the price that has to be paid by a government to get the funds it needs to implement its programs. If the benefits of these programs are sufficiently great relative to the interest on the debt, one can argue that it is worth incurring the debt.

Of course, there is likely to be great disagreement over what are the benefits of government programs. For example, some might view a government's expenditure on defense as essential to the national safety; others might think this defense expenditure is unnecessary and a waste of the government's resources.

If the interest payment on the public debt rises, increasing amounts of the revenue a government collects would have to be spent just on paying the interest. This could leave too little for other needed programs. In the US, interest rates are currently at historically low levels, keeping the interest cost of the US public debt relatively low—see the charts on the next page. As an example of how low interest rates are compared to historical levels, the first chart on the next page shows the yield on the US 10 Year Treasury. The second chart shows that the net interest payment on the US debt is a smaller fraction of GDP than it was in much of the 1990s. **Net interest** is interest paid on the **public debt**. It is the total interest on all of the government debt less the amount of interest paid on the government securities held by various agencies of the government.

There is no way to be certain of what interest rates will be in the future. But, given the historically low levels of interest rates now, it is reasonable to surmise that these rates would rise in the future as economic growth and/or inflation increase from their currently low levels. This fuels the fear that interest payment on the US public debt could reach levels that use up so much of US government revenue that too little is left for necessary government programs.

In the section **THE PUBLIC DEBT** earlier in this chapter, it was mentioned that of the $11.58 trillion of US public debt, about $5.31 trillion was held by foreigners. So just over 50 percent of the US public debt is held by US entities: citizens, corporations, banks, state and local governments, the Federal Reserve, etc.

US GOVERNMENT 10 YEAR TREASURY YIELD

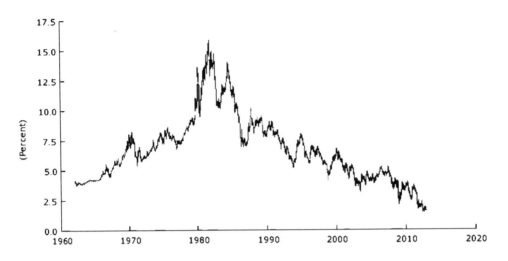

Source: Federal Reserve Bank of St. Louis (data series DGS10) &
Board of Governors of the Federal Reserve System. Accessed Dec. 30, 2012.

US GOVERNMENT NET INTEREST PAYMENT
AS PERCENT OF GDP

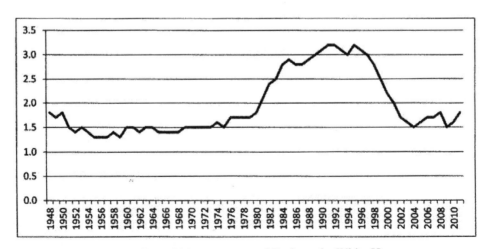

Source: Office of Management and Budget, the White House

Because of this, sometimes in the media you may encounter the argument that the interest payment on the US debt is mainly interest being paid to US entities—from one section of the US economy to another—so it is not potentially such a great burden on the US. This claim overlooks the fact that the US government has to find the interest to pay, and if this interest payment escalates, it will use up what the US government would otherwise spend on essential government programs.

Lack of policy flexibility

If an economy is headed to recession, a government would typically use fiscal policy to help offset the recessionary tendencies. Increased government spending, for example, has frequently been used to boost aggregate demand and assist recovery from recession.

However, when a government is running huge budget deficits and is heavily indebted, it could find it very difficult to borrow and increase spending to fight recessionary tendencies. Lenders might be reluctant to lend because of fears that the government would not be able to repay, and they might demand high interest rates to compensate them for the risk of a government default. The higher cost of borrowing and the limited availability of funds to borrow could severely restrict the fiscal policy options available to a government, putting at risk the government's ability to fight recessionary tendencies.

The US government has not faced difficulty borrowing and has not had to pay high interest rates in spite of huge budget deficits and rapidly rising debt. This is because US government bonds are viewed as very safe to hold, and the US government bond markets are very large and very liquid, which makes them very appealing to investors. With the Eurozone in crisis and doubts about political stability afflicting so many countries, if you are an investor and you want to put your funds into safe assets, US government bonds become the natural candidate.

Bond vigilantes

The term **bond vigilante** refers to investors who sell a government's bonds when rising government budget deficits and debt increase fears about the ability of the government to repay its debt. The selling of bonds pushes up interest rates (as explained in Chapter 6), so bond vigilantes can force a government to seek to reduce its budget deficits and debt. The term bond vigilante became prevalent during 1993 to 1994, when the US 10 Year Treasury yield went up sharply as investors sold bonds in response to what they viewed as lax US fiscal policy. This forced the US government to take strong measures to reduce the US budget deficit.

If economic conditions in Europe improve so that Eurozone bonds become increasingly attractive, and if investors become more comfortable holding bonds of countries such as China, this will give bond vigilantes stronger alternatives to holding US bonds. They will become more willing to get out of US bonds in response to concerns over US budget deficits and debt being too high, and their action will push up interest rates that must be paid by the US government when it wants to borrow. Any government that does not have prudent fiscal policies faces this risk that action by bond vigilantes can sharply raise interest rates.

BUDGET DEFICITS AND DEBT IN THE EUROPEAN UNION

The Eurozone consists of those countries that have the euro as their currency and whose monetary policies are determined by the European Central Bank (ECB). The euro was created because members of the European Union saw a common currency as a crucial element for making their "union" more meaningful. At the end of 2012 there are seventeen countries in the Eurozone: Austria, Belgium, Cyprus, Estonia, Finland, France, Germany, Greece, Ireland, Italy, Luxembourg, Malta, Netherlands, Portugal, Slovenia, Slovakia, and Spain.

Stability and Growth Pact (SGP)
To ensure that governments managed their finances well, which is essential for the stability and credibility of a common currency, the EU countries had agreed that they must adhere to guidelines on budget deficits and debt known as the Stability and Growth Pact (SGP). According to this pact, in general, a government's budget deficit should not exceed 3 % of GDP and a government's debt should not exceed 60 % of GDP.

Initially, the EU held that penalties would be imposed on countries that failed to meet these conditions. But, as worsening economic conditions caused even economically better-off countries like Germany and France to begin running fiscal deficits in excess of 3 % around 2003, the EU became more flexible. The emphasis shifted to urging EU countries that had deficits and debt above the acceptable limits to work toward deficit and debt reduction.

As the Eurozone has experienced deep crisis because of high budget deficits and debt, the EU has shifted back toward a stricter policy on these. In late 2011, six new measures were developed (called the "six pack") to give the EU Council authority to take measures to help EU members to get their budget deficits and debt under control.[103]

The table below shows the levels of budget deficit and debt in Greece, Ireland, Italy, Portugal and Spain, countries which have been hardest hit in the Eurozone crisis. It also shows data for Germany and France, the two largest Eurozone economies, and for the UK, which is not in the Eurozone but is in the EU and is constantly in the news as its government struggles to get deficit and debt reductions.

GOVERNMENT BUDGET DEFICIT AND DEBT
AS % OF GDP, SELECTED EU COUNTRIES, 2011

	Budget Deficit	Debt
Greece	9.4	170.6
Ireland	13.4	106.4
Italy	3.9	120.7
Portugal	4.4	108.1
Spain	9.4	69.3
Germany	0.8	80.5
France	5.2	86
United Kingdom	7.8	85

Source: Eurostat. (This was the data available in late 2012. Eurostat gives these data for the central government, state government, local government and social security funds combined.)

---

[103] Details of these measures can be found at the EU website at:
http://europa.eu/rapid/pressReleasesAction.do?reference=MEMO/11/898

Deficits, debt and the Eurozone crisis

The Eurozone crisis, which has featured so prominently in the news, aptly illustrates what the Stability and Growth pact was put forward to prevent. Here are some of the key strands in the crisis caused by exorbitant levels of deficit and debt racked up by some Eurozone countries.

- Fears that some Eurozone countries would not be able to meet their debt payments caused borrowing costs to shoot up in those countries.

- Anxiety developed that banks would not be repaid loans they had made to various Eurozone countries. This drove down stock prices of banks in Europe, the US, etc., pulling down stock markets and adding to the air of crisis and panic.

- Bouts of bad news on the evolving crisis fueled the view that Greece and other countries might have to leave the euro. It was felt that this would free them from the ECB determining their monetary policy, so they could then use their own monetary policy to try to fix their problems. This fear of a breakup of the Eurozone drove investors out of the euro and Eurozone assets.

- Concerns that economic growth in the Eurozone would falter made exporters to Europe, such as Japan, China, and the US, seem to have diminished growth prospects.

COULD A GOVERNMENT CONTINUALLY ROLL OVER ITS DEBT?

The **rolling over of debt** is the borrowing of new funds to repay debt that is due. If a government has to repay $10 billion of debt at the end of this month, could it issue new securities to get $10 billion to repay the $10 billion it owes, and could it do this year after year? To do so, it would have to be paying interest on each amount it borrows. So unless each year it can get revenue to pay the interest due on the amount it borrowed for that year, it will also have to borrow to pay the interest. To illustrate, if it had to pay 10 % per year interest, at the end of the first year, it would owe $11 billion (the 10 billion borrowed plus the 10 % interest). If it borrowed to repay this $11 billion, at the end of the second year, it would owe $12.1 billion, the $11 billion principal it had rolled over, plus the interest on this amount, which at 10 % would now be $1.1 billion, and so on.

With debt roll over of both the principal and the interest, the interest payments could escalate. The government debt could reach a level at which lenders might become worried about the government's ability to repay.

Of course, if the government got revenue each year to pay the interest due on its debt, it could just roll over the $10 billion each year, so this would be the amount it owed year after year. The amount of debt would be much less than if the government was rolling over both the principal and the interest. This would reduce the likelihood of lenders becoming worried about the government's ability to repay.

MONETIZING THE DEFICIT AND THE DEBT

When the bonds a government issues to finance a budget deficit are bought directly by a central bank, the central bank is said to be **monetizing the deficit**. It creates money which the government uses to pay for the deficit. Because a government budget deficit increases the government's debt, monetizing the deficit is also referred to as **monetizing the debt.** Further, if a government pays off some or all of its debt, funding this by the central bank creating money and buying bonds issued by the government, this would also be the monetizing of the debt.

In the US, the central bank (the Federal Reserve) is independent, so the government cannot compel it to monetize the deficit (debt). In the European Union, the Maastricht Treaty, which has come to be known as the Treaty of the European Union, forbids the European Central Bank (ECB) and the central banks of member states from directly buying the bonds issued by their governments (see Article 104 of the Treaty). In some countries, however, the central bank is under government influence and can be made to create money to buy bonds the government issues.

Are recent Fed policies monetizing the debt?

Policies such as QE, used by the Fed in response to the subprime/credit crunch crisis and persistent US economic weakness since 2007, have involved massive purchases of US government bonds by the Fed. This has naturally raised the question of whether the Fed is monetizing the US government debt. Responding to this question, Ben Bernanke, the Chairman of the Fed, in a speech at the Economic Club of Indiana in October 2012[104] said:

- "Monetizing the debt means using money creation as a permanent source of financing for government spending. In contrast, we are acquiring Treasury securities on the open market and only on a temporary basis, with the goal of supporting the economic recovery through lower interest rates."

- "At the appropriate time, the Federal Reserve will gradually sell these securities or let them mature, as needed, to return its balance sheet to a more normal size."

- "Moreover, the way the Fed finances its securities purchases is by creating reserves in the banking system. Increased bank reserves held at the Fed don't necessarily translate into more money or cash in circulation, and, indeed, broad measures of the supply of money have not grown especially quickly, on balance, over the past few years."

CONCLUSION

Around the world, debate rages over what are appropriate levels for government deficits and debt. This chapter has provided key concepts and a framework for evaluating issues in this debate. An underlying theme is that we should always look at the specifics of a country's situation to get a proper understanding of the dangers, if any, posed by deficits and debt.

While having a balanced budget might sound appealing, there are numerous drawbacks associated with it. It is important to be aware of the burdens posed by

---

[104] http://www.federalreserve.gov/newsevents/speech/bernanke20121001a.htm

public debt and what are the factors that have helped the United States to be able to run up huge deficits and debt without as yet becoming a victim of the bond vigilantes.

ANSWERS

EXERCISE 1

1. a

2. b

3. True. With a primary surplus, a government collects enough revenue to meet daily spending needs. So if it defaults, it doesn't have to worry that it will be left unable to fund its daily operations. If it has a primary deficit, however, it will have this worry.

4. d

EXERCISE 2

1. d

2. If Ricardian equivalence held, consumers will expect the government to increase taxes in the future to repay the $50 billion it borrowed to finance the tax cut. They will expect lower disposable income in the future, offsetting the increased income they have in the present from the tax cut. The consumers' permanent income doesn't change, the level of consumption will not change in the present and consumers will save the extra $50 billion in disposable income they have as a result of the tax cut. There will be no effect on total aggregate demand and on the output and price levels.

If Ricardian equivalence held, private saving will be higher in the amount of the tax cuts. If data shows that private saving did not increase even as a government cut taxes and borrowed to keep up its spending, this does not support Ricardian equivalence theory.

3. c

While the global economy is on a recovery path, several challenges remain. The high levels of fiscal deficits and Government debt in several of the advanced economies presents a risk to macroeconomic and financial stability and hence the sustainability of this recovery. The ensuing fiscal austerity drive and the more stringent financial regulatory measures to restore stability can be expected to see a period of slower growth in these economies.

—Dr. Zeti Akhtar Aziz, in a speech on June 17, 2010. She has been Governor of the Central Bank of Malaysia since 2000. In 2003, she was named the best central banker in the world by *The Banker* magazine, which is owned by The Financial Times Ltd.

CHAPTER 14
CONCLUDING THOUGHTS: THE PATH AHEAD

The aim of this book was to provide you with a cogent grounding in fundamental notions of macroeconomics. It deliberately avoided the approach of many textbooks that overwhelm the typical reader with a jumble of so many thoughts that he/she is unable to get a clear view of the whole. **It has given you a foundation you can readily grasp and on which you can now build to reach more sophisticated levels.**

No matter what book you read, unless you integrate the knowledge into your thinking, your insights will be vague. So I urge you to carefully go over this text to make it a part of your intellectual repertoire.

THE PATH AHEAD

There are several directions you can take from here:

a. **The very practical—**
   o **Learn about the numerous reports on the economy, called economic indicators, which come out almost daily.** Many of these deeply influence the direction of financial markets.

   o **Learn more about the financial markets**—the stock market, the bond market, foreign exchange market…. Useful information on the latter two were presented in this text. This is just a beginning. You can do a lot to build on these foundations, especially by carefully observing these markets.

In my economics seminars, for which this book is pre- and supplementary reading, I focus heavily on the two practical areas just highlighted. I show how the economic principles in this book can be extended and effectively used to better understand the daily business news and financial markets, and to profit from them.

b. **The more theoretical—**

- o If your aim is to do graduate study in economics in universities that focus on theoretical models with a heavy dose of mathematics, you should go on to texts with this orientation. The insights in this book will equip you to **think** very effectively about the notions you will encounter. You will have a distinct advantage over those who get so lost trying to grasp complex presentations that they cannot really think perceptively about how the whole macroeconomy works.

c. **A combination of approaches a and b—**

- o With this combination approach, you can play the financial markets (or at least have a keen understanding of them) and also follow the presentations of, and/or debate with, those who specialize in very abstract theory.

Bon voyage! Let the good times roll!

We study economics to learn how not to be deceived by other economists.

—Joan Violet Robinson, who made important contributions to economics and was based mainly at the University of Cambridge

My initial discussions with the Economics Department at UCLA about obtaining a Ph.D. in Economics were… pretty discouraging. I had not taken mathematics as an undergraduate primarily because I had been advised as a girl against taking any courses beyond algebra and geometry in high school. While the Economics Department encouraged me to take an outside minor in economics for my Ph.D., they discouraged any further thinking about doing a Ph.D. in economics.

—Elinor Ostrom, Nobel Prize, Economics, 2009

An economist must know, besides his subject, ethics, logic, philosophy, the humanities and sociology, in fact everything that is part of how we live and react to one another.

—Bernard Baruch, financier, statesman and advisor to eight US Presidents

END OF BOOK APPENDIX
PART I: MONEY DEMAND AND MONEY SUPPLY
(ASSOCIATED WITH CHAPTER 7)

THE DEMAND FOR MONEY

We can put into three categories the motives people have for keeping money rather than putting all their wealth into non-money forms such as bonds. The three categories are the: <u>transactions motive</u>, <u>precautionary motive</u> and <u>speculative motive</u>.

The **transactions motive** is the desire to keep an amount of money in our possession to pay for many of the items—breakfast, the newspapers, snacks, and so on—we buy each day.

The **precautionary motive** is the desire to have money on us to meet unforeseen expenses for which cash payments may be required. You may unexpectedly have to pay cash for a taxi or a laundry service. If you kept no money for such emergencies, you would be in a fix. Even if you had much wealth in assets other than money, your immediate need for money would not allow you the time and effort needed to convert these assets into money. It is necessary to always keep some money for meeting contingencies.

In addition to these motives for keeping money to pay for goods and services, people hold money because it embodies value. People face the problem of deciding how much of their wealth to hold as money and how much to hold in the form of non-money assets such as bonds. A problem of holding non-money assets is that their prices can fluctuate. For example, in Chapter 6 we saw that the current price of a bond, which is the price at which it can be sold, may be quite different from the price at which it was bought. If you buy a bond for $1000, there is no guarantee you will be able to get at least $1000 when you want to sell it. If you held $1000 in money, however, its value in terms of money would not change. If you held it in a deposit in a bank, even if that bank failed, under most circumstances there is insurance that guarantees you will get your money. The Federal Deposit Insurance Corporation (FDIC) is a US Federal agency established in 1933 that offers such insurance. Banks usually state that their accounts are FDIC insured. This generally means the FDIC will protect customers' account to a maximum of $250,000 per depositor, per insured bank.

As was mentioned in Chapter 6, principal is the amount spent to purchase an asset, and risk of principal is the risk that the selling price of an asset will decline below what was paid for it. The typical non-money asset has a risk of principal associated with it. People generally choose to hold some of their assets in the form of money because they do not wish to have all their assets subject to the risk of principal. The desire to hold some money because of the risk that the money value of other forms of assets may change is called the **speculative motive** for holding money.

The opportunity cost of holding money

If you hold $1000 in cash, you earn no interest on it. However, if you bought a bond for $1000 that had $90 per year of coupon payment, the current yield on the bond while its price was at $1000 would be (90/1000) 100 = 9 %. Some components of the money stock do earn an interest payment. For example, among bank deposits are some that earn interest. However, the interest these deposits earn is generally much less than the yield on non-money assets. Among the reasons for this are that banks seek to earn income by paying a lower interest on deposits than they charge if they have to lend money. Also, non-money assets have a risk of principal associated with them as was noted earlier. A higher yield on non-money assets is necessary to compensate people for the higher risk they take holding these assets rather than banks deposits, which generally have no risk of principal associated with them.

So when people hold money, they forego the extra yield they could earn by holding non-money assets. The yield people forego by holding money instead of higher yielding non-money assets is the **opportunity cost of holding money.**

The quantity of money demanded

There are a variety of interest rates in the economy. There are interest rates on savings accounts, interest rates on CDs (CDs were defined in the appendix to Chapter 6), the coupon interest rate of bonds, and the fed funds rate, the discount rate and the prime rate (which we learned about in Chapter 7) among others.

However, when we use the term "interest rate" or "economy's interest rate" we will mean the average yield on non-money assets. So in this model we abstract from the fact that there are a variety of interest rates in the economy and take it as if there is a single item called the interest rate. This is another example of the role of abstraction in theory building, which was discussed in Chapter 1. If we wanted to refer to some other specific interest rate—for example, the prime rate—we will use its name, or the context will make clear the specific rate being referred to.

The term **interest rate** will therefore be used to refer to the average yield on non-money assets in the economy. The higher the interest rate, the higher the yield on non-money assets people forego when they hold money, so people on the average will be inclined to hold less money. Not everyone will shift from holding money to holding more non-money assets as the interest rate rises, but on the average people will. The higher the interest rate, the smaller the quantity of money people desire to hold.

Quantity of money demanded refers to the amount of money people want (and can afford[105]) to hold at a given level of the interest rate. For example, if at an interest rate of 5 % people in the US want to hold a total of $400 million (because of their transactions, precautionary and speculative motives for holding money), then $400 million is the quantity of money demanded at the interest rate of 5 %.

The demand for money

The term **demand for money**, however, refers to the relationship between various levels of the interest rates and the quantity of money people want to hold at each interest rate. A diagram of this relationship is called the **demand curve for money** or the **money demand curve**. Because the higher the interest rate the lower the quantity of money people desire to hold, the money demand curve is negatively sloped as in Figure 1.

---

[105] The words "can afford" are included here to emphasize that we are referring to money people want to hold in the sense of being financially able to hold, not what they would wish to hold in their fantasies.

FIGURE 1

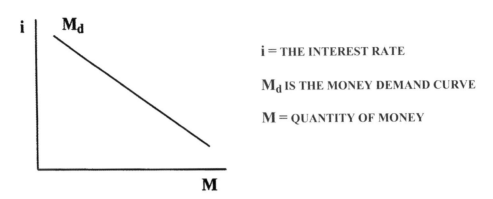

i = THE INTEREST RATE

M_d IS THE MONEY DEMAND CURVE

M = QUANTITY OF MONEY

Figure 2 shows a money demand curve for which at the interest rate i_1, the quantity of money demanded is AB. At the higher interest rate i_2, however, the quantity of money demanded is less, measured by the distance CE. As the interest rate moves above i_1, people lose more interest by holding money so they hold less money than was held at the interest rate i_1. These are examples to make you more acquainted with what the money demand curve shows.

FIGURE 2

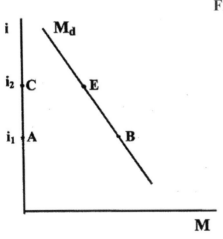

As the interest rate rises from i_1 to i_2, the quantity of money demanded falls from AB to CE.

THE QUANTITY OF MONEY SUPPLIED; THE MONEY SUPPLY

We learned in Chapter 7 that when banks give loans they increase the money stock. Generally, the higher the interest rate—which, as we noted earlier in this appendix, means the average yield on non-money assets—the higher the interest banks can charge when they make loans. But banks earn little or nothing on reserves they keep, whether as vault cash or as reserves at the central bank.[106] The higher the interest rate, the more interest income banks forego by keeping excess reserves; the higher the interest rate, the greater is the inducement banks have for taking the risks in making a loan, e.g., the risk that the loan will not be repaid. Consequently, *ceteris paribus*, the higher the interest rate, the more loans banks will make, and the greater will be the quantity of money supplied.

Since Chapter 6, we have used the terms money stock and money supply as if they meant the same thing. This is the way these terms are used in everyday speech. **Now we want to introduce a slightly different meaning of money supply** as meaning not just a single amount of money in the economy but a relationship showing the amounts of money that would be supplied in the economy at different levels of the interest rate. As we have noted, the higher the interest rate, *ceteris paribus*, the greater will be the quantity of money supplied in the economy. Suppose the amounts of money supplied at various interest rates are as in the table:

Interest rate (%)	Quantity of money supplied ($ million)
5	500
4	480
3	460
2	440

---

[106] As was noted in Chapter 7, some central banks pay interest on the reserves that banks keep at the central bank. But this is a relatively small amount, currently ¼ percent annual interest in the US. Banks can earn a much higher return by making loans.

Then the **quantity of money supplied** at the interest rate of 2 % is $440 million, the quantity of money supplied at the interest rate of 3 % is $460 million, and so on. The term **money supply,** however, would refer to the relationship between this set of interest rates and the quantity of money supplied at each interest rate.

The higher the interest rate, *ceteris paribus*, the greater will be the quantity of money supplied. So the curve representing money supply, called the money supply curve, is positively sloped. Figure 3 shows an example of a money supply curve. At the interest rate i_1, the quantity of money supplied is FG. At the higher interest rate i_2, the quantity of money supplied is HK, which is greater than FG. Evidence suggests that the money supply curve for the US is steep, as shown in Figure 3. (Some textbooks in their theory building abstract from this fact that the money supply curve is steep as depicted here and draw it as if it were vertical. When the money supply curve is vertical, the quantity of money supplied at each interest rate is the same. For example, if the quantity of money supplied at any interest rate was $400 million, the money supply curve would just be a vertical line emanating from the point corresponding to $400 million on the horizontal axis in the diagram showing money supply.)

FIGURE 3

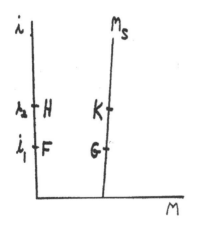

Ms is the money supply curve.
It has a positive slope—the higher
the interest rate, the greater the
quantity of money supplied.

THE EQUILIBRIUM INTEREST RATE

Figure 4 shows a money demand and a money supply curve in the same diagram. Let's say these are the relevant curves for an economy. At the interest rate i_1, the quantity of money supplied is EF, and the quantity of money demanded is also EF. The interest rate at which the quantity of money demanded equals the quantity of money supplied is called the **equilibrium interest rate**. This will be the interest rate that will prevail in the economy.

To see why this interest rate will prevail, consider the following. Suppose the interest rate is i_2, which is higher than i_1. At the interest rate i_2, the quantity of money demanded is GH but the quantity supplied is GK, which is greater than the quantity demanded. At the interest rate i_2, there is an **excess supply of money**—people have more money available to them than they want to hold.[107]

FIGURE 4

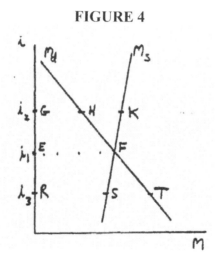

Only at the interest rate i_1 is the quantity of money supplied equal to the quantity of money demanded. i_1 is the equilibrium interest rate.

---

[107] Think of how you would behave if you felt you were holding too much money. You would be likely to use some of the money to acquire non-money assets that would earn you a higher return than if you just held the money.

They will, on the average, use the money they do not want to hold to buy non-money assets such as bonds. This desire to buy more non-money assets will push up the price of these assets and lower the yield on them—because as we learned in Chapter 6, the yield on an asset and its current price are inversely related. But the interest rate, as we have defined it in the model being presented in this appendix, is a measure of average yield. So if yield decreases, the interest rate decreases. This process continues as long as the quantity of money supplied exceeds the quantity demanded. It only stops at the interest rate i_1, where the quantity of money demanded equals the quantity supplied. The economy's interest rate declines to i_1. As long as the interest rate is above i_1, there will be this pressure for the movement of the interest rate to i_1.

Now consider what happens if the interest rate happens to be below i_1, at i_3. At the interest rate i_3, the quantity of money demanded is RT, which is greater than the quantity of money supplied, RS. There is said to be an **excess demand for money**. People have less money available to them than they want to hold. To get more money, they will, on the average, sell non-money assets such as bonds, putting downward pressure on the price of these assets. As the price of these assets fall, the yield on them rises, because of the inverse relation between the yield on an asset and its current price. But the interest rate is average yield. So the interest rate rises. This process continues as long as the quantity of money demanded exceeds the quantity supplied. It only stops at the interest rate i_1, where the quantity of money demanded equals the quantity supplied. The economy's interest rate rises to i_1. As long as the interest rate is below i_1, there will be this pressure for the movement of the interest rate to i_1.

A diagram showing money demand and money supply as in Figure 4 is called a **money market diagram**. The money market refers to the interaction of money demand and money supply in determining the interest rate. As we have learned, the money market will be in equilibrium when the quantity of money demanded equals the quantity supplied.

EXERCISE

1. Say whether each of the following is true or false and justify your response:
   a. The term "interest rate" refers to the average yield on bank deposits.
   b. The demand for money is inversely related to the interest rate.
   c. The quantity of money demanded is inversely related to the interest rate.
   d. The money demand curve can be positively sloped.
   e. If the quantity of money demanded exceeds the quantity supplied, there will be downward pressure on the interest rate.
   f. If at a given level of the interest rate, the money market is not in equilibrium and people have more money available to them than they want to hold, people will sell non-money assets and this will reduce the liquidity of their assets.

2. Draw a diagram of the money market and choose a level of the interest rate at which there is an excess supply of money. Explain how equilibrium will be reached in this money market.

3. The term money supply has two meanings. What are they?

4. If you hear in the news that "the US M2 money supply is $8,611 billion," what does this mean?

HOW CHANGES IN THE MONEY SUPPLY AFFECT THE INTEREST RATE

Because it is understood that the interest rate at which the quantity of money demanded equals the quantity supplied is the equilibrium interest rate, the word "equilibrium" is frequently omitted and this interest rate is simply called **"the interest rate,"** or the **"economy's interest rate."**

An increase in the money supply means at each interest rate the quantity of money supplied is greater than before. From what we have learned before (in Chapters 2 and 3) about shifts of curves, we know that an increase in the money supply means a rightward shift of the money supply curve. Figure 5 shows an increase in the money supply represented by a shift of the money supply curve from Ms_1 to Ms_2. When the money supply curve was Ms_1, the interest rate was i_1. After the increase in the money supply, the interest rate is i_2, because i_2 is now the interest rate at which the quantity of money supplied equals the quantity demanded. What moves the economy's interest rate from i_1 to i_2? To answer this question, recognize that after the money supply has increased to Ms_2, at the interest rate i_1 the quantity of money supplied is AC, which is greater than the quantity of money demanded, AB. People will have more money available to them than they want to hold, so they will want to buy non-money assets such as bonds. This increases the price of these assets and lowers their yield. The interest rate, which measures the average yield on non-money assets, falls. This process continues as long as the quantity of money supplied exceeds the quantity demanded, i.e., as long as the interest rate is above i_2. It only stops at the interest rate i_2, where the quantity of money demanded equals the quantity supplied. The economy's interest rate therefore falls to i_2. An increase in the money supply decreases the economy's interest rate.

FIGURE 5

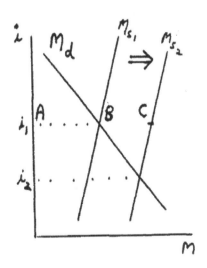

An increase in the money supply is shown by a rightward shift of the money supply curve. It decreases the economy's interest rate (from i_1 to i_2 in this figure).

A decrease in the money supply does the opposite—it increases the economy's interest rate. Figure 6 shows a decrease in the money supply increasing the economy's interest rate from i_1 to i_3. To see why the interest rate moves to i_3 after the money supply decreases, recognize that after the money supply decreases, at the interest rate i_1 the quantity of money demanded is CF, which is greater than the quantity supplied, CE. People have less money available to them than they want to hold, so they will sell non-money assets such as bonds in order to get the money they need. As they sell these assets, this puts downward pressure on the price of these assets and increases the yield. The interest rate, which measures the average yield, rises, and continues to rise as long as the quantity of money demanded exceeds the quantity supplied. This process only stops when the interest rate i_3 is reached.

FIGURE 6

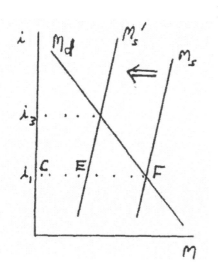

A **decrease in the money supply is shown by a leftward shift of the money supply curve. It increases the economy's interest rate (from i_1 to i_3 in this figure).**

To sum up, an increase in the money supply decreases the economy's interest rate. A decrease in the money supply increases the economy's interest rate.

FACTORS THAT CHANGE MONEY DEMAND

On average, when a person gets a higher personal disposable income (PDI, which was defined in Chapter 4), she/he increases spending and buys more expensive items. To do so, whatever is the interest rate, this person now holds more money. If at the interest rate i_1 (Figure 7) people held the amount of money AB, after a rise in PDI, they will now hold a higher amount of money AC. If at the interest rate i_2 they held the amount of money OE, now after a rise in PDI they will hold the greater amount OF. *Ceteris paribus*, a rise in personal disposable income in an economy causes an increase in money demand—a rightward shift of the money demand curve. A fall in personal disposable income, *ceteris paribus*, causes a decrease in money demand—a leftward shift of the money demand curve.

In general, we will take it in our analysis here that a rise/fall in Y, output, means a rise/fall in PDI. So we can write in symbols:

$$Y\uparrow \implies Md\rightarrow$$
$$Y\downarrow \implies Md\leftarrow$$

FIGURE 7

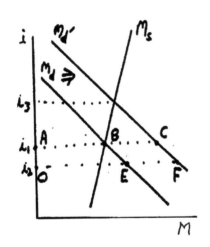

An increase in PDI causes an increase in money demand.

Similarly, if the economy's price level increases, on average people will have to pay more for the things they buy. So on average, whatever the interest rate, they will hold more money. A rise in the price level causes an increase in money demand. As you can surmise, a fall in the price level means people will need to hold less money so this causes a fall in money demand. Using symbols, we can write:

$P\uparrow \Rightarrow Md\rightarrow$

$P\downarrow \Rightarrow Md\leftarrow$

So we have learned of two factors—a change in Y (the level of output) and a change in P (the price level)—that cause a change in money demand.

It is evident from Figure 7 that a rise in money demand causes an increase in the economy's interest rate—from i_1 to i_3. Similarly, you can draw a diagram to show that a movement of the money demand curve to the left causes a fall in the interest rate.

ANSWERS

1.

    a. False. The term "interest rate" refers to the average yield on non-money assets.

    b. False. The quantity of money demanded, not the demand for money, is inversely related to the interest rate.

    c. True. The higher the interest rate, the greater the yield on non-money assets people forego by holding money. Therefore, the less money they will want to hold. So as the interest rate goes up, the quantity of money demanded goes down—an inverse relation.

    d. False. A positively sloped money demand curve would imply that the higher the yield people forego by holding money, the more money they will want to hold. This would be irrational.

    e. False. If the quantity of money demanded exceeded the quantity supplied, there will be upward pressure on the interest rate. (This corresponds to an interest rate like i_3 in Figure 4 in this appendix.)

    f. False. If people have more money available to them than they want to hold—the quantity of money supplied is greater than the quantity demanded—they will want to buy non-money assets such as bonds, not sell non-money assets. When they buy non-money assets, this will reduce the liquidity of their assets because non-money assets are less liquid than money.

2. This corresponds to an interest rate like i_2 in Figure 4 in this appendix. See the explanation in the text relating to Figure 4.

3. The term money supply is used to mean the quantity of money supplied (the money stock). It is also used in a stricter sense, as introduced in this chapter, to mean the whole relationship between various levels of the interest rate and the amount of money supplied at each interest rate. So money supply as used in this second sense would be represented by an upward sloping curve as in the line marked M_S in Figure 4 a few pages earlier. Context usually makes very clear which meaning of money supply is being used.

4. In the statement "the US M2 money supply is $8,611 billion," the term money supply is being used to mean the money stock, i.e., the quantity of money in the economy. M2 refers to one of the definitions of money, several of which were mentioned in Chapter 6.

END OF BOOK APPENDIX
PART II: MONEY AND AGGREGATE DEMAND
(ASSOCIATED WITH CHAPTER 7)

Here we consider how changes in the interest rate affect the level of investment and aggregate demand. **We continue to use the definition of the interest rate specified in the previous appendix.**

THE INTEREST RATE AND INVESTMENT ARE INVERSELY RELATED

In Chapter 2, we learned that investment comprises of investment done by businesses and the creation of new housing—residential fixed investment.[108] Investment done by businesses refers to items like spending on tools, machinery, equipment, factories and raw materials inventory.

Business people in general seek to maximize profits. If they have to borrow to fund their investments, the higher the interest rate, the higher their costs of borrowing to make investments. So, *ceteris paribus*, the higher the interest rate businesses pay to borrow to finance their investments, the lower will be the amount of their investment.

Also, before businesspersons make an investment they compare what they would earn from the investment with what they could earn by buying and holding non-money assets such as bonds. If the latter could earn them more, they would be better off holding non-money assets.

Suppose in our economy there are investment projects expected to earn a 12 % annual return, other projects expected to earn a 9 % return, and some expected to

---

[108] Recall from Chapter 2, that investment, as used in this context, should not be confused with financial investments like the purchasing of bonds or stocks (shares in a company) in the hope of getting a financial gain from these assets appreciating in value or earning you interest or dividends.

earn a 6 % return. If the interest rate—the current yield on non-money assets such as bonds—is above 12 %, none of these projects are likely to be implemented because business people could earn a higher return by purchasing non-money assets such as bonds rather than investing in the projects.

If the interest rate fell below 12 % but was higher than 9 %, the projects expected to earn a 12 % return become possible for implementation, since these projects would earn a higher rate of return than non-money assets. If the interest rate fell below 9 % but was above 6 %, the projects expected to earn a 12 % return and those expected to earn a 9 % return become feasible. If the interest rate fell below 6 %, then all the investment projects—those expected to earn a return of 12 %, 9 % and 6 %—become feasible.

The creation of new housing (residential fixed investment, which is another component of investment) is also dependent on the interest rate. Many persons take out loans (mortgages) to purchase their homes. A decrease in the interest rate they have to pay on these loans makes it cheaper to buy a home, which increases the amount of housing people will demand. This increased demand adds to the impetus for the creation of new housing. So the lower the interest rate, the higher will be residential fixed investment, *ceteris paribus*.

These illustrations show an inverse relationship between the interest rate and the level of investment—the lower (higher) the interest rate, the larger (smaller) will be the quantity of investment in the economy, *ceteris paribus*. *Ceteris paribus* is included here to make clear that with all factors, except the interest rate, that can affect investment held constant, the interest rate and investment are inversely related. For example, if at the same time the interest rate has declined, businesspersons become more pessimistic about the future, i.e., there is a decline in business confidence, they may not want to make more investment even though the interest rate has fallen. However, with other factors such as business confidence, the tax rate businesses have to pay, etc., held constant, the level of investment is inversely related to the interest rate.

A diagram of the relationship between the interest rate and the quantity of investment is called the **investment schedule**. Figure 1 shows a typical investment schedule.

FIGURE 1

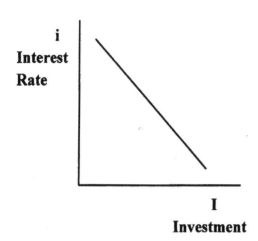

The investment schedule shows the interest rate and the level of investment are inversely related, *ceteris paribus.*

In Chapter 7, you learned the difference between the nominal interest rate and the real interest rate. When a businessperson is planning an investment, the interest rate she sees (at the bank from which she may be seeking a loan, in the news, etc.) is a nominal interest rate. When she projects what the expected inflation for the time ahead will be, she is then able to calculate what is likely to be the real interest rate on funds borrowed to make the investment. For example, if she has to borrow at a 10 % nominal interest to make an investment and expects inflation to be 4 % in the year ahead, the real interest rate will be 10 % minus 4 %, equal 6 %.[109] This is the real cost she would expect to bear. It is this real cost, the real interest rate, which will influence the level of investment she decides to make. But as long as expectations of inflation are stable, the nominal interest rate and the real interest rate will move up or down together, so for the investment schedule one can have the nominal interest rate related to the level of investment.

---

[109] As was explained in Chapter 7, the real interest rate is approximately equal to the nominal interest rate minus the expected rate of inflation.

EXERCISE 1

An economist presents data showing that as real interest rates fell, the level of investment also decreased. He claims this shows there isn't an inverse relation between the real interest rate and the level of investment. How would you respond to his claim?

HOW CHANGES IN THE MONEY SUPPLY AFFECT AGGREGATE DEMAND

We took it on faith in Chapter 2 that an increase in the money supply increases aggregate demand (causing a shift of the AD curve to the right), and that a decrease in the money supply decreases aggregate demand (causing a shift of the AD curve to the left). In Chapter 7 we elaborated on these relationships.

Here we look at these relationships in terms of how changes in the money supply affect the interest rate, which affects the level of investment and so changes aggregate demand.

We learned in the previous appendix that an increase in the money supply, *ceteris paribus*, causes a decrease in the interest rate (the average yield on non-money assets). We also learned that a decrease in the interest rate causes an increase in the quantity of investment. But an increase in the quantity of investment means more spending on tools, machinery, materials for making factories, etc., which are components of aggregate demand. This means, at any given price level, there is an increase in the quantity of aggregate demand, the total amount of desired spending on goods and services. If at any given price level there is an increase in the quantity of aggregate demand, this implies a rightward shift of the aggregate demand curve—an increase in aggregate demand. So, an increase in the money supply causes an increase in aggregate demand.

We can express the reasoning of the last paragraph in symbols as follows:

$$Ms{\rightarrow} \Rightarrow i{\downarrow} \Rightarrow I{\uparrow} \Rightarrow AD{\rightarrow}$$

We can show it with diagrams as in Figure 2.

FIGURE 2

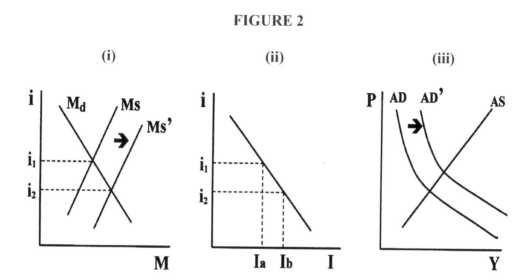

**Diagram (i):   An increase in the money supply
(a shift of the money supply curve to the right)
causes the interest rate to fall from i_1 to i_2.**

**(ii)   The fall in the interest rate causes an
increase in the quantity of investment from I_a to I_b.**

**(iii)   The AD curve shifts to the right because
the rise in investment means for any price level,
businesses want to spend more—there is an increase
in aggregate demand.**

Similarly, a decrease in the money supply causes a rise in the interest rate, a fall in
the level of investment and a decrease in aggregate demand (Figure 3).

FIGURE 3

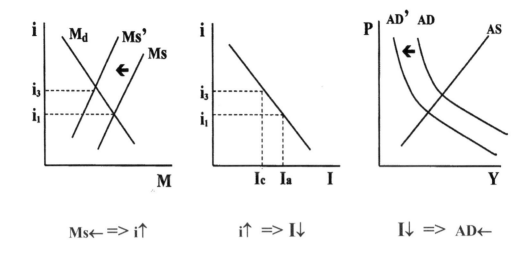

$$Ms\leftarrow \Rightarrow i\uparrow \qquad i\uparrow \Rightarrow I\downarrow \qquad I\downarrow \Rightarrow AD\leftarrow$$

EXERCISE 2

Say whether each of the following is true or false and justify your response:

a. If a country's central bank wants to see increased investment in the economy, it should buy bonds.

b. A contractionary monetary policy would lower bond prices, decrease the level of investment, and decrease aggregate demand.

THE IMPACT OF AN INCREASE
IN Ms ON THE INTEREST RATE

We have said before that:

$$Ms\rightarrow \ \Rightarrow \ i\downarrow \ \Rightarrow \ I\uparrow \ \Rightarrow AD\rightarrow \ \Rightarrow P\uparrow \,, Y\uparrow$$

Now we want to add a small complication: From the discussion in the previous appendix, we know that as P and Y are increasing, money demand (Md) increases. This pushes up the interest rate to i_3 (Figure 4) from the level i_2 to which it fell immediately after the increase in the money supply. However, i_3 will be less than i_1. We know this because for P and Y to increase, AD must increase, which means I must go up, which means i must have decreased from its original level, i_1.

So even with this complication taken into account, the increase in the money supply still causes a fall in the interest rate—from i_1 to its final level of i_3. The fall in the interest rate causes I to increase, which increases AD and so increases P and Y—just as we have learned so far.

Similarly, when Ms decreases, P and Y fall. As P and Y fall, this decreases Md and so lowers the interest rate from the level it rose to immediately after the money supply decreased. The final level of the interest rate, however, will still be above what it was before the decrease in Ms.

FIGURE 4

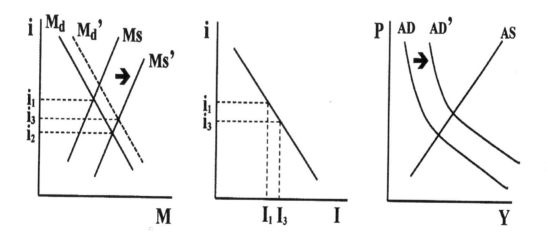

**The final effects of an increase in the
money supply on i, I and AD: i falls
from i_1 to i_3; I increases from I_1 to I_3;
AD increases from AD to AD'.**

LIQUIDITY TRAP

If the interest rate goes very low, people may not see any significant incentive to get out of cash into assets that will earn them this small rate. With the rate so little, they might, for example, feel that there is a high probability that it will increase. So if they got out of cash and bought bonds and the interest rate went up, they would suffer losses (the price of a bond decreases as the interest rate goes up). The money demand curve becomes flat at this low interest rate. See the section AB of the money demand curve in Figure 5. This is a **liquidity trap** in the sense that liquidity (cash) just gets hoarded (trapped) by people—no matter how much money is supplied, people are willing to hold on to the money they get.

In this situation, increasing the money supply as described so far in this appendix becomes ineffective. For example, increasing the money supply from Ms to Ms' (Figure 5) still leaves the economy's interest rate at the liquidity trap level, i_L.

FIGURE 5

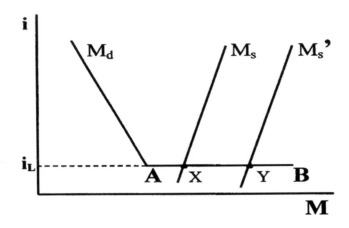

At the low interest rate i_L, there is a liquidity trap; the money demand curve has the horizontal part AB. An increase in the money supply (e.g., from Ms to Ms') does not lower the economy's interest rate, which remains at i_L after the money supply increase.

The mechanism detailed earlier in this appendix (a change in the money supply affects the interest rate, causes a change in the level of investment and so affects aggregate demand) will not work in a liquidity trap.

Keep in mind that the liquidity trap described here, which is based on notions Keynes referred to in his discussions of the Great Depression, abstracts from a lot that exists in the real world. For example, a central bank that faces a situation in which its target rate is near or at zero, and therefore does not have scope for lowering that rate further, can turn to lowering other rates in the economy. It can purchase long term bonds to lower their yields and so lower mortgage interest rates that are based on those long term bond yields. These lower mortgage interest rates would encourage people to purchase homes, and this increased demand for housing would be a mechanism for increasing aggregate demand. The policies of Quantitative Easing mentioned in Chapter 7 include long term bond purchases of the type just mentioned.

Another way a central bank can encourage people to stop hoarding cash is to create the expectation of substantially higher inflation. If people think prices will be going up, they are likely to make purchases with their cash, as cash loses purchasing power as prices rise. The central bank can create the expectation of higher inflation by declaring a clear intention to have higher inflation and then taking credible steps to inject money into the economy in a way that increases demand, such as through the long term bond buying mentioned in the previous paragraph.

ANSWERS

EXERCISE 1

The real interest rate and the level of investment are inversely related, *ceteris paribus*. If, as the real interest rate fell, other changes occurred that discouraged investment, then the level of investment could also have fallen. The economist would need to tell us what was happening to the other factors that could have influenced investment, e.g., business confidence, and check whether or not they were the cause that investment fell in spite of the real interest rate coming down.

EXERCISE 2

a. True. When the central bank buys bonds, it takes in bonds and gives out money. This increases the money supply, lowers the interest rate, and increases the level of investment.

b. True. A contractionary monetary policy raises the interest rate. There is an inverse relation between the interest rate (the yield on non-money assets) and average bond prices. So the interest rate going up implies average bond prices are going down. The level of investment is inversely related to the interest rate, so the higher interest rate will decrease the level of investment and decrease aggregate demand.

END OF BOOK APPENDIX
PART III:
THE ALGEBRA OF AN ELEMENTARY VERSION OF THE KEYNESIAN MODEL
(ASSOCIATED WITH CHAPTER 11)

INTRODUCTION

So far we have used the AD-AS model to determine whether output increases, decreases or is unchanged when factors affecting AD and/or AS change. We want to go further, however, and get insight into how to determine the amount by which output changes. This is necessary because for policy making it is sometimes not enough merely to know that output would increase or decrease if certain policies are implemented; an estimate of the amount by which output changes may be required. In your career, you may never have to deal with how these estimates are made, but it is good to have an understanding **of the thinking that underlies these calculations**. The aim of this appendix is to introduce you to these thought processes.

We want to learn the method of attempting to answer questions such as:

1. Given a certain level of aggregate demand, what will be the level of output in the economy?

2. By how much must aggregate demand be increased to attain a desired level of output?

To begin learning how to answer these questions, it is convenient to use the Keynesian model. This model has wages and prices constant, so in our calculations we can concentrate on the impact of changes in AD on output alone. This is simpler than having to also take account of how wages and prices change. Because we must learn step-by-step (walk before we can run!), it is best to begin answering these questions using the Keynesian model. Once you have a sense of how it is done, you can go on later in your studies (if you ever have a need) to learn how to get answers in more complex situations.

We can represent the Keynesian model as in Figure 1:

FIGURE 1
THE KEYNESIAN MODEL

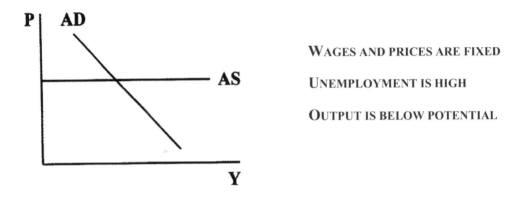

WAGES AND PRICES ARE FIXED

UNEMPLOYMENT IS HIGH

OUTPUT IS BELOW POTENTIAL

To answer the questions just posed, however, we need to move from merely drawing diagrams to doing elementary algebra.

FINDING EQUILIBRIUM INCOME

From what we learned earlier in this book, we know that the total demand for output produced in a country can be expressed as consumption C, plus investment I, plus government purchases G, plus net exports NX—as C + I + G + NX. We know that at equilibrium, the quantity of output supplied, Y, must be equal to the quantity of aggregate demand, C + I + G + NX.

Let us ignore G and NX. Including them complicates the algebra. Since we are primarily interested in the method of answering questions like 1 and 2 posed earlier, we can ignore G and NX here. Ignoring G and NX, we have that at equilibrium the quantity of output supplied, Y, equals the quantity of aggregate demand, C + I: Y = C + I, at equilibrium.

As we know from Chapter 4, if we ignore items like net income payments from abroad, depreciation, net indirect taxes, personal taxes, retained corporate profits, transfers, and so on, which cause the total value of output (GDP) and personal disposable income to differ from each other, we will have that Y = GDP = national income (NI) = personal disposable income (PDI). Let us do this to simplify the algebra and keep our focus on the method, which is what we are interested in. Once we learn the method, it is relatively easy to take account of the details we are ignoring now, if this ever becomes necessary.

We know that the amount people spend on consumption, C, depends on their personal disposable income, which equals Y here. It is reasonable to take it that C = aY, where a represents the amount of each additional dollar of income spent on consumption. For example, if C = 0.9Y, this means a = 0.9 and on the average consumers spend on consumption 0.9 of every additional dollar of their income. C = aY is called a **consumption function**. It shows consumption depending on income. When consumption is dependent on income it is said to be <u>induced</u>.

We take it here that the level of investment, I, is determined by the optimism ("animal spirits") of the business community. The greater the optimism, the higher is likely to be the level of investment. Here I is said to be **autonomous**—meaning independent of the level of income.

So we have Y = C + I = aY + I. If we get actual numbers for a and I we can immediately find Y. For example, if a = 0.8 (meaning that on the average consumers spend 0.8 of every additional dollar of their income) and I = 100, then:
Y = 0.8Y + 100

$$\Rightarrow Y - 0.8Y = 100 \quad \Rightarrow Y(1 - 0.8) = 100$$

$$\Rightarrow Y = 100/(1 - 0.8) = 100/0.2 = 500.$$

This means that at equilibrium, the level of income (or output, since here GDP = NI = PDI) would be 500 ($ million, or whatever is the appropriate unit).

So we see how we can find the equilibrium level of income in an economy depicted by this simple Keynesian model if we know the level of aggregate demand.

Another example: If we are told that a = 0.5, so that C = 0.5Y, and I = 200, then the level of aggregate demand is 0.5Y + 200. To find the equilibrium level of Y, equate Y and C + I and solve for Y:

$$Y = C + I = 0.5Y + 200 \ => Y = 0.5Y + 200 \ => Y(1 - 0.5) = 200$$

$$=> Y = 200/ (1 - 0.5) = 200/ 0.5 = 400.$$

The equilibrium level of income is 400.

MARGINAL PROPENSITY TO CONSUME; MARGINAL PROPENSITY TO SAVE

In the function C = aY, a is called the **marginal propensity to consume**, abbreviated as MPC. The MPC is the amount of each additional dollar of income that is spent on consumption. Sometimes the consumption function is of the form C = K + aY, where K and a are constants, i.e., just numbers. In this case, K is a part of consumption not dependent on current income and is said to be autonomous, meaning independent of income. For example, if a part of consumption is based on wealth accumulated in the past, it could be represented by K in C = K + aY. The part of consumption dependent on income here is aY. In the consumption function C = K + aY, a is the MPC.

We learned in Chapter 4 that personal disposable income is approximately equal to C plus personal saving. Let us say the only saving in an economy is personal saving. Generally, there would be other types of saving in an economy. For example, retained corporate profits is viewed as business saving. But since we are ignoring items like this, personal saving equals total saving and personal disposable income = C + S.

Given that in our discussion here Y is taken as equal to personal disposable income, we have Y = C + S. So, S = Y - C. If C = aY, then S = Y - C = Y - aY = (1 - a)Y. (1 - a) is the amount of each additional dollar of income that is saved. As you can readily imagine, (1 - a) is called the **marginal propensity to save** (MPS). A function relating S and Y, such as S = (1 - a)Y is called a **saving function**.

In the analysis we are doing here, the MPC + the MPS = a + (1 - a) = 1; the MPS = 1 - MPC. For example, if the MPC is 0.9, the MPS = 1 - 0.9 = 0.1.

Consider the last example we did calculating equilibrium income, where C = 0.5Y and I = 200. We found the equilibrium level of Y to be 400. The MPC = 0.5, and the MPS = 1 - MPC = 0.5. The total amount of consumption at equilibrium is C = 0.5 (400) = 200. The total amount of saving at equilibrium = Y - C = 400 - 200 = 200, or (1 - a)Y = 0.5Y = 0.5 (400) = 200.

If C = 0.9Y and I = 100, to find equilibrium income equate Y and 0.9Y + 100: Y = 0.9Y + 100, so Y - 0.9Y = 100, 0.1Y = 100 => Y = 1000.

The total amount of consumption when Y = 1000 is C = 0.9Y = 0.9 (1000) = 900. The total amount of saving when Y = 1000 is Y - C = 1000 - 900 = 100.

THE MULTIPLIER

Notice when we solved to find equilibrium, we equated Y and aY + I. This led to: Y - aY = I => Y(1 - a) = I => Y = 1/(1 - a) X I.

From Y = 1/(1 - a) X I, it follows that when I changes, **the change in Y = 1/(1 - a) times the change in I.**

1/(1 - a) is called the **multiplier**, or **Keynesian multiplier**, or **income multiplier**. It tells the amount by which income changes when autonomous spending changes by $1.

For example, if a = 0.8, the multiplier is $1/(1 - 0.8) = 5$, so if I increases by 200, the change in Y equals the multiplier times $200 = 5 \times 200 = 1000$. Y increases by 1000. Suppose I had decreased by 200. Then the decrease in Y would be $5 \times 200 = 1000$.

If C = 0.9Y (i.e., a = 0.9) and I = 100, then equilibrium income = 1000, as we saw in an earlier example. Now suppose I increases by 300. By how much does Y increase? From what we have just learned, Y increases by the multiplier times the increase in $I = 1/(1 - 0.9)$ times $300 = 10 \times 300 = 3000$. The new level of Y after I has increased is the old level of Y, 1000, plus the increase in Y, 3000 = $1000 + 3000 = 4000$.

Alternatively, to find the change in Y when I increases by 300, we can find the level of Y corresponding to I = 100 + 300 and then subtract the level of Y corresponding to I = 100. (When a = 0.9 and I = 400, Y = 4000. When a = 0.9 and I = 100, Y = 1000. The change in Y when I increases to 400 from 100 is 4000 − 1000 = 3000.)

If C = 0.9Y and I = 400, we have just seen that Y = 4000. If we want to find the amount by which I must increase to give us a level of income of 6000, i.e., an increase in income of 2000, we just use the formula "change in Y equals the multiplier times the change in I". We write 2000 = 10 (which is the multiplier here) times the change in I. The change in I is 2000/10 = 200, i.e., I must increase by 200 to cause a 2000 unit increase in Y.

THE PARADOX OF THRIFT

If C = 0.9Y, S = 0.1Y. If C then falls to 0.8Y, this implies that S has risen to 0.2Y, so people in the economy represented by these functions would now be saving more of each dollar of income—previously they were saving 0.1 of every dollar; now they are saving 0.2. If each individual attempts to save more, does it mean that total saving increases? Let's see.

When I = 100 and C = 0.9Y, equilibrium income is 1000 and total saving is 100. If C falls to 0.8Y because individuals are saving 0.2 of every dollar of income now as compared to 0.1 when C equaled 0.9Y, equilibrium income is:

$$Y = 0.8Y + 100. \text{ So } Y - 0.8Y = 100, \ 0.2Y = 100 => Y = 100/0.2 = 500.$$

The total amount of saving when income is $500 = Y - C = 500 - 0.8(500) = 100$, which exactly equals the amount of saving when each individual was saving less (0.1) of each dollar of income. So here we have a paradox, called the **paradox of thrift**: in this model, each individual seeking to save more does not cause the total level of saving to increase.

Why does this happen? It occurs because when people increase their marginal propensity to save, this decreases aggregate demand, as each individual is now spending less. This fall in aggregate demand decreases equilibrium income. So even though each individual is saving more of every dollar of income, there is now less income out of which they can save. In the situation we have just discussed, equilibrium income falls enough to cause total saving not to rise at all when each individual attempts to save more. Notice that in this simple model at equilibrium Y = C + I. But Y = C + S. So C + I = C + S, which implies S = I. In this model, the equilibrium level of S always equals I.

What does this teach us about the real world? If each of us started saving more and buying less, businesses would get less sales. They would have to cut back on their production and lay off people. This is why as the recent recession occurred in the US, politicians were eager to get Americans to spend more—to increase aggregate demand, output and employment.

If, however, people spend less on consumption but channel their saving into more investment, this prevents aggregate demand from falling since one component of aggregate demand, consumption, gets replaced by another component, investment. This possibility takes time to happen and is not considered in the simple model we have studied in this appendix because this model looks only at the more immediate effects of an attempt by people to save more.

EXERCISE

1. In a simple Keynesian model in which equilibrium income is found by equating Y and C + I, if C = 0.7Y and I = 300, what are the:
   a. MPC
   b. MPS
   c. Multiplier
   d. Equilibrium level of income
   e. Level of saving at equilibrium
   f. Change in equilibrium income if I increases by 100
   g. Change in the level of income if the MPS increases to 0.4 and I remains at 300
   h. Change in the level of saving if the MPS increases to 0.5 and I remains at 300

2. In a simple Keynesian model in which equilibrium income is obtained by equating Y and C + I, if C = 0.5Y and I = 400, what are the:
   a. Equilibrium level of income
   b. Level of saving at equilibrium
   c. Equilibrium income if I doubles
   d. Multiplier

CONCLUSION

In this section of the appendix, you got fundamental notions on how economic models are used to calculate the level of output in an economy, how much output will change in response to changes in various causal factors, etc. The aim was to give you a notion of what technicians do when they have to use large economic models to make these calculations. If you are a typical person, it is unlikely that you will ever have to do these calculations yourself, so it is enough just to have an understanding of the thought processes involved. You also became familiar with some commonly used terms such as marginal propensity to consume, marginal propensity to save, Keynesian multiplier and paradox of thrift, which, deftly used, can entertain guests at cocktail parties! So let the party begin!

ANSWERS 1

1.

   a. MPC = 0.7.

   b. MPS = 1 – MPC = 0.3.

   c. Multiplier = 1/(1 – MPC) = 1 / (1 – 0.7) = 10/3.

   d. At equilibrium, Y = C + I => Y = 0.7Y + 300, so 0.3Y = 300, Y = 1000.

   e. The level of saving at equilibrium is MPS times the equilibrium level of income = 0.3 x 1000 = 300. Or, we know it is equal to the level of I, so it will have to be 300.

   f. The change in equilibrium income when I increases by 100 = the multiplier times 100 = 10/3 x 100 = 1000/3.

   g. If the MPS increases to 0.4, the MPC falls to 0.6. At equilibrium, Y = C + I = 0.6 Y + 300 => 0.4 Y = 300. Therefore, Y = 750. Y has decreased by 250 from the level it was at before the MPS increased (see the answer at d).

   h. From the paradox of thrift, we know that if the MPS increases but the level of investment remains the same, total saving will not change. The change in saving is zero.

2.

   a. At equilibrium, Y = C + I. Here Y = 0.5Y + 400 => 0.5Y = 400. Y = 800 is the equilibrium level of income.

   b. The level of saving at equilibrium is the MPS times the equilibrium level of income = 0.5 x 800 = 400. Or, we know it is equal to the level of I, so it will have to be 400.

   c. If I doubles, then at equilibrium Y = 0.5Y + 800. So 0.5Y = 800, Y = 1600.

   d. The multiplier = 1/(1 – MPC) = 1/(1 – 0.5) = 2.

Index

Made in the USA
Columbia, SC
27 July 2017